ARCHAEOLOGY and the PEOPLE of the BIBLE

TITUS KENNEDY

HARVEST HOUSE PUBLISHERS
EUGENE, OREGON

Cover design by Studio Gearbox

Cover images © Sytilin Pavel, 1777177 / Shutterstock; Classical Numismatic Group / Wikipedia Commons (license: https://creativecommons.org/licenses/by-sa/3.0/deed.en); remainder of cover images are from the author's collection.

Interior design by KUHN Design Group

All photos and illustrations are © Titus Kennedy with the exceptions noted below.

Photos on pages 28, 36, 52, 100, 101, 111, 115, 127, 155, 160, 164, 182, 184, 188, 209, 214, 229, 238, 247 (second photo), 259, 292, and 324 are in the public domain.

Photos on pages 254 (both), 278, and 279 are © Paradiso and used with permission.

For bulk, special sales, or ministry purchases, please call 1-800-547-8979.
Email: CustomerService@hhpbooks.com

This logo is a federally registered trademark of the Hawkins Children's LLC. Harvest House Publishers, Inc., is the exclusive licensee of this trademark.

Archaeology and the People of the Bible

Published by Harvest House Publishers
Eugene, Oregon 97408
www.harvesthousepublishers.com

ISBN 978-0-7369-9027-1 (pbk)
ISBN 978-0-7369-9028-8 (eBook)

Library of Congress Control Number: 2025937053

Printed in Colombia

25 26 27 28 29 30 31 32 33 34 / NI / 10 9 8 7 6 5 4 3 2 1

"Titus Kennedy uses a rigorous methodology to demonstrate that the Bible is a book about real people. Far too often, Bible readers just skip over hard-to-pronounce names, assuming they must be uninteresting or unimportant. *Archaeology and the People of the Bible* builds a bridge from the present to the distant past and illuminates and contextualizes the inspired ancient narratives."

Scott Stripling, PhD, Provost and VP of Donor Relations,
President, Near East Archaeological Society

"This book correlates a significant number of ancient individuals who are present in both the archaeological record and the biblical text. In addition, it has plentiful background information on the individuals discussed. As such, it is an excellent source to verify the historical record of the Bible and to help readers to better understand the historical context of Scripture. In effect, it is both an apologetics asset and a commentary rolled into one book. Highly recommended."

Dr. Michael J. Caba, independent scholar

"Titus Kennedy has established himself in biblical archaeology not only by his excellent fieldwork but also for his production of outstanding contributions in publications. His books have especially been helpful to those seeking to understand how the science of archaeology can reveal the historical accuracy of the Bible. This book, then, will be a revelation to many who may see, for the first time, the large corpus of personal names of biblical figures in the archaeological, and thus historical, record. It should remind every reader that if the biblical writers took pains to include such details as these, and they were accurate to their place and time, that the spiritual, even supernatural, things they recorded must also be regarded as carefully recorded facts of history."

Randall Price, PhD, Ret. Distinguished Professor of Biblical
and Judaic Studies, John Rawlings School of Divinity,
Liberty University; author, *The Stones Cry Out*

"Are the events reported in the Bible myth or history? *Archaeology and the People of the Bible* answers this question by compiling classical sources and the latest archaeological discoveries that provide independent, detailed evidence for the existence of more than 120 people—the elites as well as the incidentals—recorded in the Bible. This is an exceptional and thorough treatment of persons with the same title, position, family name, living in the same time period, and geographical location as those mentioned in the Bible. Moreover, each entry includes primary literature citations, photographs, an identification rating (most are firm), and gives additional historical details about the person and their activities beyond what is found in the Bible. A must-have reference for scholars and students who want to flesh out (literally) the real people whom we independently can identify behind the real events in Bible history."

John A. Bloom, PhD, PhD, MDiv, Founding Director, MA Science and Religion Program and Emeritus Professor of Physics, Biola University

Oh that my words were written!
Oh that they were inscribed in a book!
That with an iron stylus and lead
they were engraved in the rock forever!
As for me, I know that my Redeemer lives,
and at the last He will take His stand on the earth.

Job 19:23-25

𐤌𐤉 𐤉𐤕𐤍 𐤀𐤐𐤅
𐤅𐤉𐤊𐤕𐤁𐤅𐤍 𐤌𐤋𐤉
𐤌𐤉 𐤉𐤕𐤍 𐤁𐤎𐤐𐤓
𐤅𐤉𐤇𐤒𐤅
𐤁𐤏𐤈 𐤁𐤓𐤆𐤋 𐤅𐤏𐤐𐤓𐤕
𐤋𐤏𐤃 𐤁𐤑𐤅𐤓
𐤉𐤇𐤑𐤁𐤅𐤍
𐤅𐤀𐤍𐤉 𐤉𐤃𐤏𐤕𐤉
𐤂𐤀𐤋𐤉 𐤇𐤉
𐤅𐤀𐤇𐤓𐤅𐤍 𐤏𐤋 𐤏𐤐𐤓
𐤉𐤒𐤅𐤌

CONTENTS

PART 1: OLD TESTAMENT PEOPLE (CHRONOLOGICAL ORDER)

PART 2: NEW TESTAMENT PEOPLE (CHRONOLOGICAL ORDER)

INTRODUCTION

Over the last several decades, archaeological projects and research have uncovered new discoveries directly related to many of the people named on the pages of the Bible. While scholars generally acknowledge that the Bible may contain accurate geographical information, when it comes to the existence and lives of specific individuals named in the Bible, opinions about the historical nature of these figures and their positions have varied drastically due to presuppositions and limited archaeological data.

The idea that the Bible is primarily a mythological work composed as religious and political propaganda rather than an accurate retelling of the past continues to be widespread. This viewpoint implies that if mythology, the Bible may describe real locations but the events and even people are largely fictional rather than historical.

A comparison with the Bible has often been made with the *Iliad* of Homer, an epic poem with mythological elements composed in ancient times around the 8th century BC but probably set in the 12th century BC. Although the city of Troy is now known to have existed and was likely even destroyed as a result of a war similar to what Homer described, no evidence for any of the people named in the poem—such as Achilles, Hector, Agamemnon, Priam, Helen, or Paris—has ever been found in contemporary archaeological sources. Discussions of the gods and supernatural events connected to ancient Greek religion and mythology are prevalent throughout the text, and even though a few historical elements can be identified in the poem, the *Iliad* has been classified as a traditional work of historical fiction or myth.

This Bible as mythology and fiction position would therefore argue that simply because Jerusalem and the temple existed and were probably destroyed after being defeated by the Babylonians, this does not mean that David, Isaiah, Sargon, Hezekiah, Jehoiachin, Nebuchadnezzar, and Belshazzar were real people who held the titles and performed the deeds the Bible claims.

Indeed, the existence of a city and evidence for a battle in a similar chronological context does not mean that the events and people mentioned in the book are historical. And yet archaeological discoveries have now demonstrated the historical existence of these people and many others, indicating that the narratives accurately reflect and record historical reality with detailed precision.

Certainly many names that appear in the Bible have also been found in a variety of archaeological sources. Even more people might potentially be identified or proposed, but those who are only referred to in the Bible using a title or association are excluded. These speculative cases based only on information from their title and time period would include pharaohs or kings whose names are not specified and therefore can only be suggested identifications based on circumstantial evidence and parallels. Names appearing similar to the names of rulers from distinct cultural and chronological settings but lacking definitive links have also been excluded, including the intriguing examples of Chedorlaomer a possible Elamite king, Amraphel a possible Mesopotamian king, and Tidal a possible Hittite king.

Further, many others clearly named in records from antiquity dating to a later time period are also excluded. For example, although Lot is mentioned on a stone inscription from the Byzantine period at the Cave of Lot, and the cave had a long and ancient tradition along with archaeological materials dating to the Early and Middle Bronze Ages, the inscription does not come from the Bronze Age and therefore does not qualify as contemporary attestation of the person Lot.

The information must be thoughtfully evaluated and consistent criteria applied in each instance to avoid misidentifying the use of a name as unambiguous attestation for a biblical person. In antiquity as today, numerous people often shared the same name—especially those from similar cultural contexts and time periods. And even if there is an overlap of name, time, and place, the difference between possibility and certainty must be acknowledged. In order to associate an archaeological attestation of an individual with a person named in the Bible, multiple categories of information need to be present and match—name, family, time period, location, title, or profession.

The first and most obvious is that the names must be the same and not a speculative nickname or unknown additional name. Second, if any family names are known, those must also match and be in the correct relationship, such as grandfather, father, son; grandmother, mother, daughter; brother, sister; husband, wife; or another relative. Third, the chronological setting for the archaeological person and the biblical person must be within the same time frame and restricted to a reasonable lifespan, if that exact degree of timing is possible.

Fourth, the geographic setting or location must be consistent between the two sources, such as a particular city, region, or kingdom. Fifth, if there is any supplemental data such as title, occupation, place of origin, attribute, achievement, or association, then these must either match or be plausible. Finally, the archaeological source—a stele, statue, coin, tablet, manuscript, mosaic, ostracon, seal, bulla, ossuary, or any other artifact with writing containing a name and specific information about an individual—should be verified as authentic. Numerous scholars have objected to the study, publication, and use of unprovenanced artifacts—discoveries that cannot be traced to a controlled archaeological excavation, but instead are found in a collection, on the antiquities market, or on the surface of the ground by a pedestrian visiting an ancient site. While these unprovenanced artifacts lack archaeological context and should be scrutinized with a critical and skeptical posture, the current ability to analyze artifacts through rigorous scientific tests and evaluation by multiple experts has made forgeries almost impossible to escape detection. Therefore, many scholars consider unprovenanced artifacts that have been sufficiently examined to be worthy of discussion, publication, and inclusion in the archaeological record.

Ideally, all five of the aforementioned categories of information would be present and the artifact would have been discovered and clearly documented in a controlled archaeological excavation, making the association and identification certain. Lacking one or more of these conditions, identifying the person may still be possible, but a rating of probable, tentative, or speculative may be necessary. Circumstances are not always perfect in archaeology, and in many situations, the quantity and clarity of the information presently available is sufficient only to classify the identification as tentative or speculative. The objective in these cases is to provide information about identifications that are unclear or debated so that the reader is aware of both the possibility of attestation and the current problems or lack of data, understanding that the archaeological evidence exists, but might be inconclusive or disputed. The level of confidence or lack thereof can be noted for each potential person, but simply because an identification is speculative does not mean it should always be disregarded or excluded, for one new piece of data might solve the puzzle in the future.

By applying these five categories and examining every case of a named person in the Bible who appears to be attested by archaeological artifacts and ancient manuscripts, approximately 130 candidates emerge across both the Old and

New Testaments combined. The classification of each person as firm, probable, tentative, or speculative is based on evaluation with the five categories of information and the assessments of various scholars, whether or not the provenance of the discovery can be traced. Ultimately, however, there are identifications that will be disputed due to the weighing of evidence and different perspectives.

Readers will notice that the more recent time periods have a greater frequency of named people of the Bible attested in the archaeological record. This is due to the ravages of time and depth of excavation skewing results, along with variances in writing and recording practices between different cultures and time periods. Nevertheless, as new discoveries are made and past data is researched and assessed, the picture emerges that the Bible is not an ancient mythological book set in real places filled with fictional characters but a historically accurate source recording the lives and details of real people whose existence continues to be verified by archaeology.

PART 1

OLD TESTAMENT PEOPLE

(CHRONOLOGICAL ORDER)

DANEL

Epic of Aqhat

Name: Danel

Time Period: 2nd Millennium BC (Bronze Age)

Geographical Area: Levant

Biblical Reference(s): Ezekiel 14:14-20; 28:3

Ancient Source(s): Epic of Aqhat; The Rephaim

Identification Rating: Probable (B)

The man named Danel, whose life is set in far-off ancient times during the Bronze Age in Ugaritic tablets and in the book of Ezekiel may be the same person. The Epic of Aqhat was discovered on three tablets of the 14th century BC recovered in excavations at the ancient city of Ugarit, while a fourth tablet probably existed but has not yet been discovered (KTU 1.17-1.19). Although the text is incomplete due to damage and a missing tablet, the story focuses on a man named Danel ("God/El is judge") and his son Aqhat.

The protagonist, Danel, is described as pious and just, and his actions imply that he is wise. Danel is also called "man of the Rephaim" and "man of Haranam," and the text relates that he was a judge who advocated for widows and orphans, while also making it clear that he was a prominent hero and influential man.

The story reveals that Danel initially has no son and heir, so he makes a divine appeal through ritual and prayer and El blesses him with a son named Aqhat. Later, a special bow and arrows are delivered to Danel, and he instructs his wife to prepare a lamb to honor the guest who brought these weapons. Danel then gives the bow and arrows to Aqhat. Unfortunately, due to the evil and covetousness of the goddess Anat, Aqhat is murdered because he would not sell his special bow to her even though she offered silver, gold, and immortality.

According to the story, while out hunting, Aqhat is killed by Yatipan, the mercenary acting on the orders of Anat, and the bow is accidentally broken. At the instigation of his daughter Paghit, who sees a foreboding sign, Danel begins searching for Aqhat, eventually learns of his son's death, and finds his remains. He then buries Aqhat at the shores of Kinneret (Galilee), giving an important geographic marker as to the location of the events. Although the tablet dates to the 14th century BC, it is surely a copy of an earlier work. Clues in the text point to the time of Danel as the Middle Bronze Age, around the time of Abraham or possibly earlier, and according to the Book of Jubilees he was the uncle of Enoch. Danel also briefly appears in another Ugaritic tablet called the Rephaim.

This man from long ago named Danel is mentioned three times by Ezekiel alongside Noah and Job and in the context of Tyre (cf. Ezekiel 28:2-3). In the Ezekiel passages, Danel is grouped with two other men whose lives are set in the long-ago Bronze Age, described as righteous and wise, and at least in the case of Job and Danel, unable to save son or daughter. While the Epic of Aqhat reflects a polytheistic worldview rather than a monotheistic viewpoint, the original story may have been adapted and redacted by Ilimilku, the high priest of Ugarit, who also wrote versions of Keret and the Baal Cycle, in order to harmonize with the ideology and theology of Ugarit. The tablets from Ugarit that preserve information on and an ancient story about Danel appear to be discussing the same man noted in the book of Ezekiel.

> *"Even though these three men, Noah, Danel and Job were in its midst, by their own righteousness they could only deliver themselves," declares the Lord God. "If I were to cause wild beasts to pass through the land and they depopulated it, and it became desolate so that no one would pass through it because of the beasts, though these three men were in its midst, as I live," declares the Lord God, "they could not deliver either their sons or their daughters"* (Ezekiel 14:14-16).

Barton, George. "Danel, a Pre-Israelite Hero of Galilee." *Journal of Biblical Literature* 60, No. 3 (1941): 213-25.

Parker, Simon. *Ugaritic Narrative Poetry*. Atlanta: Scholars Press, 1997.

BALAAM

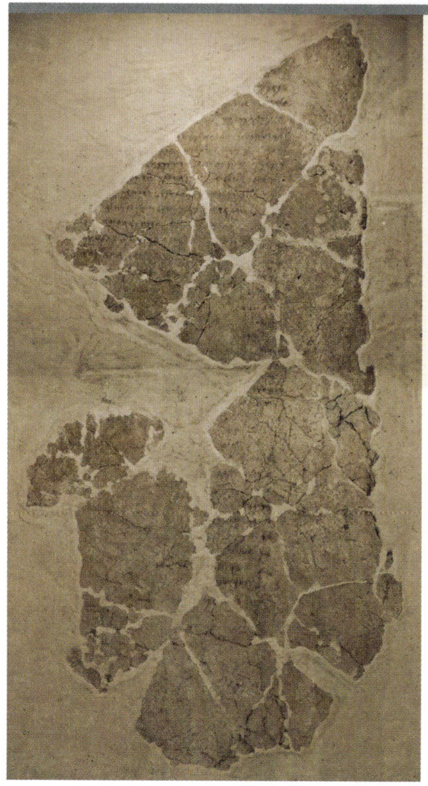
Balaam text from Deir 'Alla

Name: Balaam (son of Beor)

Time Period: 15th century BC (Late Bronze Age) and 9th century BC (Iron Age II)

Geographical Area: Mesopotamia and Moab

Biblical Reference(s): Numbers 22:5-24:25; Deuteronomy 23:3-4

Ancient Source(s): The Deir 'Alla Inscription

Identification Rating: Probable (B)

Balaam, son of Beor, from Pethor, was hired by Balak the king of Moab to curse the Israelites during their wilderness wandering. The historical context of these events places Balaam in the Late Bronze Age, coming from Mesopotamia to Moab, while an ancient Aramaic document known as the Deir 'Alla Inscription or Balaam Inscription (KAI 312) dates to the 9th century BC in the Iron Age. Discovered during excavations at the site of Deir 'Alla in Jordan (tentatively identified with ancient Succoth mentioned in Joshua 13:27), the Balaam Inscription is not strictly an inscription, but black and red ink written on plaster from an interior wall of a building. Although this poetic Aramaic text had been written on a wall around 800 BC, it appears to retell events and name an individual from centuries prior.

One of the oldest existing examples of Aramaic literature, reconstituted from 119 fragments, it relates events about Balaam. Beginning with "the book of Balaam, son of Beor, a seer of the gods," the text describes how Balaam received a divine message at night warning that darkness and chaos would be coming to the land. Balaam then attempted to appease the gods by going through various religious rituals. The people apparently rejected, condemned, and banned Balaam and his message, but specifics are difficult to understand because of missing pieces of text.

Undeciphered Late Bronze Age tablet from Deir 'Alla

Although fragmentary, this composition gives a matching name, family lineage, and profession for Balaam as a seer involved in divination, in addition to the person and events being geographically linked to the area of Moab. While the surviving text dates to the 9th century BC rather than the time of Balaam, it is possible that the information was passed down orally or adapted from an earlier written source. It is significant that a total of 15 tablets from the Late Bronze Age have been discovered at Deir 'Alla, and although difficult to decipher, the tablets demonstrate that written records existed at Deir 'Alla centuries earlier and close to the time of Balaam. Thus, Balaam, son of Beor, seems to be documented by an ancient Aramaic text from Moab, but the lapse of time means the attestation for Balaam as a historical person must be considered less than certain.

> *Balak the son of Zippor was king of Moab at that time. So he sent messengers to Balaam the son of Beor, at Pethor, which is near the River, in the land of the sons of his people, to call him, saying, "Behold, a people came out of Egypt; behold, they cover the surface of the land, and they are living opposite me. Now, therefore, please come, curse this people for me since they are too mighty for me; perhaps I may be able to defeat them and drive them out of the land. For I know that he whom you bless is blessed, and he whom you curse is cursed." So the elders of Moab and the elders of Midian departed with the fees for divination in their hand; and they came to Balaam and repeated Balak's words to him* (Numbers 22:4-7).

Hoftijzer, J. and G. van der Kooij. *The Balaam Text from Deir 'Alla Re-Evaluated.* Leiden: Brill, 1991.

BITHIA
(Daughter of Pharaoh)

Bintanath under the leg of Ramesses II

Name: Bithia (daughter of Pharaoh)

Time Period: 13th century BC (19th Dynasty)

Geographical Area: Egypt

Biblical Reference(s): 1 Chronicles 4:17-22

Ancient Source(s): Tomb QV71; Aswan Rock Stele; statue inscriptions

Identification Rating: Tentative (C)

Bithia was a daughter of Pharaoh who married an Israelite named Mered. The chronological context of Bithia places her in the period of the Judges, which overlapped with the Egyptian 19th Dynasty and the 13th century BC. One of the royal women with a tomb in the Valley of the Queens from this period was Bintanath (Bint-ʿAnat), apparently the eldest daughter of Pharaoh Ramesses II. She was the sister of the famous 13th-century BC princes Amun-her-khepeshef, Ramesses B, Khaemwese, and Merneptah, and the daughter of Isetnofret. Their father, Ramesses II, is thought to have had perhaps seven wives and an estimated 88 to 103 children, with Nefertari and Isetnofret being the two most important wives.

Bintanath, the eldest known daughter of Ramesses II, is attested by several inscriptions and artwork (Tomb QV71, Aswan Rock Stele of Ramesses II, statue at Abu Simbel, statue at Luxor). This name, Bintanath, is Semitic and not Egyptian and means "daughter of the goddess Anat." A similar name, Bithia, is in the middle of a genealogical section that also records her status as a daughter of Pharaoh, and the approximate period in which she lived (1 Chronicles 4:17-22). Bithia, or Bith-Yah, could be either a Hebrew rendering of her name or a modification containing the theophoric element "Yah" (Yahweh).

Egyptian sources do not mention that Bintanath left Egypt to marry a foreigner, but two possibilities exist. Bintanath may have left Egypt and never returned, which one could argue is suggested by the absence of her body in her tomb (QV71), and the fact that the sarcophagus found in the tomb was made for a man. Alternatively, there are indications that a younger Princess Bintanath existed, who may have been the one mentioned in the book of Chronicles instead. If Bithia and Bint-'Anat were the same person, then the name change may be reflective of editing or of her transition to a worshipper of Yahweh after becoming the wife of Mered.

Many similar examples of this are known from the Israelite period, including the changing of a female name from Baal-yada to Eli-yada, substituting El for Baal (e.g., 1 Chronicles 3:8; 14:7). Although it is possible that Bithia the daughter of Pharaoh has been identified in the archaeological record, the connection is tentative.

> *The sons of Ezrah were Jether, Mered, Epher and Jalon. (And these are the sons of Bithia the daughter of Pharaoh, whom Mered took) and she conceived and bore Miriam, Shammai and Ishbah the father of Eshtemoa* (1 Chronicles 4:17).

Dodson, Aidan and Dyan Hilton. *The Complete Royal Families of Ancient Egypt: A Genealogical Sourcebook of the Pharaohs*. London: Thames and Hudson, 2004.

DAVID

House of David on the Tel Dan Stele

Name: David, king of Israel (son of Jesse)

Time Period: 1000 BC (Iron Age II)

Geographical Area: United Monarchy of Israel

Biblical Reference(s): 1 Samuel 16:4-23; 2 Samuel 3:1; 5:1-5

Ancient Source(s): Tel Dan Stele; Mesha Stele; Shoshenq Karnak List (?)

Identification Rating: Firm (A)

David, son of Jesse, was the founder of the "house of David" and the first in a long line of the royal dynasty of Israelite kings (2 Samuel 3:1). Although David was the second king over all Israel, following Saul, it was the line of David that persisted as kings for the next four centuries until the Babylonian destruction of Jerusalem. Many of the psalms are attributed to David. He is recorded as the ancestor of the Messiah, and he is mentioned by name in 19 Old Testament books and nine New Testament books. However, until recently, many scholars considered David a mythical king because no conclusive archaeological evidence for his existence and reign had been discovered.

The first clear archaeological evidence for the existence of King David that had widespread agreement was an inscription found during excavations at the ancient city of Dan, when fragments of an Aramean victory stele from the 9th century BC were uncovered as reused building stone at the base of a wall on the edge of a plaza near the main city gate. The stele must have been erected by the Arameans to commemorate their victory over the Israelites, then smashed and used as building material after the Israelites recaptured the city

Inscribed in Aramaic, the original basalt stele was probably about 1 meter tall (3.28 feet) and 50 cm wide (19.6 inches), but currently only three fragments with 13 lines of text have been recovered. The monument was likely created around 841 BC by Hazael of Aram and relates his victories over Jehoram of Israel and Ahaziah of Judah. In the context of these Israelite kings, their lineage from the "house of David" (BYT DWD) is mentioned on line nine of the stele, demonstrating that David was an historical king and founder of the royal line who lived prior to the 9th century BC.

This phrase "house of David," referring to the dynasty that David established, is found in the books of Samuel, Kings, Chronicles, Psalms, Isaiah, Jeremiah, and Zechariah. Subsequent to the discovery of the Tel Dan Stele, it became obvious that the 9th-century BC Mesha Stele also referred to King David and contained the same phrase "house of David" on line 31 of this Moabite victory stele. Thus, two victory monuments inscribed by neighboring enemy nations of Israel—Aram and Moab—both knew about David as the founder of the Israelite royal dynasty of kings and named him in their campaign accounts from the 9th century BC (cf. 2 Samuel 5:17, etc.). A third inscription possibly referring to David, but much more speculative, comes from the 10th-century BC Karnak List of Shoshenq I, which contains a place name that has been suggested as "the heights of DWT."

In addition to 9th-century BC inscriptions of foreign nations mentioning the house of David, demonstrating widespread knowledge of King David, excavations in Jerusalem appear to have unearthed his palace. Although David began his reign over Judah ca. 1010 BC, with the capture of Jerusalem around 1003 BC,

House of David segment on the Tel Dan Stele

he established his capital there and built a new palace on the hill known as the Ophel (2 Samuel 5:4-11; 1 Chronicles 14:1; Psalm 30; 1 Kings 2:11). Excavations at the millo (terrace or earthworks) in 1923 initially discovered a large stone terrace wall constructed with cut stone. Excavations continued in the 1960s and exposed more of this massive wall, showing it to be around 18 meters (59 feet) tall, and finds such as a Phoenician-style proto-Aeolic capital and ashlar masonry indicated that a monumental building with Phoenician architecture may have been at the top of the slope. Archaeological materials indicated that it had been constructed during the Iron Age IIa around 1000–900 BC.

Then excavations beginning in 2005 revealed a massive stone building designated the "Large Stone Structure" above the terrace wall. Pottery found below the foundations of the structure dated to the 12th–11th centuries BC (Iron Age I), while the pottery above dated to the 10th century BC (Iron Age IIa). Other artifacts found within the structure included Phoenician ivory inlays and imported pottery, fitting for a palace and in agreement with the builders being Phoenician. Finds from after this period include bullae stamped with Hebrew names and titles of officials from the 7th century BC, such as Jehucal, son of Shelemiah, and Gedaliah, son of Pashhur, demonstrating that the building was used by the royal administration (Jeremiah 37:3; 38:1). Based on its location, the

Mesha Stele section mentioning house of David

monumental size of the building, the construction date, the Phoenician architecture and artifacts, and the bullae of royal officials found inside, this Large Stone Structure was probably the palace of David in Jerusalem.

Finally, the tomb of David may also have been located, although it was robbed in ancient times as most royal tombs were. Two of the nine rock-cut tombs in the City of David, T1 (Tomb 1) and T2 (Tomb 2), are the largest and most impressive. Herod the Great supposedly intended to loot the tomb of David, but he discovered it had already been robbed, and allegedly John Hyrcanus had taken 3,000 talents from the tomb of David in the 2nd century BC (Josephus, *Antiquities* 16.179-183; Josephus, *Wars* 1.61; cf. Acts 2:29). Since the book of Kings records that both David and Solomon were buried in the City of David, T1 or T2 could be the tomb of David (1 Kings 2:10; 11:43; 14:31; cf. Nehemiah 3:16).

Although until recently King David was considered a mythical character by many scholars, archaeological discoveries have now established his existence, his role as king and founder of the royal dynasty, his palace in Jerusalem, and perhaps even his tomb.

> *All the elders of Israel came to the king at Hebron, and King David made a covenant with them before the* L*ORD* *at Hebron; then they anointed David king over Israel. David was thirty years old when he became king, and he reigned forty years. At Hebron he reigned over Judah seven years and six months, and in Jerusalem he reigned thirty-three years over all Israel and Judah* (2 Samuel 5:3-5).

Biran, A. and J. Naveh. "An Aramaic Stele Fragment from Tel Dan." *IEJ* 43 (1993).

Kitchen, Kenneth. *On the Reliability of the Old Testament.* Grand Rapids: Eerdmans, 2006.

Lemaire, Andre. "House of David Restored in Moabite Inscription." *Biblical Archaeology Review* 20.3 (1994).

TAI
(King of Hamath)

Image of Taita and accompanying inscription discovered at Aleppo

Name: Tai, king of Hamath (Taita)

Time Period: 1000 BC (Iron Age IB)

Geographical Area: Hamath

Biblical Reference(s): 2 Samuel 8:9-10; 2 Chronicles 18:9-10

Ancient Source(s): Maharda Stele; Sheizar Stele; Relief of Taita

Identification Rating: Probable (B)

Tai (or Toi) the king of Hamath, a region based at Hamath (Hama) on the Orontes River in Syria, ruled around 1000 BC and overlapped with King David's reign. According to the books of Samuel and Chronicles, Tai sent David gifts of gold, silver, and bronze as thanks for defeating their mutual enemy the Arameans.

Excavations in Syria around the area of Hamath have uncovered Luwian inscriptions mentioning the kingdom of Walistin (or Palistin) and their king named Tai or Taita from just before 1000 BC. At the nearby ancient city of Sezar (modern Sheizar), a funerary stele for Queen Kupapiya was found that had also been inscribed for her husband, King Taita. Just to the southeast at Maharda, another inscription mentioning King Taita was discovered. More recently, a stone relief depicting King Taita facing the storm god and an accompanying Luwian inscription of the 11th century BC naming him have been found in a temple at the Citadel of Aleppo. The inscriptions invoke "King Taita, Hero of the Land of Walastin."

The name or names Tai and Taita are Hurrian. The King Tai (or Toi) of Hamath mentioned in the books of Samuel and Chronicles and the King Taita attested around Hamath and Aleppo appear to be the same king based on the name, title, geographic region, and time period. Scholars have suggested that the final "ta" element of the name may have been dropped from the shortened Hebrew form, and an analysis of name comparisons between Hebrew and their original language shows many similar cases of slight spelling modification.

> *Now when Toi king of Hamath heard that David had defeated all the army of Hadadezer, Toi sent Joram his son to King David to greet him and bless him, because he had fought against Hadadezer and defeated him; for Hadadezer had been at war with Toi. And Joram brought with him articles of silver, of gold and of bronze* (2 Samuel 8:9-10).

Steitler, Charles. "The Biblical King Toi of Hamath and the Late Hittite State 'P/Walas(a)tin.'" *Bibische Notizen* 146 (2010).

HIRAM

Ba'al Lebanon inscription

Name: Hiram

Time Period: 10th century BC (Iron Age II)

Geographical Area: Phoenicia

Biblical Reference(s): 1 Samuel 5:11; 1 Kings 5:1-18; 2 Chronicles 8:18

Ancient Source(s): Baal Lebanon inscription; Ahiram sarcophagus

Identification Rating: Speculative (D)

Hiram was the Phoenician king of Tyre in the 10th century BC who interacted with David and Solomon, providing them with building materials and skilled construction laborers for their palaces and the temple in Jerusalem. Although the exact dates of his reign are not known, he overlapped with both David and Solomon. As a Phoenician king, a prolific builder, and a diplomat, Hiram or his successors may have commissioned inscriptions to honor him. Although speculative, there are two Phoenician inscriptions that might refer to Hiram.

The enigmatic Ba'al Lebanon inscription, found in Cyprus and purchased after being noticed as a potentially important artifact, mentions a ruler named "Hiram, king of Sidonians" (KAI 31). The text is inscribed on bronze and appears to be a dedication to a deity called Ba'al Lebanon. It is often assigned to the 8th century BC, but as the archaeological context is unknown and the inscription is fragmentary, it could be earlier, or it could be making a historical reference to King Hiram.

Another inscription that has a possibility of mentioning King Hiram is the text on the Ahiram sarcophagus. Found in Tomb V of the royal necropolis of Byblos, this decorated sarcophagus has a Phoenician inscription mentioning "Pilsibaal, son of Ahiram, king of Gebal" (KAI 1). Yet scholars disagree on the date of this sarcophagus, with the range generally being around 1000–850 BC. Although the Phoenician name Ahiram is equivalent to Hiram, and both were kings of Phoenicia, the city and exact time period present difficulties. It is reasonable that the king of Tyre was also king of the other major Phoenician cities such as Sidon and Gebal, as was the case in later times (cf. 1 Kings 5:6). However, the unknowns of the chronological context make the connection speculative, as there may have been multiple Phoenician kings named Hiram living in the 10th and 9th centuries BC.

> *Now Hiram king of Tyre sent his servants to Solomon, when he heard that they had anointed him king in place of his father, for Hiram had always been a friend of David* (1 Kings 5:1).

Clermont-Ganneau, Charles. "Hiram, King of Tyre." *Palestine Exploration Quarterly* 12:3 (1880).

Porada, Edith. "Notes on the Sarcophagus of Ahiram." *Journal of the Ancient Near East Society* 5 (1973).

Section of the Ahiram sarcophagus and inscription

SHISHAK

Shoshenq I stele fragment from Megiddo

Name: Shishak (Shoshenq, Shoshaq, Hedjkheperre Setepenre)

Time Period: 10th century BC (22nd Dynasty)

Geographical Area: Egypt

Biblical Reference(s): 1 Kings 11:40; 14:25-26; 2 Chronicles 12:2-9

Ancient Source(s): Bubastite Portal at Karnak; Megiddo Victory Stele of Shoshenq

Identification Rating: Firm (A)

Shishak, king of Egypt, came to power during Solomon's reign and continued as pharaoh into the first several years of the divided kingdoms of Israel and Judah, ruled by kings Jeroboam and Rehoboam. Because of his name, chronological setting, and military campaign against Israel and Judah, Shishak mentioned in the books of Kings and Chronicles can be identified as Shoshenq I, a Meshwesh (Libyan) ruler of Egypt and founder of the 22nd Dynasty who reigned 21 years from about 945–924 BC.

Shoshenq I was the son of the Great Chief Meshwesh ruler named Nimlot and probably the nephew of Osorkon the Elder, the first Libyan king of Egypt. His name in the Bible, rendered as "Shishaq" (e.g., 2 Chronicles 12:2) or "Shoshaq" (1 Kings 14:25), is nearly an exact transliteration of his name in Egyptian, and Shoshenq I is written in some Egyptian inscriptions without the *n* included in his name, just as spelled in the Hebrew Bible (cf. Karnak Priestly Annals from Thebes). In Akkadian texts, his name is spelled Shwsanq—very similar to Hebrew, but with the *n* included. In the Aegyptiaca of Manetho from the 3rd century BC, the Greek spelling Sesonchis is used for Shoshenq I.

The first mention of Shishak in the Bible happens near the end of Solomon's reign, when Jeroboam had fled to Egypt and Pharaoh Shishak to escape execution, staying there until the death of Solomon (1 Kings 11:40). Perhaps as a result of Jeroboam being in Egypt for years and interacting with the pharaoh, a

12-section taxation and provisioning system with parallels to the one set up by Solomon was implemented in Egypt during the reign of Shoshenq I (cf. 1 Kings 4:7-19). Attestation of this similar system in Egypt is found on a stele from the temple of Arsaphes in Herakleopolis and ends with an invocation to Pharaoh Shoshenq I during the second half of the 10th century BC.

The primary interaction between Shishak and the kingdoms of Israel and Judah, however, occurred in the fifth year of Rehoboam, around 926 BC. According to the books of Kings and Chronicles, Shishak came with an army from Egypt and invaded Israel and Judah, ending at Jerusalem, where he forced a tribute payment but did not conquer the city (1 Kings 14:19-26; 2 Chronicles 12:1-13). The passages describe a campaign of Pharaoh Shishak against Judah during the fifth year of Rehoboam in which Shishak and his army took fortified cities of Judah and eventually arrived at Jerusalem, where a tribute was paid but the city was not attacked. Although the passages do not comment specifically on the status of the Northern Kingdom of Israel and Jeroboam during that time, the book of Kings does mention Jeroboam making war, which could in part refer to war with Pharaoh Shishak (1 Kings 14:19).

Pharaoh Shoshenq I commemorated his invasion of Israel and Judah by having it memorialized on the wall of the Bubastite Portal at the Temple of Amun in Karnak, in addition to a victory stele erected at one of the conquered cities. The topographical list of Shoshenq I records numerous locations in his expedition also known from the Bible, including Ta'anach, Shunem, Beth-Shean, Rehob, Mahanaim, Gibeon, Beth-Horon, Aijalon, Megiddo, Gath-Padalla, Bethlehem, Socoh, Penuel, Tirzah, Ezion-Geber, Arad, and Sharuhen. More than 30 percent of the place names on the list are also place names that appear in the Bible. While the name Jerusalem does not appear on the list, a place name "Yehud-melek" seems to refer to the royal seat of the Kingdom of Judah at Jerusalem. This is similar to the records of the Babylonian king Nebuchadnezzar II recounting his invasion of Judah and capture of Jerusalem, where his annals record "the city of Judah" rather than Jerusalem.

At the site of El-Hiba (Tayu-Djayet), Shoshenq I built a temple to Amun and inscribed a list of places he had conquered in his victorious campaign to western Asia, although the list is now damaged. The Karnak War stele also probably relates to this campaign of Shoshenq I. Evidence from Egyptian sources, such as the unfinished Silsila stele, indicate that the celebration of his victorious campaign to Israel and Judah occurred in year 21 of his reign, soon after returning to Egypt and not long before his death, which also accounts for the unfinished state of the stele. The location of his tomb is unknown but thought to be in Tanis or Bubastis.

Archaeological excavations found that several of the cities that appear on the Bubastite Portal list were destroyed in the 10th century BC at the time of Jeroboam, Rehoboam, and Shoshenq I. These sites include Megiddo, Taanach, Beth-Shean, Rehob, and Arad. In the southern part of the Kingdom of Judah are clear signs that the 10th-century BC city of Beersheba was also destroyed, which is compatible with the campaign of Shoshenq I. The most obvious evidence of this destructive campaign and attestation of Shoshenq I as the perpetrator comes from a late 10th-century BC destruction layer and fragmentary victory stele at Megiddo containing the cartouche of Pharaoh Shoshenq I. Jerusalem has no destruction layer from this period, as would be expected from the narrative recording a tribute payment.

The vast amount of treasure Pharaoh Shishak took from Jerusalem also appears to coincide with the financial situation in Egypt following the end of the reign of Shoshenq I. The books of Kings and Chronicles state that the pharaoh took the treasures of the palace and the temple in Jerusalem, including the many large shields of gold Solomon had made (1 Kings 14:26; 2 Chronicles 12:9). After returning to Egypt, Shoshenq I began significant temple construction projects at Thebes, Karnak, and El-Hiba.

The son and successor of Shoshenq I, Pharaoh Osorkon I, came to power when his father died perhaps two years after the end of the Israel and Judah campaign. According to ancient Egyptian records and archaeological investigations, Osorkon I spent enormous amounts of gold and silver on the temples of Egypt within the early years of his reign, specifically claiming on a temple inscription at Bubastis to have given 2.3 million deben (383 tons) of silver and gold to the gods of Egypt. If his father, Shoshenq I, had taken the treasure of Jerusalem back to Egypt, this would account for the sudden influx of gold and silver.

The evidence from the Karnak campaign list, destroyed cities, Megiddo stele, and spending and prosperity in the reign of Osorkon I demonstrates that Shoshenq I campaigned against Israel and Judah early in the reign of Jeroboam and Rehoboam, and therefore he is identified as Shishak (or Shoshaq), king of Egypt, named in the books of Kings and Chronicles.

> *It came about in King Rehoboam's fifth year, because they had been unfaithful to the* Lord, *that Shishak king of Egypt came up against Jerusalem...He captured the fortified cities of Judah and came as far as*

Jerusalem…So Shishak king of Egypt came up against Jerusalem, and took the treasures of the house of the LORD *and the treasures of the king's palace. He took everything; he even took the golden shields which Solomon had made* (2 Chronicles 12:2-9).

Kitchen, Kenneth. *The Third Intermediate Period in Egypt, 1100–650 BC*. Liverpool University Press, 1996.

Bubastite Portal and victory list of Shoshenq I at Karnak

JEROBOAM
(Son of Nebat)

Seal of Shema, servant of Jeroboam

Name: Jeroboam (son of Nebat)

Time Period: 10th century BC

Geographical Area: Northern Kingdom of Israel

Biblical Reference(s): 1 Kings 11:26–14:20; 2 Chronicles 10:2–13:20

Ancient Source(s): Seal of Shema

Identification Rating: Firm (A)

Jeroboam, king of Israel and son of Nebat, often referred to as Jeroboam I, came to power when the kingdom split following the death of Solomon and the crowning of Rehoboam in about 930 BC. During his 22-year reign, he was often at war with the Kingdom of Judah to the south against Rehoboam and then his successor Abijah. His capital was located at Tirzah (Tell el-Far'ah North), and excavations there demonstrate that in the early 10th century BC it was a substantial city. Direct evidence for Jeroboam, however, comes from another city in his kingdom.

At Megiddo, excavations recovered a jasper seal that would have been originally mounted on a ring of metal. This seal was found amid material removed from the area of the gatehouse or palace, Courtyard 1693, of the late 10th century BC. The seal is decorated with a carved lion, and painted on the sides of the lion are an ankh and palm tree. Above and below the lion is a Hebrew inscription reading "belonging to Shema, servant of Jeroboam." The owner of the seal was an otherwise unknown Shema, who served as an official in the court of King Jeroboam. Unfortunately, after the excavations concluded, the seal was lost in Istanbul or on its way to Istanbul. However, prior to this, a photograph was taken and an accurate cast of the seal was made, allowing it to be thoroughly documented. More recently, a bulla supposedly made from the original seal has been published, but epigraphers argue it is a crude forgery.

Although many scholars state that the Shema Seal naming Jeroboam is from the 8th century BC, stratigraphic evidence from the excavations at Megiddo indicates it came from a late 10th-century BC context, suggesting it was in use during the reign of Jeroboam I and attests to the existence of this king and one of his officials. However, for those who insist that the seal is from the time of Jeroboam II, who reigned ca. 793–753 BC, it would instead be the only archaeological attestation for this king yet discovered.

> *Jeroboam's wife arose and departed and came to Tirzah. As she was entering the threshold of the house, the child died. All Israel buried him and mourned for him, according to the word of the* Lord *which He spoke through His servant Ahijah the prophet. Now the rest of the acts of Jeroboam, how he made war and how he reigned, behold, they are written in the Book of the Chronicles of the Kings of Israel. The time that Jeroboam reigned was twenty-two years; and he slept with his fathers, and Nadab his son reigned in his place* (1 Kings 14:17-20).

Deutsch, Robert et al. 2024. "The Bulla of 'Shema, Servant of Jeroboam': An Embarrassing Forgery." *Gabriel: Tell this Man the Meaning of His Vision (Daniel, 8:16): Studies in Archaeology, Epigraphy, Iconography and the Biblical World in Honor of Gabriel Barkay on the Occasion of His 80th Birthday*. Archaeological Center Publications.

Ussishkin, David. "Gate 1567 at Megiddo and the Seal of Shema, Servant of Jeroboam." *Scripture and Other Artifacts*. Louisville, 1994.

BEN-HADAD I

Melqart Stele

Name: Ben-hadad I (son of Tabrimmon)

Time Period: 9th century BC (Iron Age II)

Geographical Area: Aram Damascus

Biblical Reference(s): 1 Kings 15:18-20; 2 Chronicles 16:2-4

Ancient Source(s): Melqart Stele

Identification Rating: Tentative (C)

Ben-hadad I was the son of Tabrimmon and the king of Aram, based in Damascus, reigning from approximately 885–865 BC. He interacted with both Asa of Judah and Baasha of Israel, but after King Asa paid him to revoke his support of King Baasha and provide military support, Ben-hadad I attacked and conquered several cities in the Northern Kingdom of Israel. This Ben-hadad I, or Bar-hadad I, might be mentioned on the Melqart Stele (KAI 201) found at Bureij, Syria.

The writing at the base of the Melqart Stele is slightly damaged and difficult to read in places. However, the beginning reads, "The statue which Bar-hadad, son of…king of Aram, set up for his lord, for Melqart." This text gives the name Bar-hadad, specifies that he was the son of a king of Aram and therefore probably a king of Aram himself, and states that the statue was dedicated to the god Melqart. The interpretation of this Bar-hadad has been inconsistent due to the disputed name of the father, with some scholars initially favoring Ben-hadad I, son of Tabrimmon, in the 9th century, while other scholars suggested various identities, including Ben-hadad II, or more recently, a Bar-hadad king of Arpad in the 8th century BC.

If the Melqart Stele does refer to Ben-hadad I, son of Tabrimmon, then this is the only currently known archaeological attestation of his existence. However, because of the lack of archaeological context for the stele and damage to certain letters, conclusions must be tentative.

> *Asa took all the silver and the gold which were left in the treasuries of the house of the Lord and the treasuries of the king's house, and delivered them into the hand of his servants. And King Asa sent them to Ben-hadad the son of Tabrimmon, the son of Hezion, king of Aram, who lived in Damascus, saying, "Let there be a treaty between you and me, as between my father and your father. Behold, I have sent you a present of silver and gold; go, break your treaty with Baasha king of Israel so that he will withdraw from me." So Ben-hadad listened to King Asa and sent the commanders of his armies against the cities of Israel* (1 Kings 15:18-20).

Albright, William. "A Votive Stele Erected by Ben-Hadad I of Damascus to the God Melcarth." *Bulletin of the American Schools of Oriental Research* 87 (1942).

Hackett, Jo Ann and Aren Wilson-Wright. "A Revised Interpretation of the Melqart Stele (KAI 201)." *Studies in Ancient Oriental Civilization* 73. Chicago: The Oriental Institute, 2002.

OMRI

The Mesha Stele

Name: Omri

Time Period: 9th century BC (Iron Age II)

Geographical Area: Northern Kingdom of Israel

Biblical Reference(s): 1 Kings 16:15-29

Ancient Source(s): Mesha Stele; Black Obelisk of Shalmaneser III

Identification Rating: Firm (A)

Omri was a powerful 9th-century BC king of the Northern Kingdom of Israel who established the new capital at Samaria and founded the "house of Omri" dynasty, reigning for 12 years from ca. 885–874 BC. Omri had been the commander of the army for Elah, king of Israel, but a power struggle ensued that left Omri the last man standing out of four vying for the throne. Zimri, a chariot commander, assassinated King Elah and proclaimed himself king. Then Omri brought the army and besieged the capital city of Tirzah with Zimri barricaded inside. When the city was breached, Zimri burned himself alive inside the palace, leaving Omri and Tibnah the surviving rivals who claimed the throne.

The ruins of Tirzah (Tell el-Far'ah North) have been excavated and show that a fire destroyed the 9th-century BC (Stratum VIIb) palace where Zimri ended his brief reign of seven days. Omri prevailed in the civil war that followed and became the unopposed king of Israel. After his death, his son Ahab and his grandsons Ahaziah and Jehoram ruled after him until their dynasty of approximately 48 years was eliminated by Jehu. Excavations at Samaria have uncovered a lavish 9th-century BC palace that Omri constructed, along with the probable tomb where he was buried.

Despite being a powerful monarch who achieved the throne through military victory, built a new capital city and palace, and founded a new dynasty of kings, Omri is not extensively documented in the book of Kings or through archaeological sources. However, both the Moabites and the Assyrians name Omri and make reference to him as the originator of a dynasty of Israelite kings in the 9th century BC.

In the Annals of Shalmaneser III from about 841 BC, the Assyrian king refers to Jehu as the "son of Omri." Part of the text reads "In the eighteenth year of my rule I crossed the Euphrates for the sixteenth time...At that time I received the tribute of the inhabitants of Tyre, Sidon, and of Jehu, son of Omri." Another mention of Omri is found on an impressive monument called the Black Obelisk from about 825 BC but referring to events from prior years. A panel of the obelisk describes a scene and states, "The tribute of Jehu, son of Omri" (Black Obelisk of Shalmaneser III). The phrase "house of Omri," describing the Northern Kingdom of Israel in association with the dynasty established by Omri, appears in the 8th-century BC annals of Tiglath-Pileser III and Sargon II and indicates that the Assyrians thought of the royal line of the Northern Kingdom of Israel being established by Omri.

Another neighboring nation, Moab, also named Omri as king of Israel in the 9th century BC and had a personal link to him. The Mesha Stele, inscribed in about 850–840 BC, discusses Omri as a major enemy and adversary of the Moabites: "As for Omri, king of Israel, he humbled Moab many days, for Chemosh was angry at his land. And his son followed him and he also said, 'I will humble Moab.' In my time he spoke, but I have triumphed over him and over his house, while Israel hath perished forever!"

Mesha may have been too young to have had a personal interaction with Omri, although considering that Moab was subject to Israel, it is possible that as a boy he saw Omri during a royal visit or tribute payment. However, his father, Chemosh-yat, was reigning in Moab when Omri came and defeated him, and he certainly knew Omri. The Mesha Stele is therefore a powerful first-hand attestation of the existence, position, and actions of Omri by the Moabite royal family, who was oppressed by the house of Omri for 40 years. The contemporary Assyrian and Moabite attestations of Omri, along with the ruins of his palace at Samaria, clearly identify Omri as a historical king of Israel during the 9th century BC.

> *In the thirty-first year of Asa king of Judah, Omri became king over Israel and reigned twelve years; he reigned six years at Tirzah. He bought*

the hill Samaria from Shemer for two talents of silver; and he built on the hill, and named the city which he built Samaria, after the name of Shemer, the owner of the hill (1 Kings 16:23-24).

Dahood, Mitchell. "The Moabite Stone and Northwest Semitic Philology" 429-41 in *The Archaeology of Jordan and Other Studies Presented to S.H. Horn*. Berrien Spring: Andrews University Press, 1986.

Pritchard, James, ed. *The Ancient Near Eastern Texts Relating to the Old Testament.* 3rd ed. with Supplement. Princeton: Princeton University Press, 1969.

The palace of Omri and Ahab at Samaria

AHAB

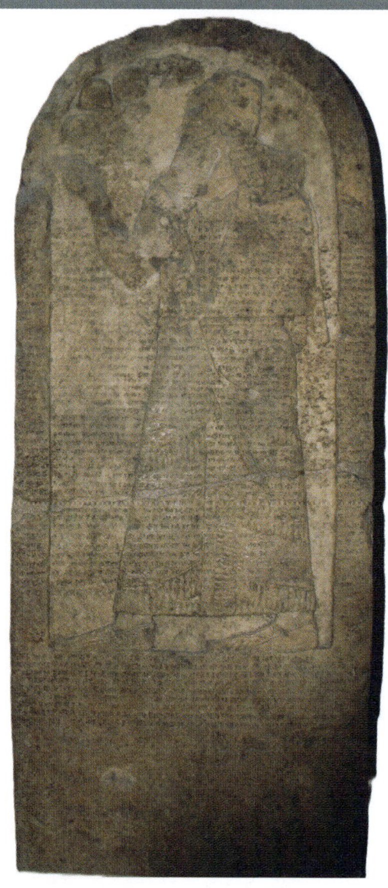
King Ahab mentioned on the Shalmaneser III Monolith Stele

Name: Ahab (son of Omri)

Time Period: 9th century BC (Iron Age II)

Geographical Area: Northern Kingdom of Israel

Biblical Reference(s): 1 Kings 16:28-33; 22:20-40

Ancient Source(s): Shalmaneser III Monolith Stele

Identification Rating: Firm (A)

Ahab was the son of King Omri and successor to the throne of the Northern Kingdom of Israel. From about 874–853 BC, Ahab reigned as the 7th king of Northern Israel for 22 years and was based in his capital city of Samaria. Notorious even among the kings of Northern Israel, Ahab promoted pagan deities, built altars and temples for Baal, persecuted faithful followers of God, and married a Phoenician princess named Jezebel with whom he had at least two sons and one daughter—Ahaziah, Jehoram, and Athaliah (1 Kings 22:40; 2 Kings 1:17; 8:26-27). The wife of Ahab, Jezebel, is attested by an inscribed Phoenician seal, while Ahab's son Jehoram is mentioned on the Tel Dan Stele and his father, Omri, is named on the Mesha Stele.

In addition to addressing religious and domestic issues, Ahab interacted on the international stage with nations including Moab, Aram, Ammon, Qedar, and Assyria. He fought in numerous battles, perhaps most often against Ben-Hadad of Aram, who is documented as fighting Ahab at Samaria, Aphek, and Ramoth-gilead (1 Kings 20:1-30; 22:20-39). However, the most significant military engagement Ahab participated in was the Battle of Qarqar around 853 BC, in which a coalition of smaller kingdoms fought against the Assyrian army under Shalmaneser III.

Metal ring inscribed with Ahab, king of Israel

In this battle, Ahab and Ben-Hadad II of Aram (Hadadezer) joined forces with other kings to stave off the threat of the dominant Assyrians. The events of the Battle of Qarqar and the people involved were recorded on an Assyrian stele referred to as the Shalmaneser III Monolith Stele, one of the two Kurkh Monoliths found at the site of Kurkh, which may have been the ancient Assyrian city of Tushhan. This Assyrian stele names "Ahab the Israelite" as one of the kings opposing Shalmaneser III and notes that Ahab brought 10,000 soldiers and 2,000 chariots. This clear and unmistakable contemporary reference to Ahab, king of Israel, is also interesting, because of all 11 kings mentioned in the coalition, Ahab had the largest chariot force. Archaeologists excavating at Jezreel, the location of one of Ahab's palaces, suggested that its large open courtyard design may have been built to accommodate his chariot force (1 Kings 21:1).

A bronze ring inscribed in archaic Hebrew with "belonging to Ahab king of Israel" might attest to the infamous Ahab, but the lack of parallels to this type of ring from the 9th century BC and questions about the forms of certain letters suggests the possibility that it was crafted centuries later. Ahab is also referenced on the Mesha Stele as the son of Omri who became king, without specifying his name, and on the fragmentary Tel Dan Stele as the father of Jehoram, but the segment containing his name was broken off in antiquity.

> *Ahab the son of Omri became king over Israel in the thirty-eighth year of Asa king of Judah, and Ahab the son of Omri reigned over Israel in Samaria twenty-two years...It came about, as though it had been a trivial thing for him to walk in the sins of Jeroboam the son of Nebat, that he married Jezebel the daughter of Ethbaal king of the Sidonians, and went to serve Baal and worshiped him* (1 Kings 16:29-31).

Luckenbill, D.D. *Historical Records of Assyria from the Earliest Times to Sargon.* Chicago: University of Chicago Press, 1926.

JEZEBEL

Seal of Jezebel

Name: Jezebel (daughter of Ethbaal)

Time Period: 9th century BC (Iron Age IIb)

Geographical Area: Northern Kingdom of Israel

Biblical Reference(s): 1 Kings 16:31; 2 Kings 9:7-37

Ancient Source(s): Seal of Jezebel

Identification Rating: Probable (B)

Queen Jezebel was a Phoenician princess and the daughter of Ethbaal, king of Sidon in the 9th century BC, eventually marrying Ahab, king of Israel. Jezebel seems to have married him around the beginning of his reign, and she survived into the first year of Jehu, meaning she held a position in the royal family from about 874–841 BC. The father of Jezebel, Ethbaal or Ithbaal I, was mentioned as the Phoenician king of Tyre by the 2nd-century BC Phoenician historian Menander of Ephesus, who copied information about the Tyrian kings from their own records (Josephus, *Apion* 1.123).

The infamous Jezebel appears to be attested by a royal seal from the 9th century BC bearing her name. The seal was carved from opal and decorated with iconography typical of the Phoenicians, such as the sphinx and the winged sun typical of royal seals in Israel and Judah, in addition to a Phoenician name inscribed with Phoenician letters. It is a seal fitting of royalty such as Jezebel. The seal is mostly intact except for part of the top where a small area is broken. The name on the seal is preserved as YZBL or Jezebel, although the spelling of her name in the book of Kings is ʻYZBL with an aleph at the beginning. This may be the Hebrew variant spelling, but more likely the missing aleph was in the broken section of the seal where the inscription begins. The inscription may also have begun with the letter *L*, meaning the entire inscription on the seal would have been ʻYZBL or LʻYZBL, translating as "belonging to Jezebel."

Although the seal does not bear the name of her father or her title, the Phoenician name Jezebel means "Where is Baal?" and seems to have been reserved only for royalty, in addition to the high quality of the seal. Further, only about 1 percent of seals from this region and period belonged to women, and in this time and place the name Jezebel appears only as the Phoenician princess who became the wife of Ahab. However, the seal was donated from a private collection, not from an excavation, and although it was subjected to rigorous analysis and research to establish its authenticity, its place and context of discovery is still unknown.

Yet it should be understood that only about 10 percent of seals and bullae come from archaeological excavations, and this particular seal is considered authentic. Thus, it is likely that this was the seal of Jezebel, wife of Ahab, and confirms her existence and position of prominence in the 9th century BC.

> *Ahab the son of Omri did evil in the sight of the* Lord *more than all who were before him. It came about, as though it had been a trivial thing for him to walk in the sins of Jeroboam the son of Nebat, that he married Jezebel the daughter of Ethbaal king of the Sidonians, and went to serve Baal and worshiped him* (1 Kings 16:30-31).

Korpel, Marjo. "Fit for a Queen: Jezebel's Royal Seal." *Biblical Archaeology Review* 34.2 (2008).

BEN-HADAD II

(Hadad-ezer)

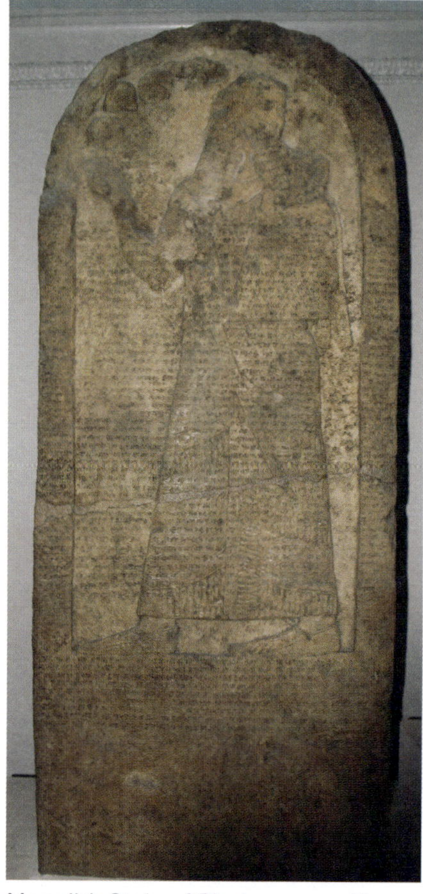
Monolith Stele of Shalmaneser III mentioning Hadad-ezer

Name: Ben-hadad II (Hadad-ezer)

Time Period: 9th century BC (Iron Age II)

Geographical Area: Aram Damascus

Biblical Reference(s): 1 Kings 20:1-34; 2 Kings 8:7-15

Ancient Source(s): Kurkh Monolith Stele of Shalmaneser III

Identification Rating: Probable (B)

Ben-hadad II, also known as Hadad-ezer (Adad-idri), was the successor and probably the son of Ben-Hadad I as the king of Aram, a contemporary of King Ahab of the Northern Kingdom of Israel, ruling about 865–842 BC from Damascus. Although no source uses both of the names Ben-hadad II and Hadad-ezer in one place, the chronological information from the Kurkh Monolith Stele of Shalmaneser III and the book of Kings indicates these names must be referring to the same king of Aram. However, a few scholars have opted to identify them as different individuals, meaning Hadad-ezer would have been a king of Aram during the time of King Ahab but not mentioned anywhere in the Bible.

This Hadad-ezer of Damascus, son of Ben-hadad I, is not to be confused with the Hadadezer king of Zobah, son of Rehob, who lived about 150 years earlier and had interactions with David (2 Samuel 8:3; 1 Chronicles 18:3). Ben-hadad II was murdered by Hazael of Aram, who became king after the assassination (2 Kings 8:7-15).

Ben-hadad II, called Hadad-ezer by the Assyrians, seems to have been the king of Aram involved in the alliance with Ahab against Shalmaneser III at the Battle of Qarqar in about 853 BC. On the Assyrian victory monument of Shalmaneser III that records details of an alliance of 12 kings defeated at Qarqar, the list of enemies begins with "1,200 chariots, 1,200 cavalry, 20,000 soldiers of Hadad-ezer of Damascus." This is the only currently known archaeological attestation of Hadad-ezer, apparently referred to elsewhere as Ben-hadad II. However, a few scholars have suggested that the Melqart Stele mention of "Bar-hadad" refers to Ben-Hadad II, although clear evidence for this specific association is lacking.

While the identification of Hadad-ezer of Aram on this 9th-century BC campaign record of Shalmaneser III is obvious, there is a slight but unlikely possibility that Hadad-ezer and Ben-hadad II were not the same person, but instead two different, successive kings of Aram based in Damascus.

A basalt statue from Assur, an inscription commissioned by Shalmaneser III, notes the death of Hadad-ezer and the subsequent usurpation of the throne by Hazael:

> I defeated Hadadezer of Damascus together with 12 princes, his allies. I stretched upon the ground 20,900 of his strong warriors...Hadadezer perished. Hazael, a son of nobody, seized the throne, called up a numerous army and rose against me. I fought with him and defeated him, taking the chariots of his camp. He disappeared to save his life. I marched as far as Damascus, his royal residence [and cut down his] gardens (RIMA 3, A.0. 102.40).

> *Now Ben-hadad king of Aram gathered all his army, and there were thirty-two kings with him, and horses and chariots. And he went up and besieged Samaria and fought against it. Then he sent messengers to the city to Ahab king of Israel and said to him, "Thus says Ben-hadad..."* (1 Kings 20:1-2).

Luckenbill, David. "Benhadad and Hadadezer." *The American Journal of Semitic Languages and Literatures*, Vol. 27, No. 3 (1911).

Pritchard, James, ed. *The Ancient Near Eastern Texts Relating to the Old Testament.* 3rd edition with Supplement. Princeton: Princeton University Press, 1969.

SHALMANESER III

Shalmaneser III and officials receiving a tribute from Sua

Name: Shalmaneser III

Time Period: 9th century BC (Neo-Assyrian Empire)

Geographical Area: Assyria

Biblical Reference(s): Hosea 10:14

Ancient Source(s): Throne Inscription; Kurkh Monolith; Black Obelisk

Identification Rating: Tentative (C)

Shalmaneser III was an Assyrian king who ruled from ca. 859–824 BC and spent much of his reign expanding the empire, engaging in campaigns to the north, south, east, and west against a variety of foes, such as Urartu, Tubal, Babylon, Elam, Aram, and Israel. In an autobiographical text he describes his lineage and titles, referring to Ashurnasirpal II and Tukulti-Ninurta II:

> (I am) Shalmaneser, the legitimate king, the king of the world, the king without rival, the "Great Dragon," the (only) power within the (four) rims (of the earth), overlord of all the princes, who has smashed all his enemies as if (they be) earthenware, the strong man, unsparing, who shows no mercy in battle, the son of Ashurnasirpal, king of the world, king of Assyria, (grand)son of Tukulti-Ninurta, likewise king of the world, king of Assyria, a conqueror from the Upper Sea to the Lower Sea (Throne Inscription of Shalmaneser III).

At the Battle of Qarqar in 853 BC, Shalmaneser III defeated a coalition of 11 kings, including Ahab of Israel, and asserted his dominance over the region (Kurkh Monolith of Shalmaneser III). Shalmaneser III also had interactions with Jehu of Israel, forcing him into a tribute that was both recorded and depicted on an Assyrian monument (Black Obelisk of Shalmaneser III).

Although unclear, Shalmaneser III might be mentioned by the prophet Hosea in the 8th century BC, long after the death of the Assyrian king. The prophet refers back to a time when "Shalman destroyed Beth-arbel" (Hosea 10:14). This may have been part of his 841 BC campaign in which he defeated Hazael of Aram and received tributes from Tyre, Sidon, and Jehu of Israel "at the mountains of Ba'li-rasi at the side of the sea" thought to be Mount Carmel (Shalmaneser III Calah Bulls Annals). However, this possible naming of Shalmaneser III by Hosea, decades after his reign, lacks definitive evidence and must remain tentative.

> *Therefore a tumult will arise among your people, and all your fortresses will be destroyed, as Shalman destroyed Beth-arbel on the day of battle, when mothers were dashed in pieces with their children* (Hosea 10:14).

Shalmaneser III depicted on his Kurkh Monolith Stele

Astour, Michael. "841 B.C.: The First Assyrian Invasion of Israel." *Journal of the American Oriental Society* Vol. 91, No. 3 (1971).

Pritchard, James, ed. *The Ancient Near Eastern Texts Relating to the Old Testament.* 3rd ed. with Supplement. Princeton: Princeton University Press, 1969.

JEHORAM
(Son of Ahab)

The Tel Dan Stele mentioning Jehoram son of Ahab, among other kings

Name: Jehoram (Joram son of Ahab)

Time Period: 9th century BC (Iron Age IIb)

Geographical Area: Northern Kingdom of Israel

Biblical Reference(s): 2 Kings 1:17; 3:1-27; 8:28–9:26; 2 Chronicles 21:1–22:7

Ancient Source(s): Tel Dan Stele

Identification Rating: Firm (A)

Jehoram of Israel was one of the sons of Ahab and ruled for 12 years from ca. 852–841 BC. Also known as Joram, he fought against Moab and Aram, had an alliance with Ahaziah of Judah, and was eventually assassinated by Jehu, who ended the line of Ahab and usurped the throne of the Northern Kingdom of Israel (2 Kings 3:1-27, 8:28–9:26; 2 Chronicles 21:1–22:7).

The military encounters Jehoram of Israel had with Hazael of Aram, mentioned in the Bible and recorded on an Aramean victory stele, is the context in which he is attested through archaeology. Alongside Ahaziah of Judah, Jehoram of Israel is recorded as having been defeated by the Aramean king, who had his victory inscribed and erected at the city of Dan. A fragmentary section of this stele from approximately 841 BC, just after the death of Jehoram, reads "[I killed Jeho]ram son [of Ahab] king of Israel, and [I] killed [Ahaz]iahu son of [Jehoram kin]g of the House of David" (Tel Dan Stele). According to the Bible and the Tel Dan Stele, both of these kings were killed as a result of the war with Aram around 841 BC. Thus, this stele corroborates part of the war mentioned in the books of Kings and Chronicles and also attests to Jehoram of Israel and his participation in a conflict that brought about his death.

Jehoram of Israel is also referenced indirectly by the Moabite king Mesha on another victory stele from the 9th century BC. King Mesha remarks that "Omri took the land of Madaba, and occupied it in his day, and in the days of his son, 40 years. And Chemosh had mercy on it in my time" (Mesha Stele).

Because in the Bible it is recorded that Jehoram of Israel, the grandson of Omri, was defeated by Mesha, then Jehoram was "his son" at the end of that 40-year period of occupation. Since Omri ruled 12 years, Ahab ruled 22 years, Ahaziah ruled 2 years, and Jehoram ruled 12 years, the 40 years Mesha refers to must have spanned from early in the reign of Omri until around the middle of the reign of Jehoram.

> *Jehu the son of Jehoshaphat the son of Nimshi conspired against Joram. Now Joram with all Israel was defending Ramoth-gilead against Hazael king of Aram, but King Joram had returned to Jezreel to be healed of the wounds which the Arameans had inflicted on him when he fought with Hazael king of Aram. So Jehu said, "If this is your mind, then let no one escape or leave the city to go tell it in Jezreel." Then Jehu rode in a chariot and went to Jezreel, for Joram was lying there. Ahaziah king of Judah had come down to see Joram...And Jehu drew his bow with his full strength and shot Joram between his arms; and the arrow went through his heart and he sank in his chariot* (2 Kings 9:14-24).

Biran, A. and J. Naveh. "The Tel Dan Inscription: A New Fragment." *IEJ* 45 (1995).

MESHA

El-Kerak Inscription mentioning Chemosh-yat, father of Mesha

Name: Mesha (son of Chemosh-yat)

Time Period: 9th century BC (Iron Age IIb)

Geographical Area: Moab

Biblical Reference(s): 2 Kings 3:4-27

Ancient Source(s): Mesha Stele; El-Kerak Inscription

Identification Rating: Firm (A)

Mesha was the king of Moab during the 9th century BC, ruling around the period of 850–840 BC for an unknown number of years and likely succeeding his father, Chemosh-yat. In the book of Kings, Mesha is mentioned in the context of the reign of Jehoram of Israel, who reigned around 852–841 BC. After being dominated by Omri and Ahab, Mesha began to rebel, and in the time of Jehoram he led a successful revolt of the Moabites against a coalition of Israel and Judah that is recorded in both the book of Kings and the Mesha Stele.

The Mesha Stele or Moabite Stone is a 9th-century BC victory monument composed of 34 inscribed lines discovered at Dibon (Dhiban) in Moab. The inscription is the longest of the few known in the Moabite language, and it identifies Mesha of Moab; his father, Chemosh-yat, who ruled for 30 years; Omri of Israel, the son of Omri (Ahab); the tribe of Gad; multiple cities, such as Dibon and Ataroth; and human sacrifice dedicated to Chemosh, the primary god of Moab:

> I am Mesha, son of Chemosh-yat, king of Moab, from Dibon. My father ruled over Moab for 30 years and I ruled after my father… Omri was king of Israel, and oppressed Moab during many days… Now Omri took the land of Madeba, and occupied it in his day, and in the days of his son, 40 years…I killed in all 7,000 men, boys, women, girls and maid-servants, for I had devoted them to destruction for Ashtar-Chemosh (Mesha Stele).

This victory monument of Mesha also has the earliest known Semitic inscription mentioning Yahweh and another important 9th century BC reference to the house of David. The Mesha Stele also gives additional chronological information that can be compared to the books of Kings and Chronicles, since it records that the oppression of Moab lasted 40 years. In the book of Kings, Jehoram of Israel, the grandson of Omri, is named as the king who fought against Mesha and therefore would have been in power at the end of that 40-year period. The 40 years referenced in the stele would include most of the 12-year reign of Omri, the 22-year reign of Ahab, the two-year reign of Ahaziah, and a few years into the 12-year reign of Jehoram.

The Mesha Stele mentioning King Mesha of Moab

The lineage of Mesha is also mentioned on a fragmentary inscription that appears to have been broken off a statue, which many scholars suggest was also commissioned by Mesha. The beginning is broken off, but part of it reads "Chemosh-yat, king of Moab, the D[ibonite in the temple of] Chemosh in sacrifice" (El-Kerak Inscription). Thus, Mesha the king of Moab is attested by his own victory stele that also records a detailed version of the oppression and conflict between Israel and Moab during the 9th century BC from his perspective, names Omri and several locations, and gives insight into the religious beliefs and practices of ancient Moab.

With his name and title on the Moabite Stone, his lineage on the El-Kerak Inscription, archaeological evidence for his kingdom in Moab, and chronological information placing his reign in the middle of the 9th century BC, Mesha is firmly established as a historical king who lived around the time of Ahab, Ahaziah, and Jehoram.

Now Mesha king of Moab was a sheep breeder, and used to pay the king of Israel 100,000 lambs and the wool of 100,000 rams. But when

Ahab died, the king of Moab rebelled against the king of Israel. And King Jehoram went out of Samaria at that time and mustered all Israel. Then he went and sent word to Jehoshaphat the king of Judah, saying, "The king of Moab has rebelled against me. Will you go with me to fight against Moab?" And he said, "I will go up; I am as you are, my people as your people, my horses as your horses."... Then he took his oldest son who was to reign in his place, and offered him as a burnt offering on the wall. And there came great wrath against Israel, and they departed from him and returned to their own land (2 Kings 3:4-7, 27).

Mykytiuk, Lawrence. *Identifying Biblical Persons in Northwest Semitic Inscriptions of 1200–539 BC.* Atlanta: Society of Biblical Literature, 2004.

Reed, William and Fred Winnett. "A Fragment of an Early Moabite Inscription from Kerak." *BASOR* 172 (1963).

Moabite relief from Redjom el A'abed depicting a deity, possibly Chemosh

HAZAEL

Hazael named on the Stele of Zakkur

Name: Hazael

Time Period: 9th century BC (Iron Age IIb)

Geographical Area: Aram Damascus

Biblical Reference(s): 1 Kings 19:15-17; 2 Kings 8:8–9:17; 10:32; 12:17-18; 13:3-25; 2 Chronicles 22:5-6; Amos 1:4

Ancient Source(s): Black Obelisk of Shalmaneser III; Stele of Zakkur; statue inscription of Shalmaneser III

Identification Rating: Firm (A)

Hazael was the king of Aram based at Damascus and ruled approximately 842–800 BC, though his exact length of reign is disputed. Although his son was his successor, his father is unknown, and according to Assyrian records and the Bible, Hazael was not in the royal line of the previous kings but an official of Bar-Haddad II, who usurped the throne by assassination and established a new dynasty in Aram. Hazael was a contemporary of other kings in the region, such as Shalmaneser III of Assyria, Zakkur of Hamath, Joram, Jehu, and Jehoahaz of Israel, and Ahaziah, Athaliah, and Joash of Judah. In the Bible, Hazael and his actions are referenced extensively in the book of Kings, while he is also briefly mentioned in the books of Chronicles and Amos.

The story of how Hazael rose to power is narrated in the book of Kings and broadly corroborated by Assyrian records. When King Bar-Hadad II was ill, Hazael, described only as a servant who had access to the king and was trusted, consulted with the prophet Elisha, who predicted the death of Bar-Hadad and the rise of Hazael. Emboldened by what he heard, Hazael took matters into his own hands and assassinated Bar-Hadad II by asphyxiation and then usurped the throne (2 Kings 8:7-15). The Assyrian records of Shalmaneser III inscribed on a basalt statue from Assur confirm his status as an official who was outside of the royal family by calling him the son of a nobody: "Hadadezer perished. Hazael, a son of nobody, seized the throne, called up a numerous army and rose against me" (RIMA 3, A.0. 102.40). Elsewhere, Shalmaneser III mentions defeating Hazael around 838 BC, recounting that he "marched to the cities of Hazael of Damascus; I captured four of his centers" (Black Obelisk of Shalmaneser III).

Ivory carving from Arslan Tash possibly depicting Hazael

During his reign, Hazael fought with and against multiple kings in the region, including conflicts with the kings of Israel and Judah. The Tel Dan Stele, inscribed around 841 BC, appears to have been a product of Hazael of Aram recording his war against Israel and Judah and records the results of a war between Aram on one side and Israel and Judah on the other side. The victory stele claims that his "father" (probably his predecessor, Bar-Hadad II) had previously fought against Israel and died and how he had been made the new king by decree of the Aramean god Hadad. The propagandistic text then describes how the king of Aram defeated and killed Jehoram of Israel and Ahaziah of Judah. According to the books of Kings and Chronicles, both kings were killed as a result of a war with Hazael of Aram (2 Kings 8:26–9:28; 2 Chronicles 22:1-9). Although the Aramean and biblical versions of the events differ in details, Hazael probably took credit for the deaths of both Jehoram and Ahaziah even if he was not directly responsible.

It is also likely that the campaign of Hazael resulting in the capture of Gath (2 Kings 12:17) is demonstrated through a siege system and destruction layer uncovered during excavations dating to the

Ivory plaque from Arslan Tash, naming Lord Hazael

9th century BC, although an inscription attributing this to Hazael has not been found at the site.

Hazael is attested on numerous other monuments and inscriptions, including a decorative ivory plaque from the Assyrian palace at Hadatu with an Aramaic dedication to "Lord Hazael" (KAI 232), bronze horse frontlets inscribed for "Lord Hazael" (KAI 311), and a victory stele from Hazrach. Hazael and his son and successor, Bar-Hadad III, are both acknowledged as kings of Aram on the Stele of Zakkur from around 800–780 BC, which notes, "Bar-Hadad, son of Hazael, king of Aram, united against me 17 kings" (KAI 202). King Hazael himself may be depicted by an ivory carving discovered at Arslan Tash, ancient Hadatu.

Therefore, Hazael is established by multiple sources as a 9th-century BC son of a nobody who became the king of Damascus and passed the throne on to his son Bar-Hadad III.

> *Hazael said, "But what is your servant, who is but a dog, that he should do this great thing?" And Elisha answered, "The* L*ORD has shown me that you will be king over Aram." So he departed from Elisha and returned to his master, who said to him, "What did Elisha say to you?" And he answered, "He told me that you would surely recover." On the following day, he took the cover and dipped it in water and spread it on his face, so that he died. And Hazael became king in his place* (2 Kings 8:13-15).

Noegel, Scott. "The Zakkur Inscription." *The Ancient Near East: Historical Sources in Translation*. Oxford: Blackwell Publishing, 2006.

Pritchard, James, ed. *The Ancient Near Eastern Texts Relating to the Old Testament*. 3rd edition with Supplement. Princeton: Princeton University Press, 1969.

Younger, K. Lawson Jr. "'Hazael, Son of a Nobody': Some Reflections in Light of Recent Study" in *Writing and Ancient Near Eastern Society*. London: T&T Clark, 2005.

Stone plaza outside the city gate at Dan

AHAZIAH

(Son of Athaliah)

Stele fragment mentioning Ahaziah of Judah

Name: Ahaziah (son of Athaliah)

Time Period: 9th century BC (Iron Age IIb)

Geographical Area: Kingdom of Judah

Biblical Reference(s): 2 Kings 8:26–9:28; 2 Chronicles 22:1-9

Ancient Source(s): The Tel Dan Stele

Identification Rating: Probable (B)

Ahaziah, son of Jehoram, was the fifth king of Judah and had a brief reign of one year from about 841–840 BC. According to the books of Kings and Chronicles, Ahaziah of Judah went to war alongside Jehoram (Joram) of Israel against Hazael of Aram. The battle, which took place at Ramoth-gilead, was a victory for Aram, and Jehoram was removed from the field of battle after being severely wounded by archers and brought to Jezreel.

Ahaziah then also went to Jezreel, where Jehu attacked both Jehoram and Ahaziah, resulting in the deaths of both kings of Israel and Judah. Jehu ascended to the throne of Israel, and Queen Athaliah assassinated many in the royal house of Judah and usurped the throne of Judah. Thus, the alliance between Jehoram of Israel and Ahaziah of Judah against Hazael of Aram had resulted in an epic disaster for the divided kingdoms—a lost battle and the death of both kings, political assassinations, and usurpations of the thrones.

Archaeology enters into the discussion of Ahaziah of Judah when an Aramean victory monument called the Tel Dan Stele is analyzed. This incredibly important stele, often referenced in connection to its mention of David, was inscribed around 841 BC in Aramaic and records the results of a war between Aram on one side and Israel and Judah on the other side. The Aramean king, who must have been Hazael of Aram based on the context, describes how his father had previously fought against Israel, had died, and how he, then, was made the new king by decree of the Aramean god Hadad.

The stele then relates how the new king, Hazael, went to war again and killed two kings identified as Jehoram of Israel and Ahaziah of Judah. Although the stele was broken in antiquity and the text is therefore fragmentary, many epigraphers argue that the partially preserved names of these two kings can be reconstructed as Jehoram and Ahaziah, since it is clear that kings of both Israel and Judah are named, the names end in "ram" (Jeho-ram) and "iahu" (Ahaz-iahu), and both were killed as a result of a war with Hazael of Aram around 841 BC. While the Aramean version of events and the biblical version of events differ slightly—the stele claims the king of Aram killed the two kings while the Bible gives a detailed account of their assassination by Jehu—the Aramean king Hazael was probably taking credit for their deaths from events he set in motion, or he may have even thought they both died in the battle or from wounds sustained in the battle. Therefore, not only does this Aramean victory text appear to substantiate a battle mentioned in the books of Kings and Chronicles, but it also seems to name Ahaziah of Judah as a participant in the battle who was ultimately killed.

> *When Ahaziah the king of Judah saw this, he fled by the way of the garden house. And Jehu pursued him and said, "Shoot him too, in the chariot." So they shot him at the ascent of Gur, which is at Ibleam. But he fled to Megiddo and died there* (2 Kings 9:27).

Lemaire, André. "The Tel Dan Stela as a Piece of Royal Historiography." *Journal for the Study of the Old Testament*, Vol. 23, Issue 81 (1998).

JEHU

Israelite tribute to Shalmaneser III

Name: Jehu (son of Jehoshaphat)

Time Period: 9th century BC (Iron Age IIb)

Geographical Area: Northern Kingdom of Israel

Biblical Reference(s): 2 Kings 9:2–10:36; 2 Chronicles 22:7-9

Ancient Source(s): Black Obelisk of Shalmaneser III; Annalistic Text of Shalmaneser III

Identification Rating: Firm (A)

Jehu became king of Israel after assassinating Jehoram of Israel and eliminating the line of Omri, establishing his own dynasty that lasted for five generations and reigning for 28 years from 841–814 BC. Jehu was the son of Jehoshaphat, son of Nimshi, not to be confused with Jehoshaphat of Judah. On his quest to obtain the throne and consolidate power, Jehu killed King Jehoram, King Ahaziah, Queen Jezebel, 70 princes of the Omri dynasty, 42 relatives of Ahaziah, and the worshippers of Ba'al (2 Kings 9:24–10:25).

During Jehu's reign, the Arameans defeated Israel and took over much of the land (2 Kings 10:32). However, at that time, the Neo-Assyrian Empire was also gaining power and influence under the leadership of Shalmaneser III. Jehu, needing an ally against Aram and other possible foes, such as Moab, Judah, and the Phoenicians, sent a tribute to Assyria that secured a powerful overlord. In year 18 of Shalmaneser, about 841 BC, his annals name Jehu and state, "At that time I received the tribute of the inhabitants of Tyre, Sidon, and of Jehu, son of Omri" (Calah Bulls, Year 18 Annalistic Text). Although Jehu was not in the line of Omri, the Assyrians often referred to the Northern Kingdom of Israel as the house of Omri, and Shalmaneser III may have been unaware that Jehu had established a new dynasty unrelated to Omri and Ahab.

On another famous monument of Shalmaneser III from Kalhu, the Assyrian king describes the tribute that Jehu gave him: "The tribute of Jehu, son of Omri: I received from him silver, gold, a golden bowl, a golden vase with pointed bottom, golden tumblers, golden buckets, tin, a staff for a king, and wooden spears" (Black Obelisk of Shalmaneser III). Below this text naming Jehu, an illustrative panel is shown with Shalmaneser III of Assyria on the left, standing under a parasol with two Assyrian officials behind him, while Jehu of Israel bows down with his face to the ground. The three adjacent panels on the obelisk show Israelites bringing the tribute described in the text. It is unlikely that the person bowing in front of Shalmaneser III is merely an emissary of Jehu, since the Assyrian king would want to showcase his dominance by illustrating foreign rulers bowing rather than an unnamed servant. This would be the oldest currently known depiction of any king of Israel or Judah. Jehu is also mentioned in two other texts of Shalmaneser III—the Kurba'il Statue and the Marble Slab of Shalmaneser.

Although the Bible does not describe any specific interactions between Jehu and the Assyrians, he is named in four contemporary documents of Shalmaneser III and depicted alongside an inscription recording his tribute.

> *Now the rest of the acts of Jehu and all that he did and all his might, are they not written in the Book of the Chronicles of the Kings of Israel? And Jehu slept with his fathers, and they buried him in Samaria. And Jehoahaz his son became king in his place. Now the time which Jehu reigned over Israel in Samaria was twenty-eight years* (2 Kings 10:34-36).

Pritchard, James, ed. *The Ancient Near Eastern Texts Relating to the Old Testament.* 3rd ed. with Supplement. Princeton: Princeton University Press, 1969.

Jehu bowing down on the Black Obelisk of Shalmaneser III

JEHOASH
(Son of Ahaziah)

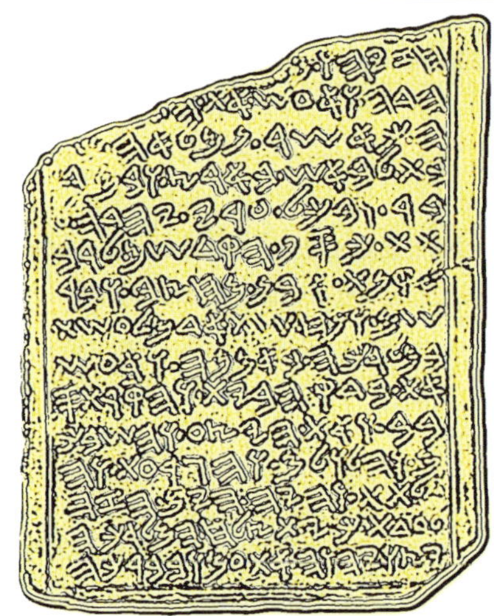

The Jehoash inscription mentioning the king and repairs to the temple

Name: Jehoash (Joash son of Ahaziah)

Time Period: 9th century BC (Iron Age IIb)

Geographical Area: Kingdom of Judah

Biblical Reference(s): 2 Kings 11:21–12:21; 2 Chronicles 24:1-27

Ancient Source(s): Jehoash Tablet; Jehoash Ostracon

Identification Rating: Tentative (C)

Jehoash of Judah was the son of Ahaziah and Zibiah, ruling for 40 years from approximately 835–796 BC. He is not to be confused with Jehoash of Israel, whose reign overlapped with his for a few years. Hazael of Aram was a contemporary of his and invaded Judah, captured Gath, and marched on Jerusalem. Before the city was attacked, Jehoash of Judah paid a tribute to Hazael so he would cease hostilities and leave Jerusalem (2 Kings 12:17-18; 2 Chronicles 24:23-24). However, the disastrous policies and actions of Jehoash near the end of his reign prompted a group of his servants to conspire and assassinate him (2 Kings 12:20-21; 2 Chronicles 24:25-26). Despite the failures later in his reign, Jehoash is known for repairing the temple of Yahweh in Jerusalem when Jehoida the priest was advising him (2 Kings 12:2-16; 2 Chronicles 24:4-14).

Outside of the Bible, Jehoash of Judah is named in an inscribed tablet that mentions the repairs to the temple during his reign and an ostracon about a donation to the temple, but scholars debate the authenticity of these artifacts. The tablet, inscribed in ancient Hebrew on gray sandstone, describes repairs to the house of Yahweh (temple of the Lord) by King Jehoash of Judah, son of Ahaziah; and it came to the attention of scholars via the antiquities market in 2001. The stone tablet, partially broken, measures 24 inches long by 12 inches wide and still includes 15 visible lines of ancient Hebrew text. The inscription mentions "I am Jehoash, son of Ahaziah, king of Judah, and I performed the work on this house…I made the repair of the Temple...May Yahweh ordain His people with blessing" (Jehoash Inscription). This tablet not only names Jehoash, his title, his lineage, and his location, but records the important event of the temple repairs he ordered and oversaw that are also mentioned in the books of Kings and Chronicles.

Jehoash of Judah may also be identified on an ostracon from a private collection, although alternatively it may refer to Josiah of Judah, and yet the authenticity has been questioned by a few scholars. The text is written in ink on a sherd of pottery and reads, "As Ashyahu the king has ordered you to give by the hand of Zecharyahu silver of Tarshish to the House of Yahweh three shekels." If this ostracon were referring to Jehoash of Judah, and if authentic, then it would appear to also name the priest Zechariah, son of Jehoida, who is mentioned during the reign of Jehoash (2 Chronicles 24:20-22).

The tablet naming Jehoash and discussing his repairs to the temple in Jerusalem was supposedly found by accident near the eastern wall of the Temple Mount of Jerusalem in a Muslim cemetery when a grave was being dug. Analysis of the stone itself indicates that it was quarried from the Jerusalem area, while residue found on the stone demonstrates its antiquity, and remnants of melted gold found on the stone suggest that it may have been in the temple area when the Babylonians burned the temple in 587 BC and caused gold to melt. Both the form of the letters and the mention of King Jehoash of Judah place its origin in the 9th century BC.

Studies conducted on the script, language, and grammar did not reach a consensus, but several experts have concluded that the inscription is either authentic or that there is no evidence to prove it is a forgery. If authentic, the Jehoash Inscription would be clear attestation of King Jehoash of Judah and one of the most important events during his reign recorded in the books of Kings and Chronicles.

> *King Jehoash called for Jehoiada the priest, and for the other priests and said to them, "Why do you not repair the damages of the house? Now therefore take no more money from your acquaintances, but pay it for the damages of the temple"... They gave the money which was weighed out into the hands of those who did the work, who had the oversight of the house of the* LORD*; and they paid it out to the carpenters and the builders who worked on the house of the* LORD*; and to the masons and the stonecutters, and for buying timber and hewn stone to repair the damages to the house of the* LORD*, and for all that was laid out for the house to repair it* (2 Kings 12:7-12).

Cohen, Chaim. "Biblical Hebrew Philology in the light of research on the new yeho'ash Royal Building Inscription" in *New Seals and Inscriptions: Hebrew, Idumean, and Cuneiform.* Sheffield: Sheffield Phoenix Press, 2007.

Eph'al, Israel and Joseph Naveh. "Remarks on the Recently Published Moussaieff Ostraca." *Israel Exploration Journal* Vol. 48, No. 3/4 (1998).

Ilani, Shimon, Amnon Rosenfeld, Howard R. Feldman, Wolfgang E. Krumbein, and Joel Kronfeld. "Archaeometric analysis of the 'Jehoash Inscription' tablet." *Journal of Archaeological Science* 35 (2008).

Area on Mount Moriah in Jerusalem where the temple of Solomon once stood

BEN-HADAD III

The Stele of Zakkur

Name: Ben-hadad III (son of Hazael)

Time Period: 800 BC (Iron Age IIb)

Geographical Area: Aram Damascus

Biblical Reference(s): 2 Kings 13:3-25

Ancient Source(s): Stele of Zakkur

Identification Rating: Firm (A)

Ben-hadad III, or Bar-hadad III, was a king of Aram and the son of King Hazael, ruling for only a short period around 800 BC or immediately after and during the time of Jehoahaz of Israel and Jehoash of Israel. This was a period in which Aram and Israel fought each other multiple times, with Israel eventually reclaiming their captured cities that Ben-hadad III had earlier conquered. In the Bible, this Ben-hadad (III) is differentiated as the son of Hazael, ruling after and from a different family than the earlier Ben-hadad (I), son of Tabrimmon, and the next Ben-hadad (II), also known as Hadadezer.

Ben-hadad III is mentioned along with his father, Hazael, on the Stele of Zakkur (KAI 202), which broadly dates to 800–780 BC and survives only partially intact. The stele was discovered at Tell Afis in Syria and originally featured an image of King Zakkur or possibly the god he invokes, Baalshamin, but now only the lower part of the legs and feet are visible. Aramaic inscriptions are found on the front below the image and both the right and left sides of the stele for a total of 48 lines of text. A section relevant to the life of Ben-Hadad III found on this Aramaic monument reads "I am Zakkur, king of Hamath and Luash… Bar-Hadad, son of Hazael, king of Aram, united against me 17 kings."

The inscription on the Stele of Zakkur demonstrates that just after 800 BC, there was a king of Aram named Bar-hadad (or Ben-hadad III) who was the son of Hazael, and that he successfully united several kings against a rival kingdom. Within the context of the biblical narrative, these events appear to fall into the reign of Jehoash of Israel, who also was at war with Ben-hadad III. Because the name of the king, the name of his father, the name of his kingdom, and his chronological placement are all given in the Stele of Zakkur, the identification of this Ben-hadad III who fought against Jehoahaz and his son Jehoash can be confirmed from archaeological data.

> *When Hazael king of Aram died, Ben-hadad his son became king in his place. Then Jehoash the son of Jehoahaz took again from the hand of Ben-hadad the son of Hazael the cities which he had taken in war from the hand of Jehoahaz his father. Three times Joash defeated him and recovered the cities of Israel* (2 Kings 13:24-25).

Hallo, W. and K. Younger, eds. *Context of Scripture*, Vol. 2. Boston: Brill, 2000.

Noegel, Scott. "The Zakkur Inscription." *The Ancient Near East: Historical Sources in Translation*. Oxford: Blackwell Publishing, 2006.

JEHOASH
(Son of Jehoahaz)

Tell al-Rimah Stele

Name: Jehoash (Joash, son of Jehoahaz)

Time Period: 8th century BC (Iron Age IIb)

Geographical Area: Kingdom of Israel

Biblical Reference(s): 2 Kings 13:10–14:16; 2 Chronicles 25:17-25

Ancient Source(s): Tell al-Rimah Stele

Identification Rating: Firm (A)

Jehoash, son of Jehoahaz, was the 12th king of the Northern Kingdom of Israel, reigning for 16 years from approximately 798–782 BC. Jehoash of Israel is also referred to by the name Joash, not to be confused with Jehoash of Judah, son of Ahaziah and Zibiah. Jehoash of Israel was a successful military leader, first achieving three victories over Aram and recovering cities that Hazael had taken from Israel (2 Kings 13:25). Later, he defeated Judah at Beth-Shemesh and captured King Ahaziah, then proceeded to Jerusalem, where he tore down 400 cubits of the city wall, looted the temple, and took hostages back to Samaria (2 Kings 14:11-14; 2 Chronicles 25:21-24).

Despite Jehoash of Israel having a substantial reign and numerous military victories, he is currently known from only one archaeological source. An Assyrian monument of Adad-Nirari III mentions a tribute sent from Jehoash, stating, "He received the tribute of Ia'asu (Jehoash) the Samarian" (Tell el-Rimah Stele). Jehoash of Israel is designated as "the Samaritan" because Samaria was the capital of the Northern Kingdom of Israel and from where Jehoash ruled, and the Assyrians often referred to this kingdom in reference to Samaria or the house of Omri. The Tell al-Rimah Stele was discovered in Nineveh Province at a site thought to be ancient Qatara or Karana, and the stele was commissioned in about 797 BC, just after the reign of Jehoash of Israel had begun.

In addition to mentioning the tribute paid by Jehoash the Samarian, the text specifically mentions subjugating Damascus. Adad-Nirari III was a contemporary of Jehoash of Israel, ruling approximately 810–783 BC, and the conquest of Damascus by a "savior" in the book of Kings prior to the time of Jehoash probably refers to this campaign of Adad-Nirari III (2 Kings 13:5).

> *In the thirty-seventh year of Joash king of Judah, Jehoash the son of Jehoahaz became king over Israel in Samaria, and reigned sixteen years* (2 Kings 13:10).

Page, Stephanie. "A Stela of Adad-nirari III and Nergal-ereš from Tell al Rimah." *Iraq* 30, No. 2 (1968).

MENAHEM

Iran Stele mentioning Menahem of Samaria, among other kings

Name: Menahem

Time Period: 8th century BC (Iron Age IIb)

Geographical Area: Kingdom of Israel

Biblical Reference(s): 2 Kings 15:14-23

Ancient Source(s): Calah Annal 13; Iran Stele; Annals of Tiglath-Pileser III

Identification Rating: Firm (A)

Menahem, son of Gadi, seized the throne and became king of Israel after killing Shallum, reigning from about 752–742 BC. Menahem is only briefly mentioned in the book of Kings, but it does record that during his reign, Pul, king of Assyria, came to Israel, and Menahem paid him a tribute of 1,000 talents of silver (2 Kings 15:19).

In the records of Tiglath-Pileser III of Assyria, not only is Menahem of Israel named, but his tribute is mentioned. From a stele set up after 737 BC in which the Assyrian king recounted various defeated kings and tributes, he stated, "I received tribute from Kushtashpi of Commagene, Rezin of Damascus, Menahem of Samaria..." (Iran Stele of Tiglath-Pileser III). A similar inscription was found at Calah that names Menahem of Samaria (Calah Annal 13). In another official text, Tiglath-Pileser III recorded that "as for Menahem I overwhelmed him [like a snowstorm] and he...fled like a bird, alone, [and bowed to my feet(?)]. I returned him to his place [and imposed tribute upon him]" (Annals of Tiglath-Pileser III). This appears to be the Assyrian version of Menahem being defeated and forced to pay a tribute to the Assyrians mentioned in the book of Kings.

Although the book of Kings uses the name Pul for the king of Assyria in the episode with Menahem, elsewhere the name Tiglath-Pileser is found, and the book of Chronicles equates the two as different names for one person (2 Kings 15:29; 16:7-10; 1 Chronicles 5:26). Many scholars regard Pul as his original name and Tiglath-Pileser III as his throne name. Others suggest Pul was the name he used in reference to his title as king of Babylon, while a few have claimed that Pul and Tiglath-Pileser III were different people. Menahem of Israel is named in only three sources of the Assyrian king Tiglath-Pileser III, but these are consistent with the period in which he reigned and include the details of being defeated by Assyria and paying a tribute.

> *Pul, king of Assyria, came against the land, and Menahem gave Pul a thousand talents of silver so that his hand might be with him to strengthen the kingdom under his rule. Then Menahem exacted the money from Israel, even from all the mighty men of wealth, from each man fifty shekels of silver to pay the king of Assyria. So the king of Assyria returned and did not remain there in the land* (2 Kings 15:19-20).

Hallo, William W. and K. Lawson Younger. *Context of Scripture*. Boston: Brill, 2000.

Pritchard, James, ed. *The Ancient Near Eastern Texts Relating to the Old Testament*. 3rd ed. with Supplement. Princeton: Princeton University Press, 1969.

UZZIAH
(Azariah)

Uzziah burial inscription

Name: Uzziah (Azariah)

Time Period: 8th century BC (Iron Age IIb)

Geographical Area: Kingdom of Judah

Biblical Reference(s): 2 Kings 15:1–32; 2 Chronicles 26:1-23; Isaiah 1:1; Hosea 1:1; Amos 1:1

Ancient Source(s): Annals of Tiglath-Pileser III; Seal of Abiyah; Seal of Shebnayaw

Identification Rating: Firm (A)

Uzziah, also known as Azariah, was a king of Judah who ruled for 52 years, perhaps about 787–736 BC, although numerous varying chronologies exist for the exact years of his reign. The son of Amaziah, his predecessor, and Jecoliah, his time as king overlapped with a tumultuous period in the Northern Kingdom of Israel that saw six different monarchs occupy the throne—Jeroboam II, Zechariah, Shallum, Menahem, Pekahiah, and Pekah. The prophets Isaiah, Hosea, and Amos also lived during the reign of Uzziah (Azariah), and the king is mentioned in their eponymous books.

During the lengthy reign of Uzziah, he oversaw building projects in Jerusalem, defeated the Philistines, exacted tribute from Ammon, and equipped an impressive army. However, Uzziah was also struck with leprosy near the end of his reign, and the nation endured a destructive earthquake around 760 BC. The time of Uzziah also saw the Neo-Assyrian empire rise to dominance under the leadership of Tiglath-Pileser III, who attacked Israel and exacted tribute from Judah. When Uzziah died, he was buried near the other royal tombs in the City of David, and his son Jotham became king of Judah.

The most controversial attestation of Uzziah (Azariah) is the mention of him in the annals of the Assyrian king Tiglath-Pileser III. In a text from year three of Tiglath-Pileser III around 743 BC, the monarch claims that during a campaign

Seal of Shebnayaw, servant of Uzziah

in the Levant, he received a tribute of "Azriyau from Yauda" (Kalhu Annals, K6205). The personal name Azriyau appears to match Azariah (or Azaryah), the place name matches the spelling used for Judah in other Assyrian documents, and the time period overlaps with Uzziah's reign. However, scholars are divided on the identification, with various explanations, including a claim that the piece of the annals should actually be connected with records of Sennacherib. Yet there is no other leader called Azariah of Judah from this period that this name could be plausibly connected to.

Another ancient inscription naming Uzziah is unquestionably referring to the monarch of Judah in the 8th century BC and discusses his burial, but the Aramaic inscription appears to have been made around the 1st century rather than the time of Uzziah. The text on the tablet notes that "the bones of Uzziah, king of Judah" had been brought there, and it seems to have been a reburial of his remains (Uzziah Tablet).

However, two Hebrew seals naming Uzziah have also been discovered, and their authenticity and connection to King Uzziah are clear. The seals, which would have been used by officials in the royal administration of Uzziah, did emerge on the antiquities market, but they were both found and documented in the middle of the 19th century, long before forgers had the knowledge and tools to emulate 8th-century BC Hebrew seals.

The seal of Abiyah was carved from agate and has Egyptian iconography in the middle, showing a kneeling Horus with horns and the sun disk on a lotus. The Hebrew text flanks each side of the figure and reads "belonging to Abiyah, servant of Uziyah."

The seal of Shebnayaw was carved from red limestone and has two different faces. Side A shows a man holding a staff with the Hebrew inscription "belonging to Shebnayaw," while Side B shows winged suns above and below two lines of Hebrew text that read "belonging to Shebnayaw, servant of Uziyah."

Despite the seals coming from the antiquities market and the identification of "Azariah of Judah" in the Assyrian text being questioned by a few, the archaeological attestation for Uzziah of Judah is compelling.

> *In the twenty-seventh year of Jeroboam king of Israel, Azariah son of Amaziah king of Judah became king. He was sixteen years old when he became king, and he reigned fifty-two years in Jerusalem; and his mother's name was Jecoliah of Jerusalem* (2 Kings 15:1-2).

Avigad, Nahman. *Corpus of West Semitic Stamp Seals.* Jerusalem: Hebrew University, 1997.

Pritchard, James, ed. *The Ancient Near Eastern Texts Relating to the Old Testament.* 3rd ed. with Supplement. Princeton: Princeton University Press, 1969.

Tadmor, Hayim. "Azarijau of Yaudi." *Scripta Hierosolymitana* 8 (1961).

ISAIAH

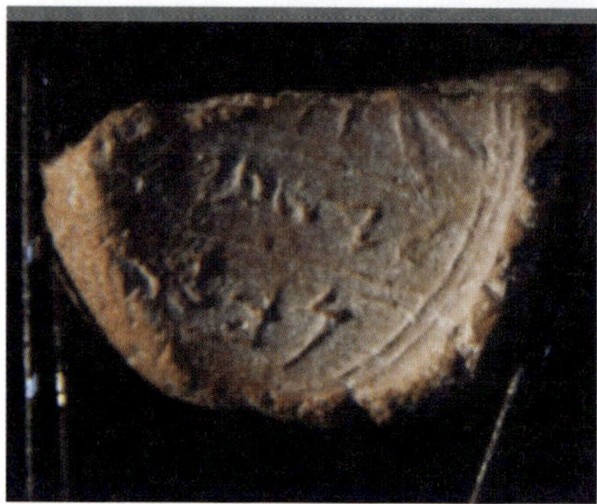
Bulla of Isaiah the prophet

Name: Isaiah (son of Amoz)

Time Period: 8th and 7th centuries BC (Iron Age II)

Geographical Area: Kingdom of Judah

Biblical Reference(s): 2 Kings 19:2–20:19; 2 Chronicles 32:20; Isaiah 1:1; 39:8

Ancient Source(s): Bulla of Isaiah

Identification Rating: Firm (A)

Isaiah was one of the most famous prophets of antiquity, living during the 8th and 7th centuries BC around 760–680 BC and functioning as a prophet about 740–686 BC during the reigns of kings Uzziah, Jotham, Ahaz, Hezekiah, and Manasseh. Isaiah was the son of Amoz and married a woman identified only as the prophetess, with whom he had two sons. Isaiah wrote one of the longest books in the Bible, the oldest copy of which is preserved on the Great Isaiah Scroll that dates to the 300s BC according to radiocarbon testing. According to later sources, Isaiah was executed by being sawn in two during the reign of Manasseh (cf. Hebrews 11:37; Yevamot 49b:8).

Despite fulfilling the role of prophet for more than 50 years, serving under multiple kings, and encountering the Assyrians, until recently there was no archaeology directly attesting to the renowned Isaiah, and at present, there is no archaeological confirmation for the prophets Hosea, Nahum, and Micah, who were contemporary with Isaiah. This all changed when excavations of an Iron Age II layer of the 8th to 7th century BC at the Ophel area in Jerusalem unearthed a seal impression. This discovery was a clay bulla about 1.3 cm in diameter impressed by a seal with the name "Isaiah" and the title "prophet" in the paleo-Hebrew script.

The seal is divided into three registers, with the top line showing an image or a symbol of what appears to be an animal and the middle and bottom lines containing Hebrew text. Although the bulla has a small piece broken off, most of the letters are preserved, and it reads "belonging to Isaiah, prophet," transliterated as L-YSAYH[W] NBY[A] (1 Kings 19:2). The suggestion that the NBY[...]

"prophet" part could be a name is extremely unlikely, since there is only one previously known and rare personal or place name associated with those first three letters, "Nebaioth," and there does not appear to be sufficient space for the additional *W* and *T* required for "Nebaioth" on the final line of the bulla (1 Chronicles 1:29; Isaiah 60:7).

Excavations in this area also discovered a bulla of one of the kings Isaiah served under, Hezekiah of Judah, along with 32 other Hebrew bullae with various names. It was found outside what has been called the "royal bakery," where royal officials and other dignitaries may have discarded old letters and the clay seals attached to those documents. Another important official bulla from the time of Isaiah was found about 100 meters to the northwest of the Western Wall in Jerusalem, inside the ruins of a large Iron Age building composed of four rooms and dated to the 7th century BC. This seal impression depicts two men facing each other with each man raising one hand, perhaps in a salute or worship, and wearing striped, knee-length garments. The archaeological context in which it was found, along with the writing style used, indicates that the seal would have been used around 700 BC. Below the illustration is a Hebrew inscription reading "belonging to the governor of the city." The position of governor of the city of Jerusalem is known from the reign of Josiah in the 7th century BC just after the time of Isaiah, with the officials Maaseiah and Joshua specifically named (2 Kings 23:8; 2 Chronicles 34:8).

These other bullae and their archaeological context demonstrate that the "Isaiah the prophet" seal impression is firmly situated around 700 BC and in the royal quarter of Jerusalem as a person who was in close association with the king and his officials. Therefore, this seal impression of Isaiah matches in name, title, time period, location, and association, indicating that Isaiah the prophet has been identified in the archaeological record.

> *The vision of Isaiah the son of Amoz concerning Judah and Jerusalem, which he saw during the reigns of Uzziah, Jotham, Ahaz and Hezekiah, kings of Judah* (Isaiah 1:1).

Mazar, Eilat. "Is This the Prophet Isaiah's Signature?" *Biblical Archaeology Review* 44.2 (2018).

JOTHAM

Ring of Jotham

Name: Jotham

Time Period: 8th century BC (Iron Age IIb)

Geographical Area: Kingdom of Judah

Biblical Reference(s): 2 Kings 15:5-16:1; 2 Chronicles 26:21-27:9

Ancient Source(s): Bulla of Ahaz; Ring of Jotham

Identification Rating: Firm (A)

Jotham was the son of Uzziah, the father of Ahaz, and the grandfather of Hezekiah, ruling as king of Judah around 750–735 BC. Jotham was given power after his father contracted leprosy, but his time recognized as sole king may not have started until after Uzziah died (2 Kings 15:5). Jotham was known for building projects in Jerusalem and elsewhere in his kingdom, and he won a victory over the Ammonites that resulted in substantial tribute payments.

Jotham is known from one bulla and possibly also named on a ring. The bulla, created when a seal of his son Ahaz was pressed into clay, dates from the 8th century BC and has a Hebrew inscription reading "belonging to Ahaz son of Jotham, king of Judah" (cf. 2 Kings 15:38). Although the bulla is from a private collection and the conditions of its discovery are unknown, it is considered to be authentic and attests to both Jotham and his son Ahaz, who succeeded him.

Another artifact bearing the name Jotham is a copper signet ring, also from the 8th century BC, decorated with the image of a ram and a Hebrew inscription reading "belonging to Jotham." The ring was found during excavations at Ezion-Geber in southern Judah. It is plausible that it was used as a royal signet ring by an official in the service of the king to mark property or correspondence of the royal house, ruled by Jotham. However, because the inscription is lacking a title or lineage, the exact identity of the owner of the Jotham ring is unknown. Regardless, Jotham of Judah is attested by the bulla of Ahaz, and therefore his name, lineage, title, and time period are confirmed.

Jotham slept with his fathers, and he was buried with his fathers in the city of David his father; and Ahaz his son became king in his place (2 Kings 15:38).

Avigad, Naaman. "A Seal of Jotham from Eilat" in *Eilat: Studies in the Archaeology, History and Geography of Eilat and the Aravah*. Jerusalem, 1995.

TIGLATH-PILESER III
(Pulu)

Stone relief of Tiglath-Pileser III from his Nimrud palace

Name: Tiglath-Pileser III (Pulu)

Time Period: 8th century BC (Neo-Assyrian)

Geographical Area: Assyria

Biblical Reference(s): 2 Kings 15:19–16:10; 1 Chronicles 5:6-26; 2 Chronicles 28:16-21

Ancient Source(s): Assyrian Eponym List; Babylonian Chronicle; Bar Rakib Inscription; Incirli Stele; Annals of Tiglath-Pileser III

Identification Rating: Firm (A)

Tiglath-Pileser III, also known as Pulu, was king of Assyria ca. 745–727 BC and king of Babylon ca. 729–727 BC, overlapping with Menahem of Israel, Pekah of Israel, Hoshea of Israel, Uzziah of Judah, Ahaz of Judah, Merodach-Baladan of Babylon, and Rezin of Damascus. Due to this substantial reign and overlap with other monarchs, his records are an important source for numerous kings, and he is attested in diverse sources. Prior to becoming king, Tiglath-Pileser III was a prominent general in the army, but because of apparent contradictions or conflicts in the ancient sources, it is unknown if he usurped the throne or was the legitimate heir of Ashur-nirari V, who may have been either his brother or father. Due to conflicting information about his lineage, a revolt in the capital city of Kalhu at the beginning of his reign, a drastic change in government officials, and that Tiglath-Pileser III claimed divine appointment, it appears likely that he was a usurper.

During the course of his reign, Tiglath-Pileser III led several victorious military campaigns and established Assyria as the most dominant empire in the ancient world. He was the first Assyrian monarch to be recognized as a king of Babylon—an important achievement and title due to the significance of Babylon in the ancient world. Aramaic also became an official language used throughout the Assyrian empire during his reign, demonstrated by a few prominent inscriptions of Tiglath-Pileser III in Aramaic. In the Bible, Tiglath-Pileser III is named in the books of Kings and Chronicles, where he is mentioned as having received a tribute from Menahem, conquering numerous cities of Israel, meeting with Ahaz and taking a payment for assisting against Aram, and capturing Damascus and killing their king, Rezin. Tiglath-Pileser III is of course attested by his own inscriptions and depicted on his wall reliefs, but he is also named in sources from Babylon, Anatolia, the Levant, and other Assyrian documents. An incredible wall painting from the palace at Masuwari (Tell Ahmar) shows Tiglath-Pileser III enthroned with his son Shalmaneser V standing in front.

Tiglath-Pileser III deporting the people of Ashtaroth

Although not consensus, the majority of scholars now agree that Tiglath-Pileser III and Pulu were the same person. Most likely, Pulu was his birth name also used in Babylon, and Tiglath-Pileser was his throne name, just as the birth name of his son also used in Babylon was Ululayu and his throne name Shalmaneser V. The equation between Tiglath-Pileser and Pulu comes primarily from three completely different sources—the Bible, the Babylonian Chronicles, and a trilingual stele of Tiglath-Pileser III.

In the Bible, both the names Pul and Tiglath-Pileser are used of an Assyrian king, but one passage mentions the names together as the king who carried away people from the Northern Kingdom of Israel into exile (1 Chronicles 5:26). In Babylonian records, Tiglath-Pileser III is recorded to have ascended the throne of Assyria in 745 BC, ruling 18 years, but also ascending to the throne of Babylon in 729 BC and ruling two years (ABC 1; cf. ABC 1B). Elsewhere, Pulu (Tiglath-Pileser III) is assigned two years as king of Babylon, immediately before the five years of his son Ululayu (Shalmaneser V), followed by 12 years of Marduk-Baladan (Babylonian King List A).

It is clear that the Babylonians understood Pulu and Tiglath-Pileser III to be the same person, just as is indicated in the book of Chronicles. However, a stele of the Danunites, recently discovered and translated, seems to make this connection certain and settle the issue. This basalt stele inscribed in Luwian, Assyrian, and Phoenician was commissioned by Awariku, king of the Danunites, and describes a grant of land from the Assyrian king. A section with both names reads "this frontier region is the gift of Tiglath-Pilesar, Puwal, king of Assyria, to the king and dynasty of the king of the Danunites" (Incirli Stele). Thus, what was the mysterious and unexplained use of both names Pul and Tiglath-Pileser in the Bible for a king of Assyria seems to have been solved through archaeological discoveries.

Among the many military campaigns of Tiglath-Pileser III was an incursion into the Levant, where he fought against numerous smaller kingdoms, including Aram, Phoenicia, Hamath, and Israel. An Aramean king named Bar Rakib and based at Sam'al (Zincirli) produced a monument in which he stated his loyalty to and named Tiglath-Pileser III, king of the four quarters of the earth (KAI 217). Another king of Sam'al, Panamuwa II, is also named alongside Tiglath-Pileser III on a stele (Panamuwa Inscription). This king Panamuwa II is recorded along with Ahaz of Judah in an inscription of Tiglath-Pileser III from Kalhu (Summary Inscription 7).

The official Assyrian records even refer to events in the reign of Tiglath-Pileser III, such as the tribute from Menahem, the payment from Ahaz, the capture of Damascus and death of Rezin, and the conquest of the Northern Kingdom of Israel (Iran Stele; Annals of Tiglath-Pileser III; 2 Kings 15:19–16:9). The Assyrian

Wall relief from Nimrud showing Tiglath-Pileser III and Shalmaneser V

campaign of Tiglath-Pileser III about 734–732 BC is not only mentioned in the Bible and the inscriptions of Tiglath-Pileser III, but alluded to in the Assyrian Eponym List and is evident from excavations at numerous archaeological sites (e.g., Summary Inscription 10, K 2649).

At Hazor, the residents built new fortifications in anticipation of the impending attack by Tiglath-Pileser III, but Hazor was destroyed and made an Assyrian administrative center. At Gezer, the 8th-century BC destruction layer is attributed to the campaign of Tiglath-Pileser III, and a stone relief from his palace at Kalhu may illustrate this capture of Gezer. Megiddo was also conquered, followed by the building of an Assyrian administrative center, and a destruction layer from the time of Tiglath-Pileser III was also found at Shechem (2 Kings 15:29; cf. Annals of Tiglath-Pileser III).

Tiglath-Pileser III died in about 727 BC, and his son Shalmaneser V ascended the throne in what appears to have been a peaceful transition of power.

> *In the days of Pekah king of Israel, Tiglath-pileser king of Assyria came and captured Ijon and Abel-beth-maacah and Janoah and Kedesh and Hazor and Gilead and Galilee, all the land of Naphtali; and he carried them captive to Assyria* (2 Kings 15:29).

Kaufman, Stephen. "The Phoenician Inscription of the Incirli Trilingual." *MAARAV* 14.2 (2007).

Pritchard, James, ed. *The Ancient Near Eastern Texts Relating to the Old Testament.* 3rd ed. with Supplement. Princeton: Princeton University Press, 1969.

AHAZ

Bulla of Ahaz, king of Judah

Name: Ahaz (Jehoahaz)

Time Period: 8th century BC (Iron Age II)

Geographical Area: Kingdom of Judah

Biblical Reference(s): 2 Kings 16:1-20; 2 Chronicles 28:19-21; Isaiah 7:1

Ancient Source(s): Summary Inscription 7 of Tiglath-Pileser III; bullae of Ahaz; bullae of Hezekiah; seal of Ushna

Identification Rating: Firm (A)

Ahaz was a king of Judah and father of the famous King Hezekiah. He reigned for 16 years from Jerusalem about 732–716 BC, although he was probably co-regent with his father, Jotham, for four years prior to this, and then possibly co-regent with his son for around 13 years. Ahaz is also called Jehoahaz, or Jehoahaz II of Judah, to distinguish him from the earlier king of Judah and the earlier Jehoahaz of Israel.

During the reign of Ahaz, the Northern Kingdom of Israel fell to the Assyrians, who were led first by Tiglath-Pileser III, followed by Shalmaneser V, and then ultimately finished by Sargon II (2 Kings 15:29; 17:3-6). Both his father and his son, Jotham and Hezekiah, are also attested by ancient inscriptions naming them as kings of Judah.

Ahaz (Jehoahaz) was a contemporary of the Assyrian king Tiglath-Pileser III (2 Kings 16:7-18; 2 Chronicles 28:19-21), and in this period of Assyrian dominance, Ahaz (Jehoahaz) was compelled to send tribute to him. An 8th-century BC Assyrian tablet probably found at Calah (K 3751) describes various rulers who paid tribute to Tiglath-Pileser III in about 729 BC, including "Jehoahaz of Judah." His payment to Tiglath-Pileser III to deliver the Kingdom of Judah from Aram and Israel may have been this tribute, or Ahaz may have sent more than one tribute to this Assyrian king. Regardless, this official Assyrian text names Ahaz as king of Judah a few years after he began his reign.

In archaeological sources from the Kingdom of Judah, the name of King

Ahaz is also found on a seal and on bullae—small pieces of clay in which a seal was impressed to make a stamp. One important Hebrew bulla from the reign of Hezekiah, discovered in excavations at Jerusalem, reads "belonging to Hezekiah, son of Ahaz, king of Judah." Another bulla that emerged on the antiquities market, but may have also been found in Jerusalem, appears to have come from the reign of Ahaz and translates as "belonging to Ahaz, son of Jotham, king of Judah." These bullae were used by the king or one of his high officials for important documents, and the Ahaz son of Jotham bulla has a fingerprint that might be that of the king himself.

Finally, a carnelian seal with the inscription "belonging to Ushna servant of Ahaz," also unprovenanced but genuine, appears to mention King Ahaz and an otherwise unknown official in his administration. Thus, Ahaz (or Jehoahaz of Judah) is attested not only in an official Assyrian inscription, but also from multiple royal and administrative seals of the Kingdom of Judah.

> *Ahaz sent messengers to Tiglath-pileser king of Assyria, saying, "I am your servant and your son; come up and deliver me from the hand of the king of Aram and from the hand of the king of Israel, who are rising up against me." Ahaz took the silver and gold that was found in the house of the* Lord *and in the treasuries of the king's house, and sent a present to the king of Assyria* (2 Kings 16:7-8).

Avigad, Nahman. *Corpus of West Semitic Stamp Seals.* Jerusalem: Hebrew University, 1997.

Pritchard, James, ed. *The Ancient Near Eastern Texts Relating to the Old Testament.* 3rd ed. with Supplement. Princeton: Princeton University Press, 1969.

Torrey, C.C. "A Hebrew Seal from the Reign of Ahaz." *Bulletin of the American Schools of Oriental Research* 79 (1940).

PEKAH

Subjugation of a foreign city by Tiglath-Pileser III in the 8th century BC

Name: Pekah (son of Remaliah)

Time Period: 8th century BC (Iron Age IIb)

Geographical Area: Kingdom of Israel

Biblical Reference(s): 2 Kings 15:25-32; 2 Chronicles 28:5-15; Isaiah 7:1-9

Ancient Source(s): Annals of Tiglath-Pileser III

Identification Rating: Firm (A)

Pekah, son of Remaliah, was a high-ranking officer in the service of King Pekahiah, son of Menahem, until he assassinated his monarch at the palace in Samaria and took the throne for himself. Pekah then ruled in the Northern Kingdom of Israel during a tumultuous time when there were rivalries for the throne and the threat of domination by the powerful Assyrian Empire. According to the book of Kings, Pekah was king for 20 years, which encompassed approximately 752–732 BC, but during part of his reign he may not have been the only person calling himself king in Israel.

A few scholars suggest that Pekah had control over the areas of Gilead and Transjordan for the duration of his reign, but he ruled over the entire kingdom for only about three years. Pekah, in an alliance with Rezin of Aram, attacked Judah, killed thousands of their soldiers, and took women and children into captivity, but failed to conquer Jerusalem (2 Chronicles 28:6-8; Isaiah 7:1). His reign came to an end when Hoshea overthrew him and became the next ruler of the Northern Kingdom of Israel.

As an ally of Aram, Pekah attempted to resist Assyrian dominance while also battling the Kingdom of Judah, but ultimately he was overpowered by Tiglath-Pileser III of Assyria (2 Kings 15:29). The only known archaeological attestation of Pekah comes from a record of Tiglath-Pileser III that describes the defeat and deportation of people from Israel, along with the death of Pekah and the installation of Hoshea:

> The house of Omri...all its inhabitants (and) their possessions I led to Assyria. They overthrew their king Pekah and I placed Hoshea as

> king over them. I received from them 10 talents of gold, 1,000 talents of silver as their [tri]bute and brought them to Assyria (Nimrud Summary Inscription 4).

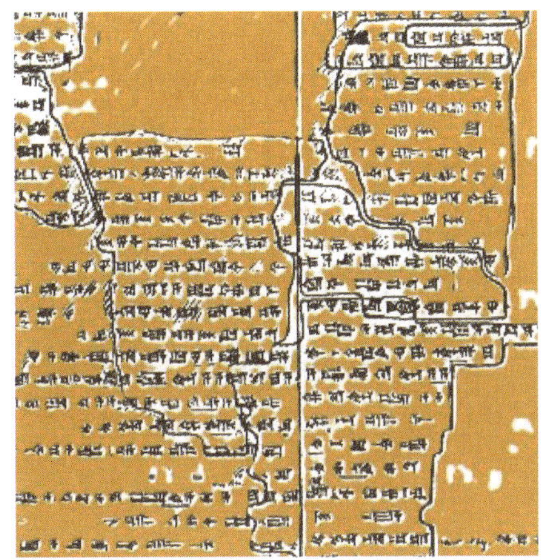

Nimrud Summary Inscription 4

Although the chronological issues for the reign of Pekah may have differing views and remain unresolved, he is clearly corroborated by official Assyrian sources as the king of Israel who was usurped by Hoshea during the time of Tiglath-Pileser III.

> *In the days of Pekah king of Israel, Tiglath-pileser king of Assyria came and captured Ijon and Abel-beth-maacah and Janoah and Kedesh and Hazor and Gilead and Galilee, all the land of Naphtali; and he carried them captive to Assyria. And Hoshea the son of Elah made a conspiracy against Pekah the son of Remaliah, and struck him and put him to death and became king in his place, in the twentieth year of Jotham the son of Uzziah* (2 Kings 15:29-30).

Pritchard, James, ed. *The Ancient Near Eastern Texts Relating to the Old Testament.* 3rd ed. with Supplement. Princeton: Princeton University Press, 1969.

REZIN

8th-century BC chalcedony seal inscribed "belonging to Hoshea"

Name: Rezin of Damascus

Time Period: 8th century BC (Iron Age IIb)

Geographical Area: Aram

Biblical Reference(s): 2 Kings 15:37–16:9; Isaiah 7:1-8

Ancient Source(s): Annals of Tiglath-Pileser III

Identification Rating: Firm (A)

Rezin was the final king of Aram based at Damascus in the middle of the 8th century BC until about 732 BC, when he was defeated by Tiglath-Pileser III and Aram was conquered and absorbed by the Assyrians. Rezin was from the town of Hadara and had established a new dynasty, according to Assyrian sources, and throughout his reign he was at war with both Assyria and Judah while allying with the Northern Kingdom of Israel.

Rezin, alongside his ally Pekah of Israel, waged a brutal military campaign against Ahaz of Judah that failed to conquer Jerusalem but killed thousands of their soldiers and took women and children into captivity (2 Kings 16:5-6; 2 Chronicles 28:6-8; Isaiah 7:1). However, the substantial losses and impending threat of Rezin and Pekah led to Ahaz pleading with and sending tribute to Assyria for assistance, resulting in Tiglath-Pileser III capturing Damascus and killing Rezin (2 Kings 16:7-9).

Rezin of Damascus is named multiple times in the official records of Tiglath-Pileser III of Assyria, including information about tributes and his ultimate defeat. An Assyrian stele from about 737 BC states:

> The kings of the land of Hatti, (and of) Aram of the western seashore, the land of Qedar (and) the land of Arabia...Rezin of Damascus...I imposed on them tribute of silver, gold, tin, iron, elephant hides, elephant tusks (ivory), blue-purple (and) red-purple garments, multi-colored garments, linen garments, camels, (and) she-camels (Iran Stele of Tiglath-Pileser III).

Elsewhere, the annals of Tiglath-Pileser III mention a tribute but then report the defeat of Rezin and the destruction of his kingdom:

> From Rezin...talents of gold, 300 talents of silver, 200 talents of...20 talents of ladanum...I received the tribute of Rezin, the Damascene, Menahem, the Samarian, Hiram, the Tyrian...Rezin [of Damascus...]. [I captured] heavy [booty] [...] his advisor [...] [(With) the blood of his] war[riors] I dyed a reddish hue the river of [...], raging [torrent]... his courtiers, charioteers and...their weapons I smashed; and...their horses...I captured his warriors, archers, shield- and lance-bearers; and I dispersed their battle array. That one (Rezin), in order to save his life, fled alone; and he entered the gate of his city [like] a mongoose. I impaled alive his chief ministers; and I made his country behold (them). I set up my camp around the city for 45 days; and I confined him like a bird in a cage. His gardens...orchards without number I cut down; I did not leave a single one...the town of Hadara, the home of the dynasty of Rezin of Damascus, [the pl]ace where he was born, I surrounded (and) captured...I destroyed 591 cities of 16 districts of Damascus like mounds of ruins after the Deluge (Nimrud Annals of Tiglath-Pileser III; cf. Summary Inscription 10).

Although the death of Rezin is not explicitly found in this Assyrian text, it is implied due to the complete destruction of Damascus, the execution of his officials, and his disappearance from history. Thus, Rezin and his final defeat at Damascus by Tiglath-Pileser III are clearly corroborated by the ancient Assyrian sources.

Annals of Tiglath-Pileser III

Ahaz sent messengers to Tiglath-pileser king of Assyria, saying, "I am your servant and your son; come up and deliver me from the hand of the king of Aram and from the hand of the king of Israel, who are rising up against me." Ahaz took the silver and gold that was found in the house of the L*ORD and in the treasuries of the king's house, and sent a present to the king of Assyria. So the king of Assyria listened to him; and the king of Assyria went up against Damascus and captured it, and carried the people of it away into exile to Kir, and put Rezin to death* (2 Kings 16:7-9).

Hallo, William W. and K. Lawson Younger. *Context of Scripture*. Boston: Brill, 2000.

Pritchard, James, ed. *The Ancient Near Eastern Texts Relating to the Old Testament*. 3rd ed. with Supplement. Princeton: Princeton University Press, 1969.

SO
(King of Egypt)

Osorkon IV on the Victory Stele of Piye

Name: So, king of Egypt (Osorkon IV, Usermaatre)

Time Period: 8th century BC (22nd Dynasty)

Geographical Area: Egypt

Biblical Reference(s): 2 Kings 17:4

Ancient Source(s): Annals of Sargon II; Victory Stele of Piye

Identification Rating: Probable (B)

The Egyptian pharaoh called by the name So is more difficult than most to identify due to the short name version that does not perfectly match any name forms of known pharaohs. However, because of the historical context mentioned in relation to this pharaoh, along with a similar name, a likely identification is possible.

According to the book of Kings, Pharaoh So was in power early in the reign of Hoshea of Israel (ca. 732–722 BC), with whom he corresponded, and around the reign of Shalmaneser V (ca. 727–722 BC) of Assyria (2 Kings 17:1-6). Matters are slightly more complicated than usual, since in this period of only a decade, there were at least five different kings in three separate areas of Egypt: Piye of the Kushite 25th Dynasty (ca. 747–714 BC), Tefnakht I (ca. 732–725 BC), Bakenranef (ca. 725–720 BC) of the 24th Dynasty based in Sais, and Osorkon IV (ca. 730–716 BC) of the Bubastite 22nd Dynasty. However, of all of these rulers, only the name Osorkon IV has similarity to "So, king of Egypt," with So appearing to be an abbreviated version of the throne name (O)so(rkon). Furthermore, Osorkon IV ruled over the eastern Nile Delta region of Egypt, which was closer to Judah than any of the other regional Egyptian kings during this period, making the connection even more probable based on geography.

Adding to the complexity of names between different languages, the Assyrians appear to have called Osorkon IV by the name Shilkanni. In the annals of

Sargon II (ca. 722–705 BC), recorded on a prism, a meeting and tribute is described between Sargon II and the pharaoh of Egypt: "I made [my army] march [the road] towards sunset...Shilkanni, king of Musri, who...the terror-inspiring glamor of Ashur, my lord, overwhelmed him and he brought as tâmartu-present 12 big horses from Musri which have not their equals in this country" (Ashur 16587). This is an event that appears to have happened after the fall of Samaria and near the end of the reign of Osorkon IV around 716 BC.

Aegis naming Osorkon IV and his mother Tadibast III

Straightforward attestation for King Osorkon IV comes from Egypt, where the Victory Stele of Piye names and depicts Osorkon IV around 728 BC, just before Hoshea of Israel sent messengers to Egypt hoping for an alliance against the Assyrians. A stone relief from the sacred lake of Mut at Tanis probably also depicts Osorkon IV and includes the royal titulary with his names "Usermaatre" and "Osorkon" in two cartouches. Osorkon IV also seems to be named in an inscription on an aegis honoring the goddess Sekhmet. The inscription appears to name him and his mother, Tadibast III, mentioning "Divine mother, King's wife Tadibast" and "Son of Ra, Osorkon, forever" (Louvre E 7167).

> *Shalmaneser king of Assyria came up against him, and Hoshea became his servant and paid him tribute. But the king of Assyria found conspiracy in Hoshea, who had sent messengers to So king of Egypt and had offered no tribute to the king of Assyria, as he had done year by year; so the king of Assyria shut him up and bound him in prison* (2 Kings 17:3-4).

Albright, William. "Further Synchronisms between Egypt and Asia in the Period 935–685 BC." *Bulletin of the American Schools of Oriental Research* 141 (1956).

Kitchen, Kenneth. *The Third Intermediate Period in Egypt, 1100–650 BC.* Warminster: Aris & Phillips, 1996.

HOSHEA

8th-century BC chalcedony seal inscribed belonging to Abdi, servant of Hoshea

Name: Hoshea

Time Period: 8th century BC (Iron Age IIb)

Geographical Area: Kingdom of Israel

Biblical Reference(s): 2 Kings 15:30; 17:1-6

Ancient Source(s): Annals of Tiglath-Pileser; Annals of Sargon II; Seal of Abdi

Identification Rating: Firm (A)

Hoshea, son of Elah, was the final king of the Northern Kingdom of Israel, reigning for nine years until the Assyrians invaded and captured Samaria in about 722 BC. Hoshea, similar to many other kings, gained power by usurping the throne through an assassination plot. While Pekah was king and the Northern Kingdom of Israel was under attack from the Assyrians led by Tiglath-Pileser III, Hoshea murdered Pekah and became king (2 Kings 15:29-30).

This appears to have happened in the final months of Jotham of Judah's reign, and then Hoshea was able to take control in Samaria by the beginning of the reign of Ahaz of Judah (2 Kings 15:30; 17:1). Although Hoshea was initially subservient to the Assyrians, paying homage to Tiglath-Pileser III and then Shalmaneser V, Hoshea stopped paying tribute and asked for an alliance with the Egyptians, resulting in his imprisonment and the capture of the capital city Samaria (2 Kings 17:3-6).

Assyrian sources name Hoshea and also corroborate major events during his reign. In the annals of Tiglath-Pileser III, the Assyrian king mentions "the house of Omri" (e.g., the Northern Kingdom of Israel) and that "all its inhabitants (and) their possessions I led to Assyria. They overthrew their king Pekah and I placed Hoshea as king over them. I received from them 10 talents of gold, 1,000 talents of silver as their [tri]bute and brought them to Assyria" (Summary Inscription of Tiglath-Pileser III). Thus, according to the Assyrians, Hoshea was installed or sanctioned as king, which may have been the conspiracy against Pekah mentioned in the book of Kings.

However, the conquest of Samaria at the end of Hoshea's reign appears to be attributed to two Assyrian kings in ancient sources. In the Babylonian Chronicle, it seems Shalmaneser V is credited with the destruction of Samaria, agreeing with the statement in the book of Kings that it was Shalmaneser V who marched on and besieged Samaria: "On the twenty-fifth of the month Tebetu, Shalmaneser in Assyria and Akkad ascended the throne. He ravaged Samaria" (ABC 1). However, Sargon II also took credit for Samaria, specifically noting that at the beginning of his reign, he conquered Samaria and deported its inhabitants. The annals of Sargon II specify:

> I besieged and conquered Samaria, led away as booty 27,290 inhabitants of it. I formed from among them a contingent of 50 chariots and made remaining (inhabitants) assume their positions. I installed over them an officer of mine and imposed upon them the tribute of the former king (Display Inscriptions of Sargon II).

Elsewhere, Sargon II claims "I conquered and sacked the towns Shinuhtu (and) Samaria, and all the house of Omri" (Annals of the Room XIV). Although there is a debate about whether Shalmaneser V or Sargon II was responsible for the conquest and destruction of Samaria, it is possible that Sargon II could have been the general commanding the Assyrian army at the time, and once he became king he credited himself for that victory.

In addition to official Assyrian inscriptions, Hoshea of Israel appears to be named on an Israelite seal of the 8th century BC. This chalcedony seal from the antiquities market, inscribed with two lines of Hebrew with a carving of a man in the center, reads "belonging to Abdi, servant of Hoshea." The owner of the seal, Abdi, was apparently an official in the royal court of Hoshea. The man shown on the seal was almost certainly Abdi, and he is depicted in Egyptian-style dress, which reflects the alliances and values of the Northern Kingdom of Israel during that period. Another 8th-century BC seal, made out of chalcedony and decorated with a winged creature wearing a crown, bears a Hebrew inscription reading "belonging to Hoshea" and could also be connected to this king. Thus, although a minor king who was a usurper and imprisoned by invaders, Hoshea is attested in archaeological sources both Israelite and Assyrian.

Annals of Sargon II

Hoshea the son of Elah made a conspiracy against Pekah the son of Remaliah, and struck him and put him to death and became king in his place, in the twentieth year of Jotham the son of Uzziah (2 Kings 15:30).

LeMaire, André. "Royal Signature: Name of Israel's Last King Surfaces in a Private Collection." *Biblical Archaeology Review* 21:6 (1995).

Pritchard, James, ed. *The Ancient Near Eastern Texts Relating to the Old Testament.* 3rd ed. with Supplement. Princeton: Princeton University Press, 1969.

SHALMANESER V

Wall painting showing Shalmaneser V standing before enthroned Tiglath-Pileser III

Name: Shalmaneser V (Ululayu)

Time Period: 8th century BC (Neo-Assyrian Empire)

Geographical Area: Assyria

Biblical Reference(s): 2 Kings 17:1-6; 18:9-11

Ancient Source(s): Babylonian Chronicle; Assyrian Eponym List; Bowl of Banitu

Identification Rating: Firm (A)

Shalmaneser V, son of Tiglath-Pileser III, was the last of five Assyrian kings who used the throne name Shalmaneser, ruling 727–722 BC. Similar to his father, he had another name that was used in reference to being the king of Babylon, and this may have been his birth name as indicated by the use of the name Ululayu in royal correspondence from the period when he was crown prince. He writes "To the king, my lord: your servant Ululayu. The best of health to the king, my lord! Assyria is well" (Nimrud Letters). This connection is primarily derived from his name Ululayu also appearing on the Babylonian King List A, where he is assigned five years after Pulu and preceded Marduk-Baladan.

In the book of Kings, Shalmaneser V is specifically named as the Assyrian king who forced Hoshea into submission and a tribute, then eventually laid siege to Samaria in the seventh year of Hoshea with the city falling after a three-year siege in about 722 BC (2 Kings 17:3; 18:9). Documentation for Shalmaneser V as king of Assyria at this time, and his attack on Samaria, is found in both the Assyrian Eponym List and the Babylonian Chronicle with an extremely brief summary of his five-year reign: "On the twenty-fifth of the month Tebetu, Shalmaneser in Assyria and Akkad ascended the throne. He ravaged Samaria. The fifth year: Shalmaneser went to his destiny in the month Tebetu. For five years Shalmaneser ruled Akkad and Assyria" (ABC 1). His reign overlapping with the time of Hoshea and his conquest of Samaria are both congruent with information recorded in the book of Kings.

Further, the Limmu list records a campaign beginning around 724 BC and

Tomb II of the queen's objects, including bowl of Banitu

going to 722 BC that is likely the siege of Samaria, but the lines are fragmentary: "During the eponomy of Bêl-Harran-bêla-usur, the governor of Guzana, campaign against...Shalmaneser [V] ascended the throne...During the eponomy of Shalmaneser, the king of Assyria, campaign against..." (Assyrian Eponym List).

For a Neo-Assyrian king of the 8th century BC with a reign of five years, the extant monuments for Shalmaneser V are surprisingly lacking. However, Shalmaneser V is elsewhere attested by eight inscribed lion weights found at Nimrud, a stamped brick from Apku (Tell Abu Marya), a bronze container and a golden bowl from Tomb II at Nimrud with inscriptions reading "belonging to Banitu, queen of Shalmaneser, king of Assyria," and a Babylonian tablet dated to year three of Shalmaneser. A wall painting discovered at Tell Ahmar, ancient Masuwari, also depicts Shalmaneser V when he was crown prince, standing in front of his father Tiglath-Pileser III on the throne.

Sources are silent about his cause of death, but a tablet of his brother Sargon II suggests that Shalmaneser V was overthrown with the excuse of sacrilege, and Sargon II portrayed himself as appointed with the favor of the gods (Assur Charter, K 1349). This would not be surprising in light of the frequency with which Assyrian kings were assassinated and the kingship usurped, even by their own family.

> *Now in the fourth year of King Hezekiah, which was the seventh year of Hoshea son of Elah king of Israel, Shalmaneser king of Assyria came up against Samaria and besieged it* (2 Kings 18:9).

Tadmor, Hayim and Shigeo Yamada. *The Royal Inscriptions of Tiglath-Pileser III (744–727 BC) and Shalmaneser V (726–722 BC), Kings of Assyria*. University Park: Eisenbrauns, 2011.

SARGON II

Kition Stele of Sargon II

Name: Sargon II (Arkeanos)

Time Period: 8th century BC (Neo-Assyrian Empire)

Geographical Area: Assyria

Biblical Reference(s): Isaiah 20:1

Ancient Source(s): Annals of Sargon; Babylonian Chronicle; Assyrian Eponym List; Kition Stele

Identification Rating: Firm (A)

Sargon II, distinguished from the Sargon of Akkad who lived 1,600 years earlier, was the king of Assyria about 722–705 BC and the father of the next king, Sennacherib. Sargon described himself as the son of Tiglath-Pileser III, meaning he would have also been a brother or half-brother of Shalmaneser V, who were his immediate predecessors to the throne. Coming to power when he was probably over 40 years old, Sargon claimed that he had been appointed by the gods, and he may have usurped the throne from Shalmaneser V.

Immediately upon ascending the throne, Sargon seems to have led military campaigns, and his reign was filled with conflicts in Urartu, Babylon, Elam, Media, Anatolia, Cyprus, and the Levant. His earliest recorded victory as king was over the Northern Kingdom of Samaria with its capital at Samaria, while later in his reign Sargon recorded that he subdued the Kingdom of Judah. In addition to expanding his empire through conquest, subduing rebellions, and sending

Sargon II standing with a royal official

an exploration expedition to Cyprus attested by a stele of Sargon II found on Cyprus, Sargon also built his new capital of Dur-Sharrukin, completed in 706 BC, which has been extensively excavated. However, the next year Sargon died on a military campaign he was leading against Tubal in Anatolia, and his son Sennacherib became king in 705 BC.

Despite being a powerful monarch with numerous military victories, constructing a new capital city, and commissioning many monuments, Sargon II was almost completely forgotten from history for over two thousand years until his building projects and inscriptions were rediscovered.

Sargon II had direct interactions with both Israel and Judah, including battles and tributes, but he is named only once in the Bible and possibly alluded to in two other passages (Isaiah 20:1; 2 Kings 17:6; 18:10-11). The first clearly documented interaction he had with Israel was the campaign that led to the fall of Samaria and the Northern Kingdom around 722 BC. In the book of Kings,

Stamped brick of Sargon II, "Sargon King of the World," from Khrosabad

Shalmaneser V is named as the Assyrian king who attacked Samaria and forced a tribute from King Hoshea, and this is also reflected in the annals of Shalmaneser V (2 Kings 17:3). However, in the annals of Sargon II, the king proclaims that he conquered Samaria and deported its residents, and his records indicate that it was his earliest military campaign.

In a rock relief carved into a mountain pass in Iran near the end of his reign, Sargon II described himself and his appointment to the kingship:

> Sargon, great king, mighty king, king of the world, king of Assyria, governor of Babylon, king of the land of [Sumer and Ak]kad, favorite of the great gods, perfect hero...pious [prince], marvelous man... shepherd...Aššur, Nabû, (and) Marduk, the gods [my] helpers, granted [me] a kingship [without] equal (Tang-i Var Inscription).

Boasts specifically about his military prowess, such as how no other ruler could be his opponent and that he had never met an opponent in battle who could overpower him, can be read in the Carchemish Cylinder. Although Sargon II did have many victories, he was by no means undefeated, and ironically his eventual death was due to being outsmarted and overpowered by an opponent during a military campaign.

Elsewhere, Sargon described his conquest of Samaria and the "house of Omri" or the Northern Kingdom of Israel, calling himself "Sargon...conqueror of Samaria and of the entire house of Omri" (Pavement Inscription 4). From the palace of Sargon II at Dur-Sharrukin (Khorsabad), he described in more detail the campaign, and that included a siege of the city, a conquest, and deportation of people also mentioned in the book of Kings:

> I besieged and conquered Samarina. I took as booty 27,290 people who lived there. I gathered 50 chariots from them. I taught the rest (of the deportees) their skills. I set my eunuch over them, and I imposed upon them the (same) tribute as the previous king (The Great Summary Inscription; cf. Sargon Prism D).

The victory over Samaria seems to be repeated multiple times, indicating that it was a notable event:

> Sargon...who subjugated the extensive land of the house of Omri, who inflicted a decisive defeat on Egypt at Raphia, and who brought

Hanunu, king of Gaza, to Aššur as a prisoner, who conquered the Tamudi, the Ibadidi, the Marsimani and the Hayappâ, of whom the remainder I removed and settled in the land of the house of Omri (Cylinder Inscription of Sargon II).

The conquest of Samaria and the Northern Kingdom of Israel was probably widely referred to by Sargon II because he participated in that siege, perhaps as the commander of the army while Shalmaneser V was still king. However, scholars often suggest that Sargon II finished the siege and conquest after Shalmaneser V died, even though others claim it might contradict ancient sources about Shalmaneser V and could be at odds with the book of Kings (ABC 1; 2 Kings 17:1-5; 18:7-11). It may be an important detail that the book of Kings refers to the conqueror of Samaria and the one who deported the people as the "king of Assyria" rather than Shalmaneser. Alternatively, a few scholars argue that Sargon II refers to a later attack on Samaria not mentioned in the Bible. However, the order of events appears to place his capture and deportation of Samaria in year one of Sargon, around 722 BC, as immediately after this event Sargon begins narrating his second regnal year (Annals of Sargon II).

Foundation tablet from palace of Sargon II

Another event mentioned in the Bible and also found in the records of Sargon II is the attack and capture of Ashdod (Isaiah 20:1). The Assyrian king stated, "With my warriors—who never leave my side in (hostile or) friend[ly terri] tory—I marched to Ashdod…I besieged (and) conquered Ashdod, Gimtu (Gath) and Ashdod-Yam" (The Great Summary Inscription). Fragments of an Assyrian stele found in a destruction layer of the 8th century BC during excavations at Ashdod further confirm this event. Sargon II also mentioned the Kingdom of Judah in one of his inscriptions, as apparently he defeated Judah or intimidated their king into giving him a tribute. Sargon calls himself "the subduer of Judah which lies far away; deporter of the land of Hamath, whose hands captured Yahubi'di, their king" (Nimrud Inscription of Sargon II).

Elsewhere, Sargon explains that "the rulers of Philistia, Judah, Ed[om], Moab (and) those who live (on islands) and bring tribute" (Sargon II Prism A). This is understandable based on what transpires with the next Assyrian king, Sennacherib. This clash between Sargon II and Judah is not found in the Bible, although it may be alluded to and could have occurred earlier in the reign of Hezekiah (Isaiah 20:6).

Both Babylonian and Assyrian sources briefly mention the fate of Sargon II in 705 BC, when he was with his army during a campaign against Tubal and died in his camp when he was attacked by a leader named Qurdi who could have been a Cimmerian. According to the Babylonian Chronicle, "[705 BC] The seventeenth year: Sargon marched to Tabalu" which is the final entry about Sargon II (ABC 1B). Assyrian sources give additional information about his fate: "[705 BC] against Qurdi the Kullumean, the king [Sargon] was killed, the camp of the king of Assyria…on the 12th of Ab, Sennacherib [became] king" (Assyrian Eponym List).

Thus, although named only once in the Bible, Sargon II was a powerful Assyrian king known from numerous monuments and texts found in Assyria, Babylon, Persia, Cyprus, and the Levant.

> *In the year that the commander came to Ashdod, when Sargon the king of Assyria sent him and he fought against Ashdod and captured it* (Isaiah 20:1).

Hallo, William W. and K. Lawson Younger. *Context of Scripture*. Boston: Brill, 2000.

Pritchard, James, ed. *The Ancient Near Eastern Texts Relating to the Old Testament*. 3rd ed. with Supplement. Princeton: Princeton University Press, 1969.

HEZEKIAH

A prism of Sennacherib (Taylor Prism) describing the attack on Judah and Hezekiah

Name: Hezekiah (son of Ahaz)

Time Period: 700 BC (Iron Age IIc)

Geographical Area: Kingdom of Judah

Biblical Reference(s): 2 Kings 18:1-20:21; 2 Chronicles 29:1-32:33; Isaiah 36:1-39:8

Ancient Source(s): Taylor Prism; Chicago Prism; Jerusalem Prism; Rassam Cylinder of Sennacherib; Bull 4 Inscription; Sennacherib Letter to God; Nebi Yunis Inscription; Bullae of Hezekiah

Identification Rating: Firm (A)

Hezekiah, son of Ahaz, was the 13th king of Judah and had a 29-year reign from Jerusalem, which is usually placed approximately 716–687 BC, although his reign may have instead dated to around 727–698 BC. The discrepancies in the dates for Hezekiah revolve around synchronisms with the fall of Samaria to Shalmaneser V during the reign of Hoshea in the 6th year of Hezekiah and the siege of Jerusalem by Sennacherib in the 14th year of Hezekiah.

Scholars have suggested various solutions, including a proposed co-regency between Hezekiah and his father, Amoz, or a co-regency between Hezekiah and his son Manasseh, or an unattested textual variant, or a slight revision of the Assyrian chronology (2 Kings 18:9-13). If Hezekiah had a co-regency with Amoz, then the year six of Hezekiah connected to the conquest of Samaria could be counting from the beginning of his co-regency, while the year 14 of Hezekiah connected to the siege of Jerusalem could be counting from his sole reign. Even without solving the chronological debates connected to Hezekiah, numerous archaeological discoveries attest to his role as king of Judah around 700 BC and corroborate many details of his reign recorded in the books of Kings, Chronicles, and Isaiah.

The archaeological attestation for Hezekiah of Judah comes primarily from Assyrian sources. In several of the official cuneiform texts of Sennacherib, including prisms, stone monuments, and tablets, Hezekiah of Judah is named. In these texts, the cities of Jerusalem, Lachish, and Azekah are also mentioned by name, showing the Assyrian awareness of the strategic and fortified cities of Judah (e.g., Prisms of Sennacherib, Lachish Reliefs, and the Sennacherib Letter to God aka Azekah Inscription).

Bulla of Hezekiah

The most famous of the Assyrian interactions with Hezekiah was officially documented and copied onto hexagonal prisms distributed throughout the empire. Three of these prisms of Sennacherib are intact, while fragments from at least eight others are known. The Taylor Prism, Chicago Prism, and Jerusalem Prism recount the third campaign of Sennacherib, launched in about 701 BC, and describe the Assyrian conquest of Judah, King Hezekiah, and a tribute paid to Sennacherib. The cuneiform text notes:

> Hezekiah of Judah, he did not submit to my yoke. I laid siege to 46 of his strong cities, walled forts, and countless small villages in their vicinity...I drove out 200,150 people...Himself I made a prisoner in Jerusalem, his royal residence, like a bird in a cage...Hezekiah himself, whom the terror-inspiring splendor of my lordship had overwhelmed and whose irregular and elite troops which he had brought into Jerusalem, his royal residence, in order to strengthen (it), had deserted him, did send me, later, to Nineveh, my lordly city, together with 30 talents of gold, 800 talents of silver...In order to deliver the tribute and to do obeisance as a slave he sent his messenger (Taylor Prism).

Sennacherib also recorded that in the past Hezekiah had gained control of the Philistine city of Ekron, whose King Padi was loyal to the Assyrians, and this king was handed over to and imprisoned by Hezekiah in Jerusalem (Taylor Prism). The book of Kings mentions this rebellion of Hezekiah against Assyrian authority and the defeat of Philistines, years prior to the campaign of Sennacherib (2 Kings 18:7-8).

These Assyrian prisms, in addition to documenting Hezekiah as king of Judah around 700 BC, give an incredibly detailed account that corroborates the narrative about Hezekiah and Sennacherib in the books of Kings, Chronicles, and Isaiah, including the invasion of Judah by Sennacherib, the conquest of all the fortified cities, the siege of Jerusalem, and even the tribute demands and payment (2 Kings 18:13–19:36; 2 Chronicles 32:1-22; Isaiah 36:1–37:37). However, this is not the only Assyrian version of the events naming Hezekiah. Other official inscriptions of Sennacherib give details about the tribute and were used to decorate the throne room at Nineveh (Bull 4 Inscription), mention the subjugation of Judah and King Hezekiah (Nebi Yunis Inscription), give a slightly different text describing the campaign (Rassam Cylinder of Sennacherib), and a shorter version of the campaign that was recorded earlier (Sennacherib Letter to God).

In addition to the Assyrian records of Sennacherib that mention Hezekiah, several bullae created from the official seal of Hezekiah have been discovered, including one excavated from a 7th-century BC layer in the royal quarter of Jerusalem. These bullae include his name, lineage, title, and nation, reading "belonging to Hezekiah, son of Ahaz, king of Judah." Although in the past these bullae had all originated on the antiquities market, the more recently discovered bulla in excavations has verified them as authentic. These pieces of stamped clay, impressed with the ring seal of Hezekiah himself, are firsthand artifacts of the king. Another unprovenanced bulla makes reference to Hezekiah as a ruler, reading "belonging to Yehozaraḥ, son of Hilkiah, servant of Hezekiah." This Yehozarah who served Hezekiah

Inscription from Nineveh describing the tribute of Hezekiah to Sennacherib

is not named in the Bible, but his father Hilkiah is mentioned, as is Eliakim, who could have been either the same person with an alternate name, his son, or even his brother (2 Kings 18:18; Isaiah 22:20).

A controversial but intriguing discovery from Jerusalem, possibly featuring the name of Hezekiah on a stone monument, is a fragmentary inscription that appears to preserve part of his name, although this must remain speculative. Hezekiah might even be depicted on a painted pottery sherd from Ramat Rahel, which would be one of the oldest artistic depictions of a king of Israel or Judah.

Painted king from Ramat Rahel

The reign of Hezekiah is also illuminated by numerous other archaeological finds, such as the Siloam Inscription and the Tunnel of Hezekiah, the Broad Wall, stamped jar handles "belonging to the king," evidence of religious reforms from Beersheva and Lachish, and destructions at many sites that were conquered by Sennacherib. Combined, these discoveries show that through archaeology, Hezekiah is one of the best attested characters in all of the Old Testament.

> *Now in the fourteenth year of King Hezekiah, Sennacherib king of Assyria came up against all the fortified cities of Judah and seized them. Then Hezekiah king of Judah sent to the king of Assyria at Lachish, saying, "I have done wrong. Withdraw from me; whatever you impose on me I will bear." So the king of Assyria required of Hezekiah king of Judah three hundred talents of silver and thirty talents of gold. Hezekiah gave him all the silver which was found in the house of the* Lord*, and in the treasuries of the king's house* (2 Kings 18:13-15).

Grayson, Kirk and Jamie Novotny. *The Royal Inscriptions of Sennacherib, King of Assyria*. University Park: Eisenbrauns, 2012.

Mazar, Eilat. *The Ophel Excavations 2009–2013*. Jerusalem: Shoham, 2015.

Pritchard, James, ed. *The Ancient Near Eastern Texts Relating to the Old Testament*. 3rd ed. with Supplement. Princeton: Princeton University Press, 1969.

SENNACHERIB

Sennacherib enthroned from the Lachish Reliefs

Name: Sennacherib

Time Period: 730–681 BC (Neo-Assyrian Empire)

Geographical Area: Assyria

Biblical Reference(s): 2 Kings 18:13–19:37; 2 Chronicles 32:1–32:22; Isaiah 36:1–37:38

Ancient Source(s): Babylonian Chronicle; Assyrian Eponym List; Sennacherib Prisms; Lachish Reliefs

Identification Rating: Firm (A)

Sennacherib was the son of his predecessor, Sargon II, and the father of his successor, Esarhaddon, ruling as the king of Assyria ca. 705–681 BC and overlapping with the reign of Hezekiah of Judah. In the books of Kings, Chronicles, and Isaiah, Sennacherib is a prominent antagonist during the reign of Hezekiah, subjugating the many cities of Judah, destroying Lachish, and laying siege to Jerusalem. Yet, he ultimately failed to conquer Jerusalem and was eventually killed by his own sons back in Nineveh. Sennacherib is attested by many of his own inscriptions and reliefs along with the Babylonian Chronicles, and his exploits are also described in the writings of Herodotus.

Immediately following the death of Sargon II during a military expedition against Tubal, "on the 12th of Ab, Sennacherib became king" of Assyria, but he soon had to deal with rebellions (ABC 1B; Assyrian Eponym List; cf. Babylonian King List A). The first known rebellion was instigated by Marduk-Baladan (Merodach-Baladan) in Babylon, but Sennacherib defeated him and commissioned a boastful description of his victory:

> At the beginning of my reign, when I had majestically ascended the throne and ruled the people of Assyria with obedience and peace, Merodach-baladan, king of Karduniash, an evil rebel, of treacherous mind...They reported these evil deeds to me, Sennacherib, who is pious in heart. I raged like a lion and gave the order to march into

> Babylonia against him…I defeated them and shattered his forces… I hurried to Babylon and entered the palace of Merodach-baladan to oversee the property and goods (stored) there (BM 113203).

This temporary defeat of Marduk-Baladan was probably achieved around 703 BC, as the Babylonian king fled the battle to regroup for a future plot against the Assyrians. Soon after, Sennacherib marched into the Levant to exert his dominance over various smaller kingdoms and force them into submission. One of these was the Kingdom of Judah that only a few years earlier had been subjugated and paid tribute to Sargon II. The account of Sennacherib invading Judah and besieging Hezekiah is described in great detail on the Prisms of Sennacherib from ca. 691 BC, with the earliest documented account of this third campaign being inscribed in about 700 BC.

The Prisms of Sennacherib were created to memorialize his accomplishments, focusing on eight campaigns of Sennacherib. The text is known from three prisms designated the Taylor Prism, Chicago Prism, and Jerusalem Prism, in addition to pieces of eight other prisms that are only fragmentary. The annals are currently known from three different cuneiform hexagonal prisms—the Taylor Prism, the Oriental Institute Prism, and the Jerusalem Prism—plus additional fragments from eight other prisms that have not survived intact.

The Taylor Prism was found in the armory at Nineveh, while the other two complete prisms both emerged on the antiquities market. Presumably, numerous copies were originally distributed throughout the Assyrian empire by order of Sennacherib. Column three, the third campaign, narrates the attack on the Kingdom of Judah in ca. 701 BC, noting the conquest of 46 fortified cities, the deportation of 200,150 people and countless animals, the siege of Jerusalem, and a massive tribute paid to Sennacherib by Hezekiah:

> In my third campaign I marched against Hatti…As for Hezekiah of Judah, who had not submitted to my yoke, I besieged 46 of his fortified walled cities and surrounding smaller towns, which were without number. Using packed-down ramps and applying battering rams, infantry attacks by mines, breeches, and siege machines, I conquered. I took out 200,150 people, young and old, male and female, horses, mules, donkeys, camels, cattle, and sheep, without number, and counted them as spoil. He himself, I locked up within Jerusalem, his royal city, like a bird in a cage. I surrounded him with

> earthworks, and made it unthinkable for him to exit by the city gate. His cities which I had despoiled I cut off from his land...I imposed dues and gifts for my lordship upon him, in addition to the former tribute, their yearly payment...Hezekiah, was overwhelmed by the awesome splendor of my lordship, and he sent me after my departure to Nineveh, my royal city...30 talents of gold, 800 talents of silver...He (also) dispatched his messenger to deliver the tribute and to do obeisance (Chicago Prism of Sennacherib).

Part of the Assyrian conquest of Judah was also found on stone reliefs adorning the walls of Room 36 in the "Palace without Rival" (Southwest Palace) of Sennacherib at Nineveh. Specifically, these carved reliefs depicted the siege, destruction, and deportation of the city of Lachish, showing details of the attack and the victorious Sennacherib along with an Assyrian inscription: "Sennacherib, king of the world, king of Assyria, seated upon the throne of judgment, the spoils of Lachish passed before him" (Lachish Reliefs).

Thus, not only did Sennacherib describe himself and his accomplishments with words and illustrations, but the details included match what was recorded in the books of Kings, Chronicles, and Isaiah, such as Hezekiah as king, the annexation of all the fortified cities of Judah, the destruction of Lachish, the tribute of 30 talents of gold and more than 300 talents of silver, the siege of Jerusalem, and Sennacherib returning to Nineveh without conquering Jerusalem (2 Kings 18:13–19:36; 2 Chronicles 32:1-10; Isaiah 36:1–37:37). Elsewhere, Sennacherib seems to summarize this campaign: "I laid waste the large district of Judah and made the overbearing and proud Hezekiah, its king, bow in submission" (Bull Inscription of Sennacherib; cf. Nebu Yunis Slab). Notably absent from the Assyrian accounts, however, is any mention of the failure to conquer Jerusalem and the death of his chief officers and mighty warriors.

Assyrian records also show that during the reign of Sennacherib, the interests of Hezekiah and Marduk-Baladan were aligned against him, without explicitly stating a meeting in Jerusalem or agreement between Hezekiah and Marduk-Baladan. Previously, Marduk-Baladan had sent gifts and a request for help against Assyria to Shutur-Nahhunte, the king of Elam, and had convinced others to join his opposition as he returned in force to rule as king of Babylon for nine months before Sennacherib defeated him and entered his palace in Babylon around 703 BC (Annals of Sennacherib). In the context of the diplomatic missions of Marduk-Baladan, sending gifts and a letter to gain the support of

The Assyrian victory at Lachish showing Sennacherib, his commander, soldiers, slaves, and defeated people of Judah

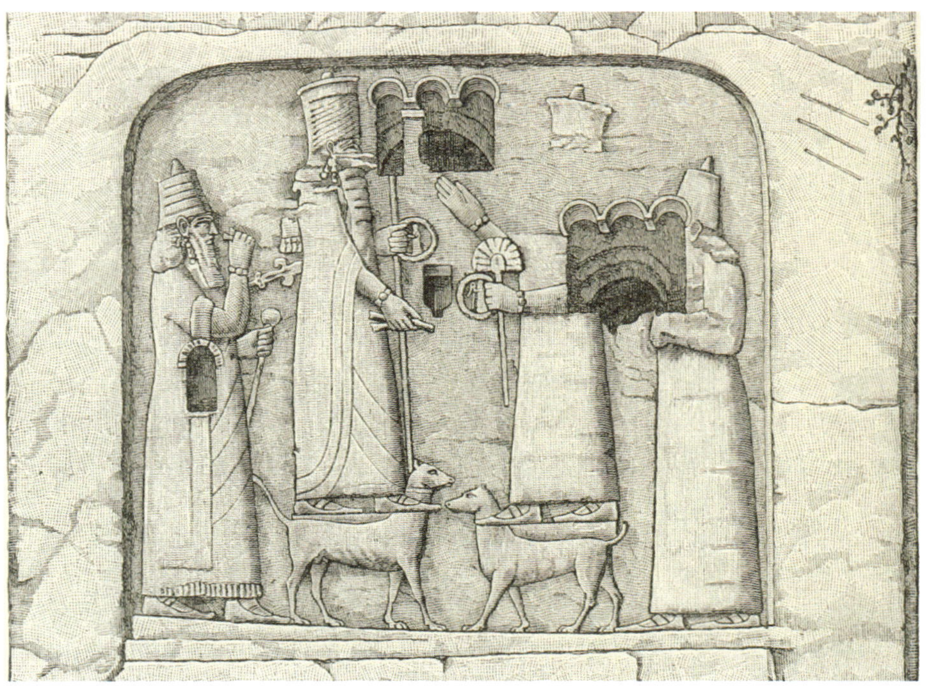

Bavian Rock Relief

Hezekiah is perfectly in line with the methods and actions of Marduk-Baladan known from Assyrian sources around this time (cf. 2 Kings 20:12-14; 2 Chronicles 32:21; Isaiah 39:1-3).

Sennacherib retaliated against revolts in Elam and another in Babylon, resulting in significant destruction of Elamite cities and the annihilation of Babylon. In about 690 BC, Sennacherib besieged the city of Babylon and eventually broke through the defenses after 15 months (in 689 BC), resulting in the death of many and the capture of a Babylonian king named Shuzubu (Bavian Rock Inscription of Sennacherib).

Sennacherib was not occupied only on the battlefield, however, as he spent much of his time building at the capital city of Nineveh, including a massive city wall and his "Palace Without Rival." This was one of the largest and most impressive in the ancient world, with over 68 rooms, numerous inscriptions, and stone-carved wall reliefs depicting Sennacherib and his military campaigns, impalement of enemies, looting, deportations, and lion hunting.

His eventful reign of 24 years came to a shameful end when he was assassinated by his sons as a result of conflict for the throne within the royal family. According to the Babylonian Chronicle:

> On the twentieth day of the month Tebetu, Sennacherib, king of Assyria, was killed by his son in a rebellion. For twenty-four years Sennacherib ruled Assyria. After the twentieth day of the month Tebetu the rebellion continued in Assyria until the second day of the month Addaru. On the eighteenth day of the month Addaru, Esarhaddon, his son, ascended the throne in Assyria (ABC 1).

Two sons of Sennacherib, Arda-Mulissu and Nabu-shar-usur (Adrammelech and Sharezer), were responsible for his assassination. His grandson, Ashurbanipal, also mentions Sennacherib and his murder involving statues of protective deities: "I smashed alive with the very same statues of protective deities with which they had smashed my own grandfather Sennacherib" (Rassam Cylinder of Ashurbanipal). Details about the death of Sennacherib are also found in the books of Kings and Isaiah, reporting that the Assyrian king was killed by his sons Adrammelech and Sharezer while worshipping in a temple in Nineveh, and Esarhaddon ascended to the throne (2 Kings 19:37; Isaiah 37:38).

Sennacherib, mentioned in the Bible more than any other Assyrian king, is extensively documented in his own inscriptions, those of his son and grandson, and in Babylonian texts that also corroborate many of the details about his life and exploits in the books of Kings, Chronicles, and Isaiah.

> *Now in the fourteenth year of King Hezekiah, Sennacherib king of Assyria came up against all the fortified cities of Judah and seized them. Then Hezekiah king of Judah sent to the king of Assyria at Lachish, saying, "I have done wrong. Withdraw from me; whatever you impose on me I will bear." So the king of Assyria required of Hezekiah king of Judah three hundred talents of silver and thirty talents of gold* (2 Kings 18:13-14).

Luckenbill, David. *The Annals of Sennacherib*. Chicago: University of Chicago, 1927.

Pritchard, James, ed. *The Ancient Near Eastern Texts Relating to the Old Testament*. 3rd ed. with Supplement. Princeton: Princeton University Press, 1969.

SHEBNA

Bulla of Yehozarah, son of Hilkiah, servant of Hezekiah

Name: Shebna the Steward

Time Period: 8th century BC (Iron Age IIc)

Geographical Area: Kingdom of Judah

Biblical Reference(s): 2 Kings 18:18-19:2; Isaiah 22:15-23

Ancient Source(s): Shebna Lintel; Shebnayahu Bulla

Identification Rating: Probable (B)

Shebna was the royal steward and a scribe during the reign of Hezekiah in the 8th century BC, prior to the Assyrian attack on Judah. Mentioned in the books of Kings and Isaiah, Shebna, "who is in charge of the royal household" (Isaiah 22:15), was rebuked by the prophet Isaiah because he had made a grand rock-hewn tomb for himself in a place of prominence overlooking the city of Jerusalem. As a consequence for his violation, he was deposed from his position and replaced by Eliakim, son of Hilkiah, and at that point Shebna may have been reassigned to the position of scribe. This Eliakim, who became an official in the service of King Hezekiah and replaced Shebna, was a son of Hilkiah and also might be attested by two bullae discovered at Lachish (2 Kings 18:18; Isaiah 36:3). Excavations of a destruction layer from ca. 701 BC, attributed to the Assyrian campaign and dating to the reign of Hezekiah, yielded two bullae impressed with a Hebrew inscription reading "belonging to Eliakim Yehozarah." The words "son of" do not appear on the bulla, but have been suggested as implied. A less likely but also possible scenario is that "brother of" could have been implied. Alternatively, the two names may have belonged to the same person, which was not uncommon in Judah during this period. Another bulla may further illuminate the identity of the Eliakim who lived around 700 BC referenced at Lachish. This bulla, unprovenanced but also from the time of Hezekiah, reads "belonging to Yehozarah, son of Hilkiah, servant of Hezekiah." Thus, Yehozarah may have been his "Yah" name and Eliakim may have been his "El" name, but he served in the royal court of Hezekiah. Alternatively, Eliakim may have been the son of Yehozarah and the "son" of Hilkiah in the sense of a grandson, or the brother of Yehozarah with both brothers serving King Hezekiah.

A tomb located in the Silwan area of ancient Jerusalem, alongside other tombs from the time of the Kingdom of Judah, was apparently carved from the limestone for Shebna based on the inscription found at the entrance. On a lintel above the opening, an inscription was found that comprises three lines of Hebrew text and dates to the 8th century BC based on epigraphic parallels to the Siloam Inscription of Hezekiah. The text translates as "This is [the sepulchre of...]yahu who is over the house. There is no silver and no gold here but [his bones] and the bones of his maidservant with him. Cursed is the man who will open this" (Shebna Lintel).

This tomb, often referred to as the Tomb of the Steward, dates to the time of Shebna (or Shebnayahu) and Hezekiah in the 8th century BC, uses the same

Bulla of Eliakim, son of Yehozarah

title of "over the house," and fits the description of the tomb mentioned by Isaiah. And although the beginning of the name is now missing, the space would perfectly accommodate the word for sepulchre or tomb, along with the four consonants for the name Shebna. The inscription probably identifies Shebna, but the missing letters in the name cast doubt on the association.

However, more recently an 8th-century BC Hebrew bulla was discovered that might have been made from the personal seal of Shebna the steward. The impression reads "belonging to Shebnayahu, servant to the king" and appears to be a more obvious attestation of the Shebna who served in the court of King Hezekiah that may have been used after he lost his position of royal steward.

> *Come, go to this steward, to Shebna, who is in charge of the royal household, "What right do you have here, and whom do you have here, that you have hewn a tomb for yourself here, you who hew a tomb on the height, you who carve a resting place for yourself in the rock?...I will depose you from your office, and I will pull you down from your station. Then it will come about in that day, that I will summon My servant Eliakim the son of Hilkiah, and I will clothe him with your tunic and tie your sash securely about him. I will entrust him with your authority, and he will become a father to the inhabitants of Jerusalem and to the house of Judah"* (Isaiah 22:15-21).

Avigad, Nahman. "The Epitaph of a Royal Steward from Siloam Village." *Israel Exploration Journal* 33, No. 3 (1953).

Deutsch, Robert. "Tracking Down Shebnayahu, Servant of the King." *Biblical Archaeology Review* 35:3 (2009).

Klingbeil, Martin G., Michael G. Hasel, and Yosef Garfinkel. "Four Judean Bullae from the 2014 Season at Tel Lachish." *Bulletin of the American Schools of Oriental Research* 381.6 (2019).

Burial lintel of Shebna

TIRHAKAH

Taharqa statuette with cartouche

Name: Tirhakah (Taharqa, Tarqu)

Time Period: 7th century BC (25th Dynasty of Egypt)

Geographical Area: Kush and Egypt

Biblical Reference(s): 2 Kings 19:9-11; Isaiah 37:8-10

Ancient Source(s): Stelae of Taharqa; Stelae of Esarhaddon and Ashurbanipal; Monumental building inscriptions; Egyptian statues; BM 25091; Pyramid of Taharqa

Identification Rating: Firm (A)

Taharqa was a king of Kush and the third pharaoh of the 25th Dynasty of Egypt, ruling as pharaoh of Egypt about 690–664 BC, partly during the reigns of Hezekiah and Manasseh. He had a long and successful reign filled with many military victories and building projects, restoring temples such as the grand temple of Amun at Jebel Barkal, adding to the Karnak temple complex at Thebes, achieving construction at Kawa, fighting the Assyrians numerous times over a period of three decades, and having the largest and most elaborate pyramid of all Kushite kings. The pyramid of Taharqa at Nuri was built near the city of Napata, and rose to about 63 meters high.

However, his ascendancy to power appears to have been fraught with conflict, and sources are unclear as to exactly what happened, with vital information missing. From his own inscriptions, Taharqa states that he became king after the death of his brother Shebitku, but elsewhere he ambiguously mentions a king who died, and afterward Taharqa was crowned king in Memphis (Kawa Stele IV and Kawa Stele V). Scholars now suggest that after the death of Shebitku, his brother Shabaka became king of Egypt and ruled for 15 years, and then finally Taharqa ascended the throne of Egypt when Shabaka died. Their family situation is unclear and the conditions of accession are still being unraveled.

What is known is that in about 706 BC, Shebitku was considered the king of Kush by the Assyrians, who mentioned King Shebitku delivering King Iamani of Ashdod to Sargon II (Great Inscription of Tang-i Var). Thus, it is possible that Taharqa succeeded Shebitku as king of Kush in 705 BC but was not crowned king of Egypt until 690 BC after the death of Shabaka. The Serapeum Stele from Saqqara names Taharqa and gives him a reign of 26 years as pharaoh of Egypt, indicating he held this position from approximately 690–664 BC.

Many other monumental statues, wall reliefs, wall paintings, and inscriptions of Taharqa have been discovered throughout Kush and Egypt, indicating that he was the most prominent of all the pharaohs from the land of Kush.

In the books of Kings and Isaiah, Taharqa is referred to as Tirhakah, king of Kush, who fought the Assyrian army under Sennacherib before the siege of Jerusalem (2 Kings 19:8-9; Isaiah 37:8-9). While the name and general time period allow for a clear identification of Tirhakah, confusion has arisen over his title as "king of Kush" at the time when Sennacherib invaded Judah around 701 BC. Because the reign of Pharaoh Taharqa is assigned to ca. 690–664 BC, the placement of Taharqa leading an army and being called king 11 years before this date has led to speculation and criticism of historical accuracy.

Named several times in Assyrian sources of the 7th century BC, Taharqa is called Tarqu, while in a Babylonian tablet discussing the reign of Šamaš-šuma-ukin (668–648 BC), "Taharqa the pharaoh" is mentioned, followed by Necho I the pharaoh (BM 25091). In Assyrian records of Esarhaddon (ca. 681–669 BC) and Ashurbanipal (ca. 669–631 BC), Taharqa is referred to with the double titles of king of Egypt and king of Kush.

In 674 BC Esarhaddon of Assyria invaded Egypt but was repelled by Taharqa. Three years later Esarhaddon returned and successfully conquered Egypt. Then in 671 BC Esarhaddon captured Memphis and established Necho I as Pharaoh in the north. The next Assyrian king, Ashurbanipal, finished Taharqa, who fled to Thebes and died there in 664 BC. These royal Assyrian texts not only name Taharqa, but specify that he held the double titles of both king of Egypt and king of Kush (e.g., Prism B of Esarhaddon; Zencirli Stele; Rassam Cylinder; Nahr el-Kalb Stele of Esarhaddon). This is important in demonstrating that the king of Kush was a separate title recognized by foreign nations such as Assyria and Judah.

When Taharqa came to the aid of Hezekiah of Judah around 701 BC, he had not yet become pharaoh, as Shabaka held the title of king of Egypt. However, just as the books of Kings and Isaiah specify, Taharqa was called the king of Kush at this time, but not the king of Egypt. Assyrian records of Sennacherib about his campaign of 701 BC that ended in the failed siege of Jerusalem mention encountering a foreign army at Eltekeh (Tel Shalaf) in western Judah:

> Hezekiah of Judah...had become afraid and had called upon the kings of Egypt and the bowmen, the chariots and the cavalry of the king of Kush, an army beyond counting. And they had come to their assistance. In the plain of Eltekeh their battle lines were drawn up against me and they sharpened their weapons...I personally captured alive the Egyptian charioteers with the princes, and the charioteers of the king of Kush" (Prism of Sennacherib).

This record indicates that the king of Kush fought against Sennacherib, but it makes no mention of the king of Egypt. Thus, Taharqa as the king of Kush was at the battle along with various Egyptian troops, but Shabaka the king of Egypt was apparently not present. Although scholars have explained this detail in Kings and Isaiah as either Taharqa functioning only as a military commander under

Pyramid of Taharqa at Nuri

Pharaoh Shabaka with an anachronistic title or simply a mistake, the Assyrian sources appear to coincide with the Hebrew sources and show that the titles king of Egypt and king of Kush were distinguished, and that the king of Kush was the leader of this army that came to Judah to oppose the Assyrians in 701 BC.

> *When he heard them say concerning Tirhakah king of Cush [Kush], "He has come out to fight against you," and when he heard it he sent messengers to Hezekiah, saying, "Thus you shall say to Hezekiah king of Judah, 'Do not let your God in whom you trust deceive you, saying, "Jerusalem will not be given into the hand of the king of Assyria"'"* (Isaiah 37:9-10).

Glassner, Jean-Jacques. *Mesopotamian Chronicles.* Atlanta: Society of Biblical Literature, 2004.

Kitchen, Kenneth. *The Third Intermediate Period in Egypt, 1100–650 BC.* Warminster: Aris & Phillips, 1996.

Pritchard, James, ed. *The Ancient Near Eastern Texts Relating to the Old Testament.* 3rd ed. Princeton: Princeton University Press, 1969.

MERODACH-BALADAN

Kudurru of Marduk-apla-iddina II

Name: Merodach-Baladan (Berodach-Baladan, Marduk-apla-iddina II)

Time Period: 8th century BC (Sealand Third Dynasty)

Geographical Area: Babylon

Biblical Reference(s): 2 Kings 20:12-18; 2 Chronicles 32:27-31; Isaiah 39:1-7

Ancient Source(s): Barrel Cylinder of Marduk-apla-iddina; Babylonian Chronicle; Annals of Sargon; Bavian Rock Inscription of Sennacherib

Identification Rating: Firm (A)

Following the period when Hezekiah of Judah was ill, a king of Babylon named Merodach-Baladan (or Marduk-Baladan, meaning "Marduk has given me an heir"), also known as Marduk-apla-iddina II from the Bit-Yakin tribe, sent letters and a gift to Hezekiah. Following this communication, Merodach-Baladan visited Hezekiah in Jerusalem and was given a grand tour of his palace, his treasury, and elsewhere in the kingdom.

This Merodach-Baladan, or Marduk-apla-iddina II, was a Chaldean prince who had rebelled against the Assyrians and acquired the throne of Babylon in ca. 721 BC. His reign in Babylon spanned approximately 721–710 BC, when Sargon II drove him out of Babylon and reconquered the area for Assyria. However, after Sargon II died and Sennacherib became king, Merodach-Baladan returned to Babylon in 703 BC and reigned for another nine months before being defeated and exiled by Sennacherib. He fled to the "Sealands" of the Babylon region and retained power in parts of southern Mesopotamia before dying a few years later.

According to Assyrian and Babylonian records, Merodach-Baladan was a prominent leader in Mesopotamia for around three decades. In his own inscriptions, he describes victory over the army of Subartu, construction of a bridge over the Nar-Banitu canal, his lineage from Yakin, and rebuilding a temple of Eanna in Uruk. Merodach-Baladan is even pictured on a Babylonian kudurru (boundary marker) where he is shown making a legal agreement with one of his vassals. In Babylonian records, he is given 12 years as king, and Sargon fought against him (Babylonian King List A; ABC 1).

Babylon garden tablet of Marduk-Baladan

The earliest mention of Merodach-Baladan is in a text of Tiglath-Pileser III from around 729 BC, when he gave a tribute and is referred to as King of the Sealand. When the transition of power between Shalmaneser V and Sargon II occurred, Merodach-Baladan took advantage and became the independent ruler of Babylon. However, Sargon II eventually defeated him and expelled him from Babylon in 710 BC, although Merodach-Baladan would return (Great Inscription of Sargon at Khorsabad; Tang-I Var Inscription).

About five years later, a lengthy inscription of Sennacherib describing events of around 705 BC notes:

> At the beginning of my reign, when I had majestically ascended the throne and ruled the people of Assyria with obedience and peace, Merodach-baladan, king of Karduniash, an evil rebel, of treacherous mind, doer of evil, for whom truth is sinful, turned to Shutur-Nahhunte, the Elamite, for help, sent him gold and silver and precious stones, requesting his help (BM 113203).

This text also shows the tactics of Merodach-Baladan that were later used on Hezekiah in an attempt to gain a new ally against Assyria. Much later in the reign of Sennacherib, the Assyrian king recounted how he defeated and captured the son of Merodach-Baladan:

> I advanced into their midst like a fierce arrow and defeated their armies. I scattered their concentrations (and) I shattered their troops. I took alive in that battle the princes of the king of Elam, together

with Nabu-shum-ishkun, son of Merodach-Baladan king of Babylon (The Bavian Rock Inscription of Sennacherib).

He seems to have lived on for several years after being chased out of Babylon, and his descendants continued to rule the Sealand for decades. Perhaps later in the reign of Hezekiah of Judah, after the Assyrian army had returned to Nineveh and Esarhaddon had succeeded Sennacherib, the Babylonian king Merodach-Baladan sent an envoy to Jerusalem to establish diplomatic relations with Hezekiah, who had also fought against the Assyrians. This may have been the final days of Merodach-Baladan, when he was in exile and attempting to find allies and support to retake this throne in Babylon.

> *At that time Merodach-Baladan son of Baladan, king of Babylon, sent letters and a present to Hezekiah, for he heard that he had been sick and had recovered. Hezekiah was pleased, and showed them all his treasure house, the silver and the gold and the spices and the precious oil and his whole armory and all that was found in his treasuries. There was nothing in his house nor in all his dominion that Hezekiah did not show them* (Isaiah 39:1-2).

Frame, Grant. *Rulers of Babylonia: From the Second Dynasty of Isin to the End of Assyrian Domination (1157–612 BC)*. Toronto: RIMB 2, 1995.

Gadd, C.J. "Inscribed Barrel Cylinder of Marduk-Apla-Iddina II." *Iraq* 15.2 (1953).

AMARIAH
(Son of Hezekiah)

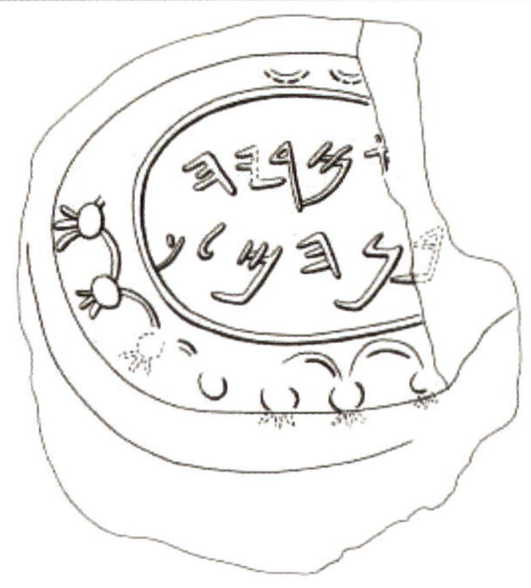

Bulla of Amariah

Name: Amariah (son of Hezekiah)

Time Period: 700 BC (Iron Age IIc)

Geographical Area: Kingdom of Judah

Biblical Reference(s): Zephaniah 1:1

Ancient Source(s): Bulla of Amaryahu

Identification Rating: Tentative (C)

Amariah was a son of King Hezekiah in the 8th and 7th centuries BC and an ancestor of the prophet Zephaniah who lived in the time of Josiah. A bulla from the Kingdom of Judah dated to around 700 BC may identify this prince. The bulla, impressed from a seal, was decorated with images of pomegranates encircling the Hebrew text, which reads "belonging to Amaryahu, son of thc king." Since the only known Amaryahu or Amariah who was a prince during this period was the son of Hezekiah mentioned in the book of Zephaniah, it is plausible to connect the bulla to Amariah, son of Hezekiah. However, due to the king not being named, the identification must remain tentative.

> *The word of the* Lord *which came to Zephaniah son of Cushi, son of Gedaliah, son of Amariah, son of Hezekiah, in the days of Josiah son of Amon, king of Judah* (Zephaniah 1:1).

Deutsch, Robert and Peter van der Veen. "The Bulla of Amaryahu Son of the King, the Ancestor of the Prophet Zephaniah?" in *Bible et Proche-Orient. Mélanges André Lemaire III* (Transeuphratène 46). Paris, 2014.

MANASSEH

Prism of Esarhaddon, which discusses the restoration of Babylon and includes the name Manasseh

Name: Manasseh (son of Hezekiah)

Time Period: 7th century BC (Iron Age IIc)

Geographical Area: Kingdom of Judah

Biblical Reference(s): 2 Kings 21:1-18; 2 Chronicles 32:33–33:20; Jeremiah 15:4

Ancient Source(s): Esarhaddon Prism B; Rassam Cylinder; Seal of Manasseh

Identification Rating: Firm (A)

Manasseh was the son of Hezekiah and the longest ruling king of Judah, holding the throne for 55 years about 697–643 BC. Recorded as the most corrupt of all the kings of Judah, who overturned many of the reforms ordered by Hezekiah, the books of Kings, Chronicles, and the prophet Jeremiah all condemn his evil deeds (Jeremiah 15:4). Near the end of his reign, Manasseh built additional defensive walls in Jerusalem, stationed soldiers in all of the fortified cities of Judah, and removed idols from the temple (2 Chronicles 33:14-16).

However, prior to this drastic change, Manasseh had been captured by the Assyrians, had a hook put in his flesh, and was taken in chains to Babylon temporarily (2 Chronicles 33:11-13). This brutal and humiliating practice of putting a hook in an enemy king and force-marching him in chains was a method by which the Assyrians attempted to intimidate and dominate other nations and was often done in tandem with tribute payments. This event is not known from Assyrian records, but it may relate the aftermath of the rebellion by Shamash-shum-ukin of Babylon against his brother Ashurbanipal of Assyria, which was crushed and Babylon defeated in 648 BC.

Other interactions of Manasseh with Assyria, however, are known from official sources of the Assyrian kings. During the reign of Manasseh, which spanned the reigns of Sennacherib, Esarhaddon, and Ashurbanipal of Assyria, the Kingdom of Judah was under threat and dominated by the Assyrians. In an official document of Esarhaddon, the Assyrian king names Manasseh along with other kings of the region and even describes how he forced them to transport construction materials to his capital at Nineveh:

> I called up the kings of the country Hatti and (of the region) on the other side of the river: Ba'lu, king of Tyre, Manasseh, king of Judah... all these I sent out and made them transport under terrible difficulties, to Nineveh, the town where I (exercise) my rulership, as building material for my palace (Esarhaddon Prism B).

The next Assyrian king, Ashurbanipal, also mentions Manasseh and a tribute, but adds that he forced these kings to accompany him and his army:

> Ba'al, king of Tyre, Manasseh, king of Judah...together 12 kings from the seashore, the islands and the mainland; servants who belong to me, brought heavy gifts to me and kissed my feet. I made these kings accompany my army over the land as well as the sea-route with their armed forces and their ships (Rassam Cylinder).

The Rassam Cylinder of Ashurbanipal

While the episode of Manasseh being brought to Babylon with hook and chains

Prism of Ashurbanipal mentioning Manasseh

has not been found in Assyrian records, it is consistent with their practices, and he is named in the official annals of two contemporary kings. Further, Manasseh is attested by his own seal from the time when his father, Hezekiah, was still king. This stone seal, carved from conglomerate, depicts a winged beetle at the top with two lines of Hebrew below. This winged beetle iconography is also found on the seals of Hezekiah and royal jar handle stamps attributed to the reign of Hezekiah. The Hebrew inscription on the seal reads "belonging to Manasseh, son of the king." Although it was found on the antiquities market, analysis by archaeologists and epigraphers indicates that it is an authentic seal from 8th-century BC Jerusalem and therefore attests to Manasseh when he was the crown prince of Judah.

> *Therefore the* L*ORD* *brought the commanders of the army of the king of Assyria against them, and they captured Manasseh with hooks, bound him with bronze chains and took him to Babylon* (2 Chronicles 33:11).

Hallo, William W. and K. Lawson Younger. *Context of Scripture*. Boston: Brill, 2000.

Pritchard, James, ed. *The Ancient Near Eastern Texts Relating to the Old Testament*. 3rd ed. with Supplement. Princeton: Princeton University Press, 1969.

ADRAMELECH

Crown prince Arda-Mulissu from the southwest palace of Sennacherib at Nineveh

Name: Adramelech (Arda-Mulissu)

Time Period: 7th century BC (Neo-Assyrian)

Geographical Area: Assyria

Biblical Reference(s): 2 Kings 19:37; Isaiah 37:38

Ancient Source(s): ABL (Assyrian and Babylonian Letters)

Identification Rating: Firm (A)

Adramelech (or Adrammelech), rendered in Assyrian sources as Arda-Mulissu, was one of the sons of King Sennacherib and a prince of Assyria. Living primarily in the 7th century BC during the Neo-Assyrian period, Adramelech participated in or even orchestrated the assassination of his father, Sennacherib, on the day of 20 Tebet in 681 BC with the help of his brother Sharezer. The brothers then fled west to the nearby kingdom of Urartu, and another one of their brothers, Esarhaddon, took the throne of Assyria.

At this time, Adramelech was the current eldest son and would have been heir to the throne. But Esarhaddon had replaced him as crown prince in 684 BC, likely due to the influence of his mother, Naqia. It seems that Adramelech had planned to take the throne through violence, assassinating his father, and as eldest son, naming himself king. But his younger brother Esarhaddon successfully outmaneuvered him. A few scholars have suggested that Esarhaddon was actually the assassin, but this is contrary to the testimony of the ancient sources and makes little sense since Esarhaddon was already the crown prince and designated heir and had no need to usurp the throne.

Instead, Adramelech was forced to flee to the "land of Ararat" (Urartu) and apparently never returned. Previously, Urartu had been attacked by the Assyrians under Sargon II with Sennacherib as the main commander, and although a peace had been made after Sennacherib became king of Assyria, the Urartian king Argishti II must have been wary of his Assyrian neighbors, probably held a grudge for the invasion decades ago, and was ready to take any advantageous opportunity available. The brothers, Adramelech and Sharezer, apparently thought they could seek refuge in Urartu and might be welcomed with open arms after killing Sennacherib. Based on the timeline, this happened at the very end of the reign of Argishti II, and they may have arrived in Urartu at the beginning of the reign of Rusa II.

Multiple sources discuss this plot and the culpability of sons of Sennacherib, although the primary blame appears to have been placed on Adrammelech. The Babylonian Chronicles refer to the assassination of Sennacherib by one son without specifying a name: "On the twentieth day of the month Tebêtu, Sennacherib, king of Assyria, was killed by his son in a rebellion" (Chronicle of Nabonassar). The records of Esarhaddon, who ascended the throne after Sennacherib died and he won the battle for succession, relate that at least two of his brothers had been opposing his appointment as crown prince and wanted the throne for themselves:

> Esarhaddon, the great king...Of my elder brothers their younger brother was I...(my) father who begat me exalted me in all due right amid all my brothers, and thus (he spoke): Is this the son of my succession?... the true fact of (my succession was brought home to my brothers, and the (way) of the gods they abandoned and to their own violent deeds trusted, plotting evil, evil tongue, lying slander, against the will of the gods, they set afoot against me and (with) unholy disloyalty behind my back they planned rebellion with each other (Esarhaddon Prism A).

The naming of Adramelech and his direct connection to the conspiracy is found in an Assyrian letter to the king, discovered at Nineveh (Kuyunjik), that describes an appeal to the king in which a man comes to warn the king of Assyria that his son Arda-Mulissu is planning to kill him. Although this cuneiform tablet is fragmentary with the beginning and end missing, the main body of the text has been preserved and relays important information and context, naming a particular son of Sennacherib, Arda-Mulissu (Adramelech), and describing knowledge of the planned assassination before it occurred:

> "[What] is your appeal to the king ab[out]?" He (answered): "It is about Arda-[Mullissi]." Th[ey covered] his face with his cloak and made him

> stand before Arda-Mul[lissi himself], saying: "Look! [Your appeal] is being granted, say it with your own mouth!" He said: "Your son Arda-[Mullissi] will kill you" (Assyrian Letter to Esarhaddon ABL 1091).

Sennacherib died ca. 681 BC, assassinated by his sons, and this was recorded in Assyrian sources as being primarily the work of Arda-Mulissu with his accomplice, who appears to have been Sharezer (cf. Berossus). Esarhaddon, the heir and crown prince, then took the throne.

> *It came about as he was worshiping in the house of Nisroch his god, that Adrammelech and Sharezer his sons killed him with the sword; and they escaped into the land of Ararat. And Esarhaddon his son became king in his place* (Isaiah 37:38).

Reynolds, Frances. *The Babylonian Correspondence of Esarhaddon and Letters to Assurbanipal and Sin-Šarru-Iškun from Northern and Central Babylonia.* State Archives of Assyria, Vol. 18. Helsinki: Helsinki University Press, 2003.

Stele of Rusa II in Urartu, where Adramelech fled

ESARHADDON

Esarhaddon and Queen Naqia

Name: Esarhaddon (Assur-ahu-iddina)

Time Period: 7th century BC (Neo-Assyrian)

Geographical Area: Assyria

Biblical Reference(s): 2 Kings 19:36-37; Ezra 4:2; Isaiah 37:38

Ancient Source(s): Esarhaddon Prism B; Samal Stele of Esarhaddon; Letter to Ashurbanipal; Chronicle of Nabonassar

Identification Rating: Firm (A)

Esarhaddon was a king of Assyria, coming to the throne after the murder of his father, Sennacherib, and reigning approximately 681–669 BC during the period of the Neo-Assyrian Empire. Originally, his eldest brother Aššur-nādin-šumi had been the heir to the throne, but when he was captured and killed by the Elamites in ca. 694 BC, Arda-Mulissu, the second eldest, was elevated to the position of crown price. However, he fell out of favor with Sennacherib, and in ca. 684 BC Esarhaddon was designated as the new heir and crown prince. Jealousy, anger, or lust for power led to Arda-Mulissu playing a major role in the overthrow of his father, and in 681 BC he was part of a plot that resulted in the assassination of Sennacherib.

Following a power struggle for the throne with his brothers, which Esarhaddon ultimately won, his assassin brothers Arda-Mulissu (Adrammelech) and Nabu-shar-usur (Sharezer) fled to the kingdom of Urartu (cf. 2 Kings 19:36-37). In addition to Assyrian sources and the Bible, this plot and the ascension of Esarhaddon was also recorded in Babylonian sources:

> On the twentieth day of the month Tebêtu, Sennacherib, king of Assyria, was killed by his son in a rebellion. For 24 years Sennacherib ruled Assyria. After the 20th day of the month Tebêtu the rebellion continued in Assyria until the 2nd day of the month Addaru. On

> the 18th day of the month Addaru Esarhaddon, his son, ascended the throne in Assyria (Chronicle of Nabonassar).

Esarhaddon is only briefly mentioned in the Bible, naming him as the successor to Sennacherib following the assassination and informing that Esarhaddon had settled people in Israel who were ancestors of the Samaritans (Isaiah 37:38; Ezra 4:1-2). Esarhaddon seems to be referenced as the king of Assyria who captured Manasseh, although his name is not specified (2 Chronicles 33:11). This campaign appears to be recorded in his records, stating:

> Property of Esarhaddon, great king, legitimate king, king of the world, king of Assyria, regent of Babylon...I called up the kings of the Hatti-land and the other side of the river (Euphrates); Ba'al, king of Tyre, Manasseh, king of Judah, Qaushgabri, king of Edom, Musuri, King of Moab, Sil-Bel, king of Gaza, Metinti, king of Ashkelon, Ikausu, king of Ekron...a total of 22 kings of the Hatti-land...I sent all of these to drag with pain and difficulty to Nineveh, the city of my dominion, as supplies needed for my palace (Esarhaddon Prism B).

After gaining control of the kingship, Esarhaddon then proceeded to occupy his time with military campaigns and building projects. He was especially interested in restoring old temples, including the Esagila temple of Marduk in Babylon and the Esharra temple of Ashur in the city of Ashur. And he rebuilt the city of Babylon that his father had destroyed, documenting this in his inscriptions and characterizing himself as the chosen servant of Marduk (BM 91027). He also constructed his own palace in Nineveh, which was discovered underneath the Nabi Yunus shrine.

From a military perspective, Esarhaddon was inconsistent, and although he won victories against the Cimmerians, the king of Sidon, the Kingdom of Judah, and Egypt, he was unable to conquer Urartu, and his armies were defeated by the Elamites and the Egyptians. His second campaign against Egypt was successful, and on the way from Assyria to Egypt, he received a prophecy that probably made him overconfident: "Esarhaddon entered and placed the crowns onto his head, and the following was proclaimed: 'You shall go forth and conquer the world!'" (Esarhaddon Letter to Ashurbanipal).

On one of his victory stelae, he identifies himself as "Esarhaddon, the great king, the mighty king, the king of the universe, king of Assyria, viceroy of

Samal Stele of Esarhaddon

Babylon, king of Sumer and Akkad, king of Karduniash…I am all powerful, I am a hero, I am gigantic, I am colossal, I am honored, I am magnified, I am without equal among all kings" and eventually goes on to describe his victory over Taharqa, king of Egypt and Kush in 671 BC (Samal Stele).

However, when Egypt launched a counter offensive in 669 BC and Esarhaddon traveled west to fight Taharqa once more, he died at Harran, and his son Ashurbanipal became king of Assyria. Although only briefly mentioned in the Bible, those events in the reign of Esarhaddon and the king himself are also attested in Assyrian and Babylonian records.

> *It came about as he was worshiping in the house of Nisroch his god, that Adrammelech and Sharezer killed him with the sword; and they escaped into the land of Ararat. And Esarhaddon his son became king in his place* (2 Kings 19:37).

Hallo, William W. and K. Lawson Younger. *Context of Scripture*. Boston: Brill, 2000.

Pritchard, James, ed. *The Ancient Near Eastern Texts Relating to the Old Testament*. Princeton: Princeton University Press, 1969.

ASHURBANIPAL

Lion hunt relief depicting Ashurbanipal in action

Name: Ashurbanipal (Osnappar)

Time Period: 7th century BC (Neo-Assyrian)

Geographical Area: Neo-Assyrian Empire

Biblical Reference(s): Ezra 4:10; cf. 2 Chronicles 33:11-13

Ancient Source(s): Assyrian Inscriptions and Reliefs of Ashurbanipal

Identification Rating: Probable (B)

Ashurbanipal, or Ashur-bani-apli, was the king of Assyria from 669–631 BC, enjoying the longest reign of any king in the Neo-Assyrian Empire. His most notable accomplishment was probably what has come to be known as the Library of Ashurbanipal in Nineveh, which contained tablets and copies of tablets from important texts of the Sumerians, Akkadians, Babylonians, and Assyrians in a vast array of subjects, numbering more than 30,000 tablets found in the palace of Ashurbanipal and the palace of Sennacherib. The contents of the tablets span many subjects, including legal, diplomatic, religious, astronomical, mathematical, medical, lexical, historical, literary, and mythological.

Because of this impressive collection of Ashurbanipal, many ancient writings have survived that would otherwise be unknown, and the king often communicated his interest in scholarship and the preservation of ancient tablets in his own inscriptions:

> I, Ashurbanipal, king of the universe, on whom the gods have bestowed intelligence, who has acquired penetrating acumen for the most recondite details of scholarly erudition (none of my predecessors having any comprehension of such matters), I have placed these tablets for the future in the library at Nineveh. I, Ashurbanipal, learned the wisdom of Nabu [the god of writing], laid hold of scribal practices of all the experts, as many as there are.

> I learnt the lore of the wise sage Adapa, the hidden secret of all scribal art. I can recognize celestial and terrestrial omens and discuss (them) in the assembly of the scholars. I can deliberate upon the series "If the liver is a mirror image of heaven" with able experts in oil divination. I can solve complicated multiplications and divisions which do not have an obvious solution. I have studied elaborate composition[s] in obscure Sumerian and Akkadian which are difficult to get right. I have inspected cuneiform sign[s] on stones from before the flood, which are cryptic, impenetrable and muddled up (Ashurbanipal Inscription L from Nineveh).

In numerous texts, Ashurbanipal names himself and uses the titles king of Assyria and king of the world, often invoking his predecessor kings or the deities of the Assyrian pantheon. He is also depicted in a variety of artwork from his reign, including the stone reliefs found at the North Palace in Nineveh and known as the Lion Hunt of Ashurbanipal, where the king is shown hunting and killing lions.

Although Ashurbanipal was a powerful and successful monarch who left behind many monuments and inscriptions detailing and depicting events from his reign, he was probably named only once in the Bible. This singular and contested mention comes from the book of Ezra and describes an earlier time when Osnappar or Asenappar (Ashurbanipal) was involved in the resettlement of peoples to Samaria. Because Ashurbanipal did conduct military campaigns in Elam and Babylonia, including an attack on the city of Susa, and predecessor kings such as Sargon II did resettle conquered people in areas such as Samaria, the events recounted in Ezra are consistent with the reign of Ashurbanipal.

Further, Asenappar could be a variant version of his name, and it is therefore plausible that the letter in the book of Ezra does refer to Ashurbanipal. Elsewhere, in the book of Chronicles, he seems to be described but not named when the "commanders of the army of the king of Assyria" captured Manasseh with hooks. Ashurbanipal may have been the king of Assyria referred to there, although it is likely that Esarhaddon was king at the time and Ashurbanipal was a commander of the army.

> *Then wrote Rehum the commander and Shimshai the scribe and the rest of their colleagues, the judges and the lesser governors, the officials, the secretaries, the men of Erech, the Babylonians, the men of Susa, that is,*

the Elamites, and the rest of the nations which the great and honorable Osnappar deported and settled in the city of Samaria, and in the rest of the region beyond the River (Ezra 4:9-10).

Jeffers, Joshua, and Jamie Novotny. *The Royal Inscriptions of Ashurbanipal (668–631 BC), Aššur-Etel-Ilāni (630–627 BC), and Sîn-Šarra-Iškun (626–612 BC), Kings of Assyria, Part 2. Royal Inscriptions of the Neo-Assyrian Period,* Vol. 5/2. University Park: Eisenbrauns, 2023.

Luckenbill, Daniel. *Ancient Records of Assyria and Babylonia*, Vol. II. Chicago: University of Chicago Press, 1927.

Millard, Alan. "Assyrian Royal Names in Biblical Hebrew." *Journal of Semitic Studies* XXI (1976).

JOSIAH

Name: Josiah, son of Amon (Yoshiyahu)

Time Period: 7th century BC (Iron Age II)

Geographical Area: Kingdom of Judah

Biblical Reference(s): 2 Kings 21:26–23:30; 2 Chronicles 25:3; Jeremiah 25:3

Ancient Source(s): Moussaieff Ostracon

Identification Rating: Speculative (D)

The "Three Shekels" ostracon possibly referencing Josiah

Josiah ascended to the throne of Judah when he was only eight years old, and he ruled for a total of 31 years about 640–609 BC. Josiah was known for his religious reforms and the reinstitution of the celebration of Passover after Hilkiah the priest rediscovered the Book of the Law in the 18th year of his reign around 622 BC (2 Kings 23:23). Years later in about 609 BC, Josiah rode out to battle against Pharaoh Necho II as an ally of the Babylonians, but he was mortally wounded by archers and taken back to Jerusalem, where he died and was buried.

It is possible that Josiah is named in a Hebrew ostracon, dated on epigraphic grounds to approximately the 8th or 7th century BC based on parallels from other ostraca, but there has been considerable debate about the authenticity of the artifact and the king to whom it refers. The text translates as "Ashyahu the king has ordered you to give by the hand of [Ze]charyahu silver of Tarshish to the house of YHWH three shekels" (Moussaieff Ostracon No. 1). The Bible does indeed discuss Josiah in the context of the temple, and the name on the ostracon could be that of Josiah the king, but it also could be Jehoash, whose reign ended in the early 8th century BC. The mention of a Zechariah in the context of the Jerusalem temple further suggests an identification with Jehoash and Zechariah the priest. However, due to the questions about the artifact and the names, its connection to Josiah should be understood as speculative.

Now in the eighteenth year of King Josiah, the king sent Shaphan, the son of Azaliah the son of Meshullam the scribe, to the house of the Lord saying, "Go up to Hilkiah the high priest that he may count the money brought in to the house of the L*ORD* *which the doorkeepers have gathered from the people. Let them deliver it into the hand of the workmen who have the oversight of the house of the* L*ORD*, *and let them give it to the workmen who are in the house of the* L*ORD* *to repair the damages of the house"* (2 Kings 22:3-5).

Eph'aland Naveh. "Remarks on the Recently Published Moussaieff Ostraca." *IEJ* 48 (1998).

MESHULLAM

Name: Meshullam

Time Period: 7th century BC (Iron Age IIc)

Geographical Area: Kingdom of Judah

Biblical Reference(s): 2 Kings 22:3

Ancient Source(s): Azaliah seal

Identification Rating: Probable (B)

Meshullam was the father of Azaliah, the grandfather of Shaphan, and the great-grandfather of Gemariah. All four of the men in this family lineage appear to be attested by seals and bullae from the Kingdom of Judah. According to the book of Kings, Meshullam seems to have been a scribe perhaps serving in the 7th century BC under Amon and into the reign of Josiah, and his descendants continued in this role of serving the kings of Judah for many decades.

The name and lineage of Meshullam is found on a Hebrew seal inscribed with two lines divided by a lotus bud and reading "belonging to Azaliah son of Meshullam." The seal was made of a red stone, and although its whereabouts are currently unknown, an impression created from the seal has preserved the information. The type of seal matches the time period of Meshullam and Azaliah around the 7th century BC, and the names in the lineage are correct, although the seal does not make reference to their profession or the name of a king.

> *In the eighteenth year of King Josiah, the king sent Shaphan, the son of Azaliah the son of Meshullam the scribe, to the house of the* Lord*...* (2 Kings 22:3).

Avigad, Nahman. *Corpus of West Semitic Stamp Seals*. Jerusalem: Hebrew University, 1997.

AZALIAH

Name: Azaliah

Time Period: 7th century BC (Iron Age IIc)

Geographical Area: Kingdom of Judah

Biblical Reference(s): 2 Kings 22:3; 2 Chronicles 34:8

Ancient Source(s): Azaliah bulla

Identification Rating: Tentative (C)

According to the books of Kings and Chronicles, a scribe known as Azaliah belonged to a family of scribes in Jerusalem, including his father Meshullam, his son Shaphan, and his grandson Gemariah. Azaliah seems to have lived during the time of King Josiah and probably the previous kings Amon and Manasseh in the 7th century BC, although detailed information is sparse.

A seal impression from a now-lost red stone seal may have belonged to this Azaliah the scribe. The Hebrew inscription reads "belonging to Azaliah son of Meshullam" and features a lotus bud that divides the two lines of text. Since it is of the type of bullae and seal attributed to the 8th to 6th centuries BC, and the names and relationships are a match, it may be archaeological attestation of the scribes Azaliah and his father, Meshullam, although the currently limited data makes a definitive conclusion impossible.

> *In the eighteenth year of King Josiah, the king sent Shaphan, the son of Azaliah the son of Meshullam the scribe, to the house of the* Lord*...* (2 Kings 22:3).

Avigad, Nahman. *Corpus of West Semitic Stamp Seals*. Jerusalem: Hebrew University, 1997.

SHAPHAN

Bulla belonging to Gemariah, son of Shaphan

Name: Shaphan the Scribe

Time Period: 7th century BC (Iron Age IIc)

Geographical Area: Kingdom of Judah

Biblical Reference(s): 2 Kings 22:3-14; 2 Chronicles 34:8-21; Jeremiah 36:10-12

Ancient Source(s): Bulla of Gemariah; Bulla of Ahiqam

Identification Rating: Firm (A)

Shaphan was a scribe or secretary during the reign of Josiah in the 7th century BC, and multiple members of his family who were involved in serving the royal house for generations seem to be attested by seals and bullae. Four generations of his family are mentioned in connection with the government of Judah during the 7th and 6th centuries BC—his father, Azaliah; Shaphan himself; his sons Gemariah and Ahiqam; and his grandson Gedaliah the governor.

Two artifacts—one from Jerusalem and one from an unknown location—mention the name Shaphan and two of his sons known from the books of Kings, Chronicles, and Jeremiah. A 6th-century BC bulla excavated from Stratum X, the 587 BC destruction layer of the City of David in Jerusalem, contains two lines of Hebrew text and appears to attest to Shaphan the Scribe and one of his sons, reading "belonging to Gemariah [son of] Shaphan." A similar Hebrew bulla, although found on the antiquities market but likely genuine, seems to attest to Shaphan and his other son Ahiqam, named in the books of Kings and Jeremiah, reading "belonging to Ahiqam son of Shaphan."

Although Shaphan's occupation or title of scribe is not mentioned, the two bullae together present compelling evidence for the identification and attestation of Shaphan based on name, time period, location, and family lineage.

Moreover, Shaphan the scribe told the king saying, "Hilkiah the priest has given me a book." And Shaphan read it in the presence of the king. When the king heard the words of the book of the law, he tore his clothes.

Then the king commanded Hilkiah the priest, Ahikam the son of Shaphan, Achbor the son of Micaiah, Shaphan the scribe, and Asaiah the king's servant… (2 Kings 22:10-12).

Schneider, Tsvi. "Six Biblical Signatures." *Biblical Archaeology Review* 17.4 (1991).

Remains of a house in Jerusalem destroyed by the Babylonians in 587 BC

HILKIAH
(the Priest)

Seal of Hanan, son of Hilkiah the priest

Name: Hilkiah (the Priest)

Time Period: 7th century BC (Iron Age IIc)

Geographical Area: Kingdom of Judah

Biblical Reference(s): 2 Kings 22:4-23:24; 1 Chronicles 6:13; 9:11; 2 Chronicles 34:9-22

Ancient Source(s): Seal of Hanan; Bulla of Azariah

Identification Rating: Firm (A)

Hilkiah, son of Shallum, was the high priest during the reign of Josiah (ca. 640–609 BC). Hilkiah was instrumental in the religious reforms of King Josiah, as not only did he assist in reforms and restoration but was credited with rediscovering the Book of the Law in the Jerusalem temple during the 18th year of Josiah (2 Kings 23:24; 2 Chronicles 34:14). According to the book of Chronicles, Hilkiah the priest had a son named Azariah who also became a priest (1 Chronicles 6:13).

Two inscribed artifacts found in Jerusalem connect to Hilkiah the priest and his family. A ring seal of the 7th century BC may be the most compelling evidence for Hilkiah the priest, and it includes the name of a son previously unknown. The seal has a three-line inscription in Hebrew that translates as "belonging to Hanan, son of Hilkiah, the priest." While belonging to a son of Hilkiah and not Hilkiah himself, it does designate him as a priest and places him around the 7th century BC, which due to the priestly lists narrows the identification to only one possible Hilkiah.

However, a second artifact naming Hilkiah appears to further support his existence as a prominent person in Jerusalem during the 7th century BC. Excavated in a 7th-century BC layer from roughly the reign of Josiah, Jehoahaz, or

Jehoiakim (Eliakim) prior to the Babylonian destruction of the city, a bulla stamped with the name of Hilkiah and another son may attest to two people named in the Old Testament. The impression on the bulla reads "belonging to Azariah, son of Hilkiah." Although this seal impression does not give the occupation of the bearer, it was certainly the property of a prominent official in Jerusalem during the late 7th century BC, gives the basic family lineage, and therefore appears to have belonged to the Azariah who is named as the son and successor of Hilkiah the priest (1 Chronicles 6:13; Ezra 7:1). Thus, the ring seal and bulla together provide substantive evidence for the existence of Hilkiah the priest and his sons around 600 BC.

> *Moreover, Josiah removed the mediums and the spiritists and the teraphim and the idols and all the abominations that were seen in the land of Judah and in Jerusalem, that he might confirm the words of the law which were written in the book that Hilkiah the priest found in the house of the* L*ORD* (2 Kings 23:24).

Elayi, Josette. "New Light on the Identification of the Seal of Priest Hanan, Son of Hilqiyahu." *Bibliotheca Orientalis* 5/6 (1992).

JEREMIAH

Lachish Letter 16

Name: Jeremiah the prophet (son of Hilkiah)

Time Period: 7th century BC (Iron Age IIc)

Geographical Area: Kingdom of Judah

Biblical Reference(s): 2 Chronicles 35:25; 36:12-22; Jeremiah 1:1

Ancient Source(s): Lachish Ostraca

Identification Rating: Tentative (C)

Jeremiah the prophet was the son of Hilkiah the priest and came from the town of Anathoth just northeast of Jerusalem, prophesying during the reigns of Josiah, Jehoahaz, Jehoiakim, Jehoiachin, and Zedekiah from about 627–587 BC (Jeremiah 1:1-3). A few years after the fall of Jerusalem and the assassination of Gedaliah the governor, Jeremiah relocated to Egypt with a group that included Baruch and members of the royal family (Jeremiah 43:5-7).

Although he was the major prophet in the Kingdom of Judah for about four decades and two books of the Bible are attributed to him, it is generally thought that Jeremiah the prophet is unattested in the archaeological record. No seal or bulla of Jeremiah has been found in Jerusalem or Judah, and although he lived his final years in Egypt and may have even gone to Elephantine, where a significant cache of 5th-century BC Aramaic papyri and ostraca were found that discuss officials and priests in Jerusalem and a community of diaspora Jews in Elephantine, no reference to Jeremiah has been found in those documents.

Yet the letters discovered at Lachish from the time of the Babylonian conquest of Judah just before 587 BC may refer to Jeremiah the prophet and perhaps even specify him by name. One letter that clearly reads "Mibtahyahu son of Jeremiah" cannot be Jeremiah the prophet because he had no children (Jeremiah 16:2), and further information about the identity of this Jeremiah is unknown (Lachish Letter 1). However, other letters may relate to Jeremiah the prophet. A letter about a mission to Egypt, also noted in the book of Ezekiel and alluded to in the book of Jeremiah, mentions a warning from the prophet (Ezekiel 17:15; cf. Jeremiah 37:5). The letter states, "As for the letter of Tobiah, servant of the king, which came to Shallum son of Jaddua through the prophet, saying, 'Beware! Your servant has sent it to my lord'" (Lachish Letter 3). Although the name of the prophet is not specified, by historical context and process of elimination it can be inferred that this would be a reference to Jeremiah.

While there were two other prophets in Judah during the life of Jeremiah, Uriah and Hananiah, both had died years before these Lachish letters were written. Thus, Jeremiah is the only known remaining candidate for this prophet. Uriah, son of Shemaiah, was executed during the reign of Jehoiakim, and Hananiah died in the 4th year of Zedekiah around 594 BC (Jeremiah 26:23; 28:1-17). This "Hananiah, son of Azzur, the prophet who was from Gibeon" might also be attested by a 7th-century BC inscribed seal (Jeremiah 28:1). The blue chalcedony seal has a two-line Hebrew inscription reading "belonging to Hananiah son of Azzur" that is surrounded by a pomegranate border. However, it was purchased on the antiquities market, Hananiah was a fairly common name around the 7th century BC, and because no other information besides the name of the father is known, the identification must be speculative.

Further, the name of Jeremiah the prophet may appear in two other letters from Lachish. One fragmentary letter records "[...i]ah the prophet" on line five, while on line three of another poorly preserved ostracon the name "[Je]remiah" can be read (Lachish Letter 16 and 17).

This phrase "Jeremiah the prophet" occurs in the books of Chronicles, Daniel, and Jeremiah, indicating that he was widely known and associated with this title. The connection is possible, considering the fragmentary name fits Jeremiah, the person is identified as the prophet, and the political and chronological context suggests the only known identification could be Jeremiah the prophet, although his attestation must remain tentative at this time.

Lachish Letter 3

The word that came to Jeremiah from the L*ORD* *in the tenth year of Zedekiah king of Judah, which was the eighteenth year of Nebuchadnezzar. Now at that time the army of the king of Babylon was besieging Jerusalem, and Jeremiah the prophet was shut up in the court of the guard, which was in the house of the king of Judah, because Zedekiah king of Judah had shut him up, saying, "Why do you prophesy, saying, 'Thus says the* L*ORD,* *"Behold, I am about to give this city into the hand of the king of Babylon, and he will take it"'"* (Jeremiah 32:1-3).

Ahituv, Shmuel. *Echoes from the Past: Hebrew and Cognate Inscriptions from the Biblical Period.* Carol Stream: Tyndale House, 2015.

Avigad, Nahman. *Corpus of West Semitic Stamp Seals.* Jerusalem: Hebrew University, 1997.

ASAIAH

Gedaliah son of Ahikam—seal of Jaazniah, servant of the king

Name: Asaiah (Asayahu)

Time Period: 600 BC (Iron Age IIc)

Geographical Area: Kingdom of Judah

Biblical Reference(s): 2 Kings 22:12-14; 2 Chronicles 34:20

Ancient Source(s): Seal of Asayahu

Identification Rating: Tentative (C)

Asaiah was a servant of King Josiah who lived during the 7th century BC in Judah, and he was associated with other officials such as Hilkiah the priest, Ahikam, and Shaphan the scribe. He was designated as "Asaiah the king's servant" (2 Kings 22:12). A stone seal decorated with the image of a horse, with Hebrew text below and above, may have belonged to this individual. Dated to the 7th century BC, the inscribed Hebrew seal reads "belonging to Asayahu, servant of the king."

Since name, title, date, and geographic region are a match, it is plausible that this seal belonged to Asaiah, the servant of King Josiah. However, as the name of the king is not specified and no additional information is present, this identification is tentative.

> *The king commanded Hilkiah the priest, Ahikam the son of Shaphan, Achbor the son of Micaiah, Shaphan the scribe, and Asaiah the king's servant...* (2 Kings 22:12).

Heltzer, Michael. "The Seal of Asayahu," in Hallo, William W. and K. Lawson Younger. *Context of Scripture*, Vol. 2. Boston: Brill, 2000.

AHIQAM

Name: Ahiqam (Ahikam)

Time Period: 600 BC (Iron Age IIc)

Geographical Area: Kingdom of Judah

Biblical Reference(s): 2 Kings 22:12; 25:22; 2 Chronicles 34:20; Jeremiah 26:24

Ancient Source(s): Bulla of Ahiqam

Identification Rating: Probable (B)

Ahiqam, or Ahikam, was a son of Shaphan and an official in the royal court of Judah during the 7th and 6th centuries BC. He served under the kings Josiah and Jehoiakim and was an ally of the prophet Jeremiah. His son, Gedaliah, was appointed the governor of Judah after the Babylonian conquest of Nebuchadnezzar. A bulla, partially damaged, appears to have been impressed by a Hebrew seal inscribed with "belonging to Ahiqam son of Shaphan."

The clay bulla was supposedly found with two other bullae dating to the period around 600 BC, and it may have originated in Jerusalem. As it appeared on the antiquities market rather than documented in an official excavation, however, its provenance remains speculative. But the bulla does contain the correct father and son names, these seals and their bullae were typically used by government officials, it comes from the kingdom of Judah, and it dates to the period in which Ahiqam served. Thus, while not definitive, it appears likely that the bulla was created by an official seal that belonged to the Ahiqam mentioned in the books of Kings, Chronicles, and Jeremiah.

> *The king commanded Hilkiah the priest, Ahikam the son of Shaphan, Achbor the son of Micaiah, Shaphan the scribe, and Asaiah the king's servant…* (2 Kings 22:12).

Avigad, Nahman. *Corpus of West Semitic Stamp Seals.* Jerusalem: Hebrew University, 1997.

SHELEMIAH

Name: Shelemiah, father of Jehucal (son of Shebi)

Time Period: 7th and 6th centuries BC (Iron Age IIc)

Geographical Area: Kingdom of Judah

Biblical Reference(s): Jeremiah 37:3; 38:1

Ancient Source(s): Bulla of Jehucal

Identification Rating: Firm (A)

Shelemiah lived around the 7th and 6th centuries BC and is mentioned only in reference to his son Jehucal (Jucal), who served in the royal court of Zedekiah leading up to the time of the Babylonian capture and destruction of Jerusalem in 587 BC. During excavations in Jerusalem, a 6th-century BC Hebrew bulla was found that names both father and son. The impression reads "belonging to Jehucal, son of Shelemiah, son of Shebi."

Although the grandfather, Shebi, is not mentioned in the Bible, the names, relationship, location, time period, and status all indicate that the seal used to make the bulla belonged to Jehucal and also attests to his father, Shelemiah.

> *Now Shephatiah the son of Mattan, and Gedaliah the son of Pashhur, and Jucal the son of Shelemiah, and Pashhur the son of Malchijah heard the words that Jeremiah was speaking to all the people…* (Jeremiah 38:1).

Mazar and Ben-Arie. *The Summit of the City of David Excavations 2005–2008.* Jerusalem: Shoham, 2015.

NECHO II
(King of Egypt)

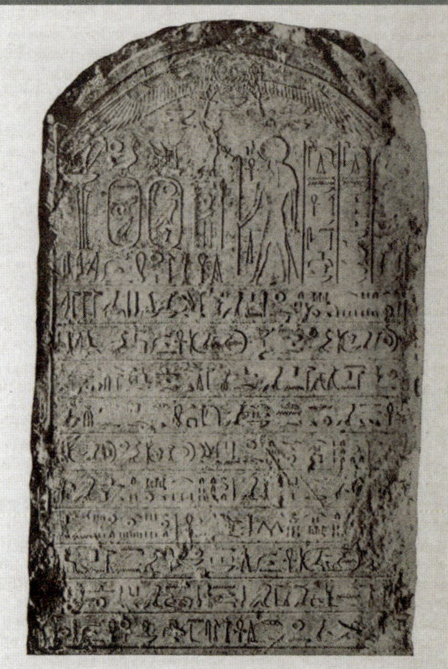

Apis Stele of Necho II

Name: Necho II, king of Eygpt (Neco, Wahe-ib-re)

Time Period: 600 BC (26th Dynasty of Egypt)

Geographical Area: Egypt

Biblical Reference(s): 2 Kings 23:29-35; 2 Chronicles 35:20–36:4; Jeremiah 46:2

Ancient Source(s): Egyptian monuments; Babylonian Chronicle; Herodotus

Identification Rating: Firm (A)

Necho II, or Neco, was the pharaoh of Egypt about 610–595 BC, when Jeremiah was a prophet in Judah and the Babylonian kings Nabopolassar and Nebuchadnezzar II were asserting dominance over western Asia. The Bible mentions Necho II by name in three books—Kings, Chronicles, and Jeremiah—describing the victory of Necho II over Josiah at the battle of Megiddo in 609 BC, appointing Eliakim (Jehoiakim) as the new king of Judah, and the victory of the Babylonians over Necho II at the battle of Carchemish in 605 BC. Necho II appears to have had extensive interaction with other nations and kings, including the Assyrians, Babylonians, and Judeans.

While Necho II is specified by name in the Hebrew Bible and on numerous Egyptian monuments, in Babylonian records only the "army of Egypt" that helped Ashur-uballit II of Assyria is mentioned, while Assyrian sources have either not survived or do not refer to him. There is another Necho, king of Egypt, mentioned in Assyrian texts such as the Rassam Cylinder of Ashurbanipal and the Esarhaddon Chronicle. But this is in reference to Necho I (ca. 672–664 BC), who reigned about 55 years before Necho II.

The Babylonian Chronicle ABC 3 (BM 21901) mentions the army of Egypt without specifying the name of its leader, Pharaoh Necho II: "In the seventeenth year...Ashur-uballit [II], king of Assyria, with a large army from Egypt crossed the river Euphrates and marched against Harran to conquer it." This conflict was subsequent to the battle of Megiddo, where Josiah foolishly decided to fight in support of the Babylonians against Necho II. Josiah was fatally wounded by arrows and then taken back to Jerusalem, where he died and was buried (2 Kings 23:29-30; 2 Chronicles 35:20-24).

ABC 4 Babylonian Chronicle

This battle at Megiddo may also be briefly mentioned by Herodotus in the 5th century BC, who records that Necho II was victorious at "Magdolus" without naming Josiah (Herodotus, *Histories* 2.159). Herodotus also noted that Necho II began digging a canal from the Nile River near Bubastis to the Red Sea, and that later he sent a sailing expedition of Phoenicians that circumnavigated Africa in nearly three years (Herodotus, *Histories* 2.159, 4.158-159).

Jasper seal belonging to Jehoahaz, son of the king

On his way home to Egypt after he and Ashur-uballit II failed to defeat the Babylonians, Necho II captured Jehoahaz and appointed Eliakim (Jehoiakim) as king of Judah in his place. This Jehoahaz, son of king Josiah, reigned for only three months before he was taken prisoner (2 Kings 23:31-34). Jehoahaz III may be attested on an unprovenanced jasper seal from around the 7th century BC, reading "belonging to Jehoahaz son of the king" and decorated with a rooster, similar to the image on the seal of Jaazaniah. This seal would have been from the period when Jehoahaz III was a prince, but since the name of the king is not specified on the seal, the identification cannot be certain. A few years later, the army of Pharaoh Necho II was obliterated by Nebuchadnezzar II at the battle of Carchemish

Fall of Nineveh Chronicle

in ca. 605 BC, as recorded in both the Babylonian Chronicle and the book of Jeremiah.

> Nebuchadnezzar...crossed the river to go against the Egyptian army which lay in Carchemish. They fought with each other and the Egyptian army withdrew before him. He accomplished their defeat and beat them to non-existence. As for the rest of the Egyptian army which had escaped from the defeat so quickly that no weapon had reached them, in the district of [Battle of Hamath] the Babylonian troops overtook and defeated them so that not a single man escaped to his own country (ABC 5; cf. Jeremiah 46:2).

Following this battle, the Assyrian Empire disintegrated, and the Egyptians received a blow from which their kingdom never recovered. However, Necho II survived, and about two years later he was asked to help against the "king of Babylon," who was Nebuchadnezzar. The Adon Papyrus (KAI 266), which was probably written around 603 BC from a local king in the Levant, possibly located at Aphek, asks for military intervention from the "Lord of Kings Pharaoh," who at the time was Necho II.

Although foreign sources give the most information about events during the reign of Necho II, various inscriptions and monuments from Egypt also attest to his presence and role as pharaoh, including a stele from Elephantine, a building at Sais, and his cartouche found on numerous objects and a statue. Necho II was obviously a pharaoh of Egypt around 600 BC who had considerable involvement in international affairs, although many of his endeavors were unsuccessful.

> *That which came as the word of the* L*ORD* *to Jeremiah the prophet concerning the nations. To Egypt, concerning the army of Pharaoh Neco king of Egypt, which was by the Euphrates River at Carchemish, which Nebuchadnezzar king of Babylon defeated in the fourth year of Jehoiakim the son of Josiah, king of Judah...* (Jeremiah 46:1-2).

Grayson, Albert. *Assyrian and Babylonian Chronicles*. University Park: Eisenbrauns, 2000.

Porten, Bezalel. "The Identity of King Adon." *The Biblical Archaeologist* Vol. 44, No. 1 (1981).

NEBUCHADNEZZAR II

Tower of Babel Stele

Name: Nebuchadnezzar II, son of Nabopolassar (Nebuchadrezzar)

Time Period: 642–562 BC (Neo-Babylonian Empire)

Geographical Area: Babylon

Biblical Reference(s): 2 Kings 24:1–25:22; 2 Chronicles 36:6-16; Ezra 5:12; Nehemiah 7:6; Esther 2:6; Jeremiah 21:2-7; 39:1-11; Ezekiel 29:19; Daniel 1:1–4:37

Ancient Source(s): Babylonian Chronicle; East India House Inscription; Ishtar Gate Inscription; Tower of Babel Stele; Building Cylinders of Nebuchadnezzar

Identification Rating: Firm (A)

Nebuchadnezzar II was the second king of the Neo-Babylonian Empire and the son of Nabopolassar, ruling for 43 years from 605–562 BC and establishing Babylon as the dominant power in the ancient Near East for decades. Born in about 642 BC before his father became king, Nebuchadnezzar served as general of the army before ascending to the throne when Nabopolassar died.

In the Bible, Nebuchadnezzar is named in the books of Kings, Chronicles, Ezra, Nehemiah, Esther, Jeremiah, Ezekiel, and Daniel. Significant events of his reign described in the biblical texts include the deportation of people from Judah, imprisonment of kings, installation of new kings, attacks on Jerusalem, the conquest and destruction of Jerusalem, looting and destruction of the temple, victory over Egypt, building projects in Babylon, construction of a massive statue, and a period of madness;—are all described in the biblical texts.

The archaeological attestation for Nebuchadnezzar is overwhelming, so only a select few artifacts need to be mentioned that firmly establish his existence and key events from his life. Just prior to becoming king, Nebuchadnezzar commanded the forces of Babylon in a victory against Necho II and the Egyptians at the Battle of Carchemish in 605 BC. Recorded in the Chronicle of Nabopolassar, it notes:

> The king of Akkad [Nabopolassar] stayed home (while) Nebuchadnezzar, his eldest son and crown prince mustered. He took his army's lead and marched to Carchemish, which is on the bank of the Euphrates. He crossed the river at Carchemish...They did battle together. The army of Egypt retreated before him. He inflicted a (defeat) upon them and finished them off completely (ABC 5; cf. ABC 4 and Jeremiah 46:2).

The death of Nabopolassar and the ascension of Nebuchadnezzar are recorded next, in addition to an attack on the Levant that included the subjugation of Judah in 605 BC when Jehoiakim was king:

> For 21 years Nabopolassar had been king of Babylon, when on 8 Abu he went to his destiny; in the month of Ululu Nebuchadnezzar returned to Babylon and on 1 Ululu he sat on the royal throne in Babylon. In the accession year Nebuchadnezzar went back again to the Hatti-land and until the month of Šabatu marched unopposed through the Hatti-land. In the month of Šabatu he took the heavy tribute of the Hatti-territory to Babylon (ABC 5; cf. Chronicle 23; 2 Kings 24:1).

The most detailed existing Babylonian account about Nebuchadnezzar and Judah, however, records the time when he besieged Jerusalem, captured Jehoiachin, and installed Zedekiah on the throne in 598 BC:

> In the seventh year, the month of Kislîmu, the king of Akkad mustered his troops, marched to the Hatti-land, and besieged the city of Judah [Jerusalem] and on the second day of the month of Addaru he seized the city and captured the king [Jehoiachin]. He appointed there a king of his own choice [Zedekiah], received its heavy tribute and sent to Babylon (ABC 5; cf. 2 Kings 24:8-17).

In his capital city of Babylon, Nebuchadnezzar carried out extensive construction and remodeling projects, including the Ishtar Gate, his palace, temples, and the great ziggurat. The cuneiform inscription on the Ishtar Gate gives biographical information about Nebuchadnezzar and a few of his construction projects with aggrandizing language about the monarch:

> Nebuchadnezzar, King of Babylon, the pious prince appointed by the will of Marduk, the highest priestly prince, beloved of Nabu...constantly concerned with the well being of Babylon and Borsippa, the wise, the humble, the caretaker of Esagila and Ezida, the first born son of Nabopolassar, the King of Babylon, am I...I pulled down these gates and laid their foundations at the water table with asphalt and bricks and had them made of bricks with blue stone on which wonderful bulls and dragons were depicted (Ishtar Gate Inscription of Nebuchadnezzar).

Numerous clay cylinders and bricks of Nebuchadnezzar describe the building of his royal palace in Babylon or repairs and expansion of his palace in Babylon (cf. Daniel 4:28-30). An odd passage in an expedition inscription of Nebuchadnezzar even refers to a statue of himself with an accompanying identification, reminiscent of the golden image of Nebuchadnezzar mentioned in the book of Daniel:

Ishtar Gate Inscription

> Beside my statue as king...I wrote an inscription mentioning my name...I erected for posterity. May future [kings] res[pect the monuments], remember the praise of the gods (inscribed thereupon). [He who] respects...my royal name, who does not abrogate my statutes (and) not change my decrees, shall be secure (Wadi Brisa Inscription; cf. Daniel 3:1-6).

Another impressive text of Nebuchadnezzar repeats biographical information and notes his building of a temple for Marduk:

> I am Nebuchadnezzar, king of Babylon, the exalted prince, the favorite of the god Marduk, the beloved of the god Nabu...the son of Nabopolassar, king of Babylon...By thy command, merciful Marduk, may the temple I have built endure for all time and may I be satisfied with its splendor (East India House Inscription).

Although Nebuchadnezzar is extensively documented in Babylonian sources, information from the middle of his reign is lacking, and the only known image of him appears on a stele that records reconstruction of the great ziggurat of Babylon: "Etemenanki the ziggurat of Babylon, I made it, the wonder of the people of the world, I raised its top to heaven, made doors for the gates, and I covered it with bitumen and bricks" (Tower of Babel Stele).

Nebuchadnezzar died in 562 BC, apparently of natural causes, and one of his sons, Amel-Marduk, became his successor for two years until he was assassinated. Nebuchadnezzar, one of the most frequently referenced foreign kings in the Bible, is also one of the most widely known kings of the ancient world through archaeological discoveries.

> *Nebuchadnezzar the king of Babylon came to the city, while his servants were besieging it. Jehoiachin the king of Judah went out to the king of Babylon, he and his mother and his servants and his captains and his officials. So the king of Babylon took him captive in the eighth year of his reign...So he led Jehoiachin away into exile to Babylon; also the king's mother and the king's wives and his officials and the leading men of the land, he led away into exile from Jerusalem to Babylon...Then the king of Babylon made his uncle Mattaniah king in his place, and changed his name to Zedekiah* (2 Kings 24:11-17).

East India House Inscription

Glassner, Jean-Jacques. *Mesopotamian Chronicles*. Atlanta: Society of Biblical Literature, 2004.

Pritchard, James, ed. *The Ancient Near Eastern Texts Relating to the Old Testament*. 3rd ed. with Supplement. Princeton: Princeton University Press, 1969.

AZARIAH

Name: Azariah

Time Period: 7th and 6th centuries BC (Iron Age IIc)

Geographical Area: Kingdom of Judah

Biblical Reference(s): 1 Chronicles 6:13-15; Ezra 7:1

Ancient Source(s): Bulla of Azariah

Identification Rating: Tentative (C)

Azariah, the son of Hilkiah the priest and the ancestor of Ezra, is mentioned along with his family lineage in both the book of Ezra and the book of Chronicles. A Hebrew bulla reading "belonging to Azariah son of Hilkiah" was found in excavations in the City of David area of Jerusalem and dates to around 600 BC, prior to the Babylonian attack on the city. Azariah, like his father, Hilkiah, was a priest in Jerusalem, and therefore this bulla might name two priests around 600 BC.

Another bulla of Hilkiah the priest is related and suggests the plausible identification of these two men as the priests mentioned in Chronicles and Ezra. Further, the bulla of Gemariah, son of Shaphan, a scribe around 605 BC when Azariah was priest and just after the time Hilkiah was high priest, was found in this same bullae hoard indicating a chronological connection in addition to connections of geography and names. However, because no title is present on this particular bulla, and both Azariah and Hilkiah were popular names in ancient Judah, the identification of Azariah as priest and ancestor of Ezra must be tentative.

> *Shallum became the father of Hilkiah, and Hilkiah became the father of Azariah, and Azariah became the father of Seraiah, and Seraiah became the father of Jehozadak; and Jehozadak went along when the* Lord *carried Judah and Jerusalem away into exile by the hand of Nebuchadnezzar* (1 Chronicles 6:13-15).

Schneider, Tsvi. "Six Biblical Signatures: Seals and seal impressions of six biblical personages recovered." *Biblical Archaeology Review* 17:04 (1991).

GEMARIAH

Bulla belonging to Gemariah, son of Shaphan

Name: Gemariah (son of Shaphan)

Time Period: 600 BC (Iron Age IIc)

Geographical Area: Kingdom of Judah

Biblical Reference(s): Jeremiah 36:10-25

Ancient Source(s): Bulla of Gemariah

Identification Rating: Firm (A)

Gemariah, the son of Shaphan, was a scribe who served in the court of King Jehoiakim of Judah and is specifically mentioned in year five around 604 BC. It was in his chamber in the Jerusalem temple complex that Baruch read the words of Jeremiah on a scroll to many of the people. When the scroll was later read to the king, Gemariah and two others pleaded with him to not destroy it. But Jehoiakim rejected the words and their counsel and cut and burned the scroll before the reading was even finished.

A bulla impressed with the Hebrew inscription "belonging to Gemariah son of Shaphan" was discovered in the "House of Bullae" in Jerusalem at the base of the Stepped Stone Structure, found in the destruction layer from the Babylonian conquest of the city around 587 BC. This bulla was almost certainly created by a seal belonging to Gemariah the scribe, the son of Shaphan, who served under Jehoiakim.

> *Baruch read from the book the words of Jeremiah in the house of the* Lord *in the chamber of Gemariah the son of Shaphan the scribe, in the upper court, at the entry of the New Gate of the* Lord*'s house, to all the people* (Jeremiah 36:10).

Avigad, Nahman. *Corpus of West Semitic Stamp Seals*. Jerusalem: Hebrew University, 1997.

Schneider, Tsvi. "Six Biblical Signatures: Seals and seal impressions of six biblical personages recovered." *Biblical Archaeology Review* 17:04 (1991).

JERAHMEEL

Name: Jerahmeel (son of Jehoiakim)

Time Period: 7th century BC (Iron Age IIc)

Geographical Area: Kingdom of Judah

Biblical Reference(s): Jeremiah 36:26

Ancient Source(s): Bulla of Jerahmeel

Identification Rating: Firm (A)

Jerahmeel, son of Jehoiakim, was a prince of Judah and one of three known sons of Jehoiakim near the end of the 7th century BC. He was named along with two royal officials being commanded to apprehend Jeremiah and Baruch, while two of his brothers, Jeconiah and Zedekiah, are mentioned elsewhere (Jeremiah 36:26; 1 Chronicles 3:16).

A 7th-century BC bulla of Jerahmeel was found among a hoard of 255 bullae impressed with 211 different seals that came to light on the antiquities market all at the same time. This bulla was impressed by a seal that had the inscription "belonging to Jerahmeel, son of the king" (Bulla No. 414). The names and titles of the people represented in the bulla hoard from the time of Jeremiah include five royal officials, three sons of the king, and Baruch the scribe.

Because the bulla includes the name of Jerahmeel along with his status as son of the king, and the bulla is placed chronologically at the time of Jeremiah and Baruch in the 7th century BC, it clearly attests to the existence of this prince during the reign of Jehoiakim.

> *The king commanded Jerahmeel the king's son, Seraiah the son of Azriel, and Shelemiah the son of Abdeel to seize Baruch the scribe and Jeremiah the prophet, but the* LORD *hid them* (Jeremiah 36:26).

Avigad, Nahman. "Baruch the Scribe and Jerahmeel the King's Son." *IEJ* 18 (1978).

JEHOIACHIN

(Jeconiah)

Babylonian ration tablet naming king Yaukin of Judah

Name: Jehoiachin (Jeconiah or Coniah, son of Jehoiakim)

Time Period: 6th century BC (Iron Age IIc)

Geographical Area: Judah and Babylon

Biblical Reference(s): 2 Kings 24:6-15; 25:27-30; 1 Chronicles 3:17-18; 2 Chronicles 36:8-10; Jeremiah 22:24-30; 52:31-34; Ezekiel 1:2

Ancient Source(s): Babylon Ration Tablets

Identification Rating: Firm (A)

Jehoiachin, also known as Jeconiah, was the son of Jehoiakim and the second to last king of Judah, reigning only three months until he was taken prisoner by the Babylonians in ca. 598 BC. After Jehoiachin was defeated and brought to Babylon, he was imprisoned until Amel-Marduk (Evil-merodach) became king and freed him in the first year of his reign around 561 BC. In addition to releasing Jehoiachin from prison, Amel-Marduk gave him daily meals and an allowance. Although it is not specified in any known document why Amel-Marduk treated Jehoiachin with kindness and gave him a position of honor above the other exiled kings in Babylon, they had both been imprisoned by Nebuchadnezzar and may have become friends during that time.

Jehoiachin is mentioned by name, along with his title as king of Judah and reference to his sons, in four cuneiform tablets discovered in a library of official documents in the northeast part of the palace, near the Ishtar Gate in Babylon. These tablets were part of approximately 300 official documents from the time of Nebuchadnezzar and Amel-Marduk, around 595–560 BC. The ration tablets, originating from the brief reign of Amel-Marduk, state that ten sila of oil (8 liters) is designated for the king of Judah, Jehoiachin (Yaukin), and two and a half sila of oil is designated for the sons of the king of Judah (Ration Tablets, Babylon 28122, 28178, 28186). Three of the tablets appear to have similar content, while the fourth tablet mentions the sons of the king of Judah and rations for various craftsmen (cf. 2 Kings 24:14).

Although none of Jehoiachin's sons are specified by name in the tablets, the book of Chronicles records the names of seven of them (1 Chronicles 3:17-18). One of these sons of Jehoiachin, Pedaiah, is known from a Hebrew seal. These Babylonian tablets—naming Jehoiachin as the king of Judah, his sons, and his daily allowance in Babylon—attest to the historical character of Jehoiachin and the historical accuracy of the short narratives about his life.

> *Now it came about in the thirty-seventh year of the exile of Jehoiachin king of Judah, in the twelfth month, on the twenty-seventh day of the month, that Evil-merodach king of Babylon, in the year that he became king, released Jehoiachin king of Judah from prison; and he spoke kindly to him and set his throne above the throne of the kings who were with him in Babylon. Jehoiachin changed his prison clothes and had his meals in the king's presence regularly all the days of his life; and for his allowance, a regular allowance was given him by the king, a portion for each day, all the days of his life* (2 Kings 25:27-30).

Pritchard, James, ed. *The Ancient Near Eastern Texts Relating to the Old Testament.* 3rd ed. with Supplement. Princeton: Princeton University Press, 1969.

PEDAIAH

Seal of Pedaiah, son of the king

Name: Pedaiah (son of Jehoiachin)

Time Period: 6th century BC (Iron Age IIc)

Geographical Area: Kingdom of Judah

Biblical Reference(s): 1 Chronicles 3:16-19

Ancient Source(s): Seal of Pedaiah

Identification Rating: Probable (B)

Pedaiah of Judah was one of the sons of Jehoiachin (Jeconiah), the penultimate king of Judah who reigned for only three months, ca. 599–598 BC. Pedaiah is listed third among his brothers Shealtiel, Malchiram, Shenazzar, Jekamiah, Hoshama, and Nedabiah, who were all apparently taken into exile in Babylon with their father when Nebuchadnezzar subjugated Jerusalem in 598 BC.

One of the sons of Pedaiah was Zerubbabel, the governor of Yehud Province, who oversaw a return of exiles to Jerusalem and the completion of the rebuilding of the temple in 517 BC during the reign of Darius the Great (1 Chronicles 3:19; Ezra 5:2). The sons of Jehoiachin (Jeconiah) are mentioned but not specified by name in the Babylonian Ration Tablets that recorded the daily allowance received by Jehoiachin king of Judah and his sons.

However, Pedaiah is named on a Hebrew seal of this period that appears to have been his personal property. The seal is made of red granite and decorated on the top with a proto-Aeolic capital. It has two lines of text underneath that read "belonging to Pedaiah, son of the king." Although the seal does not name Jehoiachin as his father, this is the only known Pedaiah who was a prince, and the identification is likely.

The sons of Jeconiah, the prisoner, were Shealtiel his son, and Malchiram, Pedaiah, Shenazzar, Jekamiah, Hoshama and Nedabiah. The sons of Pedaiah were Zerubbabel and Shimei. And the sons of Zerubbabel were Meshullam and Hananiah, and Shelomith was their sister (1 Chronicles 3:17-19).

Avigad, Nahman. *Corpus of West Semitic Stamp Seals.* Jerusalem: Hebrew University, 1997.

NATHAN-MELECH

Bulla, "Belonging to Nathan-melech, servant of the king"

Name: Nathan-melech

Time Period: 7th century BC (Iron Age IIc)

Geographical Area: Kingdom of Judah

Biblical Reference(s): 2 Kings 23:11

Ancient Source(s): Bulla of Nathan-melech

Identification Rating: Probable (B)

Nathan-melech was an official who served in the court of King Josiah during the second half of the 7th century BC. According to the brief information in the book of Kings, Nathan-melech had duties associated with the temple in Jerusalem, as his chamber was described as being in the temple precincts near the entrance to the house of the Lord. Excavations in Jerusalem, south of the temple area and in the western part of the City of David, recovered a bulla of the 7th or 6th century BC buried in the ruins of a two-story public building amongst fallen stones, pottery sherds, burnt wooden beams, and ash, which was a result of the ca. 587 BC fiery destruction of Jerusalem by the Babylonians under Nebuchadnezzar II. It was recovered in the same context as a blue agate seal inscribed with "belonging to Ikar son of Matanyahu."

This Mattanyahu, or Mattaniah, was the name of the final king of Judah, Zedekiah, before he was appointed as ruler and renamed by Nebuchadnezzar around 598 BC. The discovery of these artifacts in the area of Jerusalem where the palace once was, and the mention of the king, indicates association with the royal family. The bulla had been impressed with a Hebrew seal bearing an inscription for the owner that read "belonging to Nathan-melech, servant of the king." Previously, another Nathan-melech bulla had surfaced on the antiquities market, but because its provenance was unknown, its authenticity, date, and context were questioned. Even without the name of King Josiah specified, because of the match between the time period, location, occupation, and a unique name, the identification of the Nathan-melech attested on this bulla with the person mentioned in the book of Kings appears likely.

He did away with the horses which the kings of Judah had given to the sun, at the entrance of the house of the Lord, *by the chamber of Nathan-melech the official, which was in the precincts; and he burned the chariots of the sun with fire. The altars which were on the roof, the upper chamber of Ahaz, which the kings of Judah had made, and the altars which Manasseh had made in the two courts of the house of the* Lord, *the king broke down; and he smashed them there and threw their dust into the brook Kidron* (2 Kings 23:11-12).

Mendel-Geberovich, Anat et al. "A Newly Discovered Personal Seal and Bulla from the Excavations of the Giv'ati Parking Lot, Jerusalem." *IEJ* 69/2 (2019).

ZEDEKIAH
(Mattaniah)

Seal belonging to Ikar, son of Mattaniah

Name: Zedekiah (Mattaniah)

Time Period: 6th century BC (Iron Age IIc)

Geographical Area: Kingdom of Judah

Biblical Reference(s): 2 Kings 24:17–25:7; 2 Chronicles 36:10-11; Jeremiah 1:3

Ancient Source(s): Seal of Mattaniah; Seal of Ikar

Identification Rating: Speculative (D)

Mattaniah was the name of ten different people mentioned in the Bible, with the most famous being the Mattaniah who was appointed king by Nebuchadnezzar around 598 BC and had his name changed to Zedekiah. This Mattaniah was the son of Josiah and Hamutal, and although he had numerous sons and daughters, only his son Malchijah is named (Jeremiah 38:6).

Zedekiah is attested indirectly in the Jerusalem Chronicle, which records the installation of Zedekiah without using his name, stating that Nebuchadnezzar "besieged the city of Judah and on the second day of the month of Addaru he seized the city and captured the king [Jehoiachin]. He appointed there a king of his own choice [Zedekiah], received its heavy tribute and sent to Babylon" (ABC 5).

Several seals and bulla, some found in Jerusalem while others appearing on the antiquities market, have been found with the name Mattaniah on them as either the owner or the father. Only two of these might have any possible connection to the Mattaniah that became King Zedekiah. A round gemstone seal carved from dark agate was discovered in Jerusalem during excavations of a public building on the western side of the City of David that had been destroyed in the 587 BC Babylonian conquest of the city. The Hebrew seal was inscribed with "belonging to Ikar, son of Mattanyahu." While the location, date, and name of the father match for this seal, the name Ikar is unknown.

Another seal—oval shaped, carved of black stone, and inscribed with two lines of Hebrew text divided by a lotus bud—reads "belonging to Malikyahu, son of Mattan." The names match those of Mattaniah (Zedekiah) and his son Malchijah, but the seal surfaced on the antiquities market, and therefore the exact date and place of discovery are unknown. While not impossible, the connection of either of these seals to Zedekiah is speculative, and definitive attestation for Zedekiah remains to be discovered.

> *The king of Babylon made his uncle Mattaniah king in his place, and changed his name to Zedekiah* (2 Kings 24:17).

Avigad, Nahman. *Corpus of West Semitic Stamp Seals.* Jerusalem: Hebrew University, 1997.

Mendel-Geberovich, Anat et al. "A Newly Discovered Personal Seal and Bulla from the Excavations of the Giv'ati Parking Lot, Jerusalem." *IEJ* 69/2 (2019).

JEHUCAL

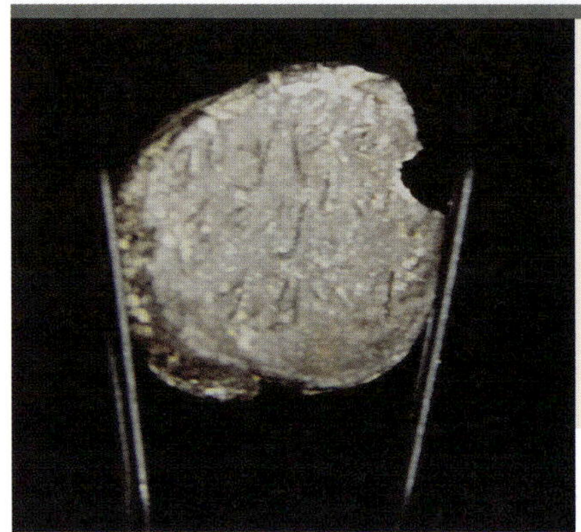

Bulla of Jehucal, son of Shelemiah, son of Shebi

Name: Jehucal (Jucal, son of Shelemiah)

Time Period: 6th century BC (Iron Age IIc)

Geographical Area: Kingdom of Judah

Biblical Reference(s): Jeremiah 37:3; 38:1-4

Ancient Source(s): Bulla of Jehucal

Identification Rating: Firm (A)

Jehucal, also known as Jucal, was the son of Shelemiah and a court official or prince serving King Zedekiah, the last monarch of Judah prior to the Babylonian destruction of Jerusalem that occurred in 587 BC (Jeremiah 38:1-4). A 6th-century BC bulla impressed with his seal was discovered in the royal quarter of Jerusalem from a layer destroyed by the Babylonians. The Hebrew text reads "belonging to Jehucal, son of Shelemiah, son of Shebi."

Nearby, the bulla of another person mentioned with Jehucal in the book of Jeremiah, the official Gedaliah, son of Pashhur, was discovered. This seal impression records his name and lineage and was found in the correct chronological and geographical context, demonstrating that the bulla had been created by the seal of Jehucal named in the book of Jeremiah.

> *King Zedekiah sent Jehucal the son of Shelemiah, and Zephaniah the son of Maaseiah, the priest, to Jeremiah the prophet, saying, "Please pray to the Lord our God on our behalf"* (Jeremiah 37:3).

Mazar, Eilat and Reut Ben-Arie. *The Summit of the City of David Excavations 2005–2008*. Jerusalem: Shoham, 2015.

GEDALIAH
(Son of Pashur)

Belonging to Gedaliah, servant of the king

Name: Gedaliah (son of Pashhur)

Time Period: 6th century BC (Iron Age IIc)

Geographical Area: Kingdom of Judah

Biblical Reference(s): Jeremiah 38:1-6

Ancient Source(s): Bulla of Gedaliah

Identification Rating: Firm (A)

Gedaliah, son of Pashhur, was minister in the royal administration of King Zedekiah of Judah, who reigned for 11 years, ca. 598–587 BC. This Gedaliah was also one of the officials who opposed the prophet Jeremiah because his advice conflicted with their views, and as a result they put Jeremiah in a cistern hoping he would die. Excavations in Jerusalem at the City of David, in the context of other bullae and material from just before the 587 BC destruction of Jerusalem, discovered a bulla that had been imprinted by a Hebrew seal inscribed with "belonging to Gedalyahu son of Pashhur."

Although only briefly mentioned in the book of Jeremiah, this Gedaliah is clearly attested by a bulla that was stamped with his official seal bearing his name and the name of his father.

> *Now Shephatiah the son of Mattan, and Gedaliah the son of Pashhur, and Jucal the son of Shelemiah, and Pashhur the son of Malchijah heard the words that Jeremiah was speaking to all the people* (Jeremiah 38:1).

Mazar, Ẹilat. *The Palace of King David: Excavations at the Summit of the City of David: Preliminary Report of Seasons 2005–2007*. Jerusalem and New York: Shoham, 2009.

NERIAH

Bulla of Baruch, son of Neriah

Name: Neriah (son of Mahseiah)

Time Period: 7th century BC (Iron Age II)

Geographical Area: Kingdom of Judah

Biblical Reference(s): Jeremiah 32:12; 51:59

Ancient Source(s): Bullae of Baruch; Seal of Seriah

Identification Rating: Probable (B)

Neriah, son of Mahseiah, was the father of Seriah the quartermaster and Baruch the scribe of Jeremiah, living during the time when the Babylonians were dominating the Kingdom of Judah. Neriah is mentioned only alongside his sons, and he may not have been alive during the reign of Zedekiah in the 6th century BC.

Neriah is named on two bullae that designate him as the father of Baruch and a seal that names him as the father of Seriah. The bullae read "belonging to Baruch, son of Neriah, the scribe" and the seal reads "belonging to Seriah, son of Neriah." Presumably the two bullae were created by the seal of Baruch in the 6th century BC, but a few scholars have questioned their authenticity because they were sourced on the antiquities market. The seal of Seriah was carved from red jasper, and the name Neriah appears on the second of two lines.

The bullae and seals appear to attest to Neriah, father of Baruch and Seriah, due to the match in name, family lineage, and chronological context, although doubts may linger because they were not discovered in official excavations.

> *I signed and sealed the deed, and called in witnesses, and weighed out the silver on the scales. Then I took the deeds of purchase, both the sealed copy containing the terms and conditions and the open copy; and I gave the deed of purchase to Baruch the son of Neriah, the son of Mahseiah, in the sight of Hanamel my uncle's son and in the sight of the witnesses who signed the deed of purchase, before all the Jews who were sitting in the court of the guard* (Jeremiah 32:10-12).

Avigad, Nahman. *Corpus of West Semitic Stamp Seals*. Jerusalem: Hebrew University, 1997.

Schneider, Tsvi. "Six Biblical Signatures." *Biblical Archaeology Review* 17.4 (1991).

BARUCH THE SCRIBE

Bulla of Baruch, son of Neriah the Scribe

Name: Baruch the Scribe (Baruchyahu)

Time Period: 600 BC (Iron Age II)

Geographical Area: Kingdom of Judah

Biblical Reference(s): Jeremiah 36:18-32

Ancient Source(s): Bullae of Baruch son of Neriah

Identification Rating: Probable (B)

Baruch was the scribe of Jeremiah the prophet, serving in this role for decades, from before the Babylonian conquest of Judah until after Jeremiah relocated to Egypt. Baruch was the son of Neriah and the brother of Seriah the quartermaster of King Zedekiah, so his family members also seem to have served in administrative roles.

Two bullae (clay seal impressions) are known that read "belonging to Baruchyahu son of Neriah the scribe" in paleo Hebrew script. Each of the impressions are divided into three lines, with the first being the name Baruch (Baruchyahu), the second being his lineage, and the third being his profession. Both appear to have come from a signet seal that would have been the personal seal of Baruch.

One of the bullae was probably discovered inside the "Burnt House" in Jerusalem, which was destroyed along with the rest of the city by the Babylonians in 587 BC, but it subsequently came to light on the antiquities market. The second bulla had the same inscription, but also a fingerprint impression. Both bullae have been criticized by a few scholars as being forgeries, but more recent research and analysis has shown that the bullae could be authentic. The seal impressions, which specify the profession of Baruch and the name of his father, appear to date to the period around 600 BC, when Jeremiah functioned as a prophet in Judah. If even one of the bullae are authentic, then the details of the inscription and its owner, along with the geographic and chronological context, would attest to the existence of Baruch the scribe of Jeremiah and evidence left behind by him stamping documents he wrote or was responsible for.

Other seals and clay stamp impressions of people mentioned in the book of Jeremiah have also been discovered, including "Jehucal son of Shelemiah" (Jeremiah 38:1), "Gedalyahu ben Pashur" (Jeremiah 38:1), and a seal of "Baalyisha king of the Ammon" (Jeremiah 40:14).

> *In the fourth year of Jehoiakim the son of Josiah, king of Judah, this word came to Jeremiah from the LORD, saying, "Take a scroll and write on it all the words which I have spoken to you concerning Israel and concerning Judah, and concerning all the nations, from the day I first spoke to you, from the days of Josiah, even to this day... Then Jeremiah called Baruch the son of Neriah, and Baruch wrote on a scroll at the dictation of Jeremiah all the words of the LORD which He had spoken to him* (Jeremiah 36:1-4).

Van der Veen, Peter, Robert Deutsch, and Gabriel Barkay. "Reconsidering the Authenticity of the Berekhyahu Bullae: A Rejoinder." *Antiguo Oriente* 14 (2016).

SERAIAH

Name: Seraiah, son of Neriah

Time Period: 6th century BC (Iron Age IIc)

Geographical Area: Kingdom of Judah

Biblical Reference(s): Jeremiah 51:59-61

Ancient Source(s): Seal of Seraiah

Identification Rating: Tentative (C)

Seraiah was the son of Neriah and the brother of Baruch, and he served as quartermaster under King Zedekiah during the 6th century BC. According to the book of Jeremiah, the prophet sent a message with Seraiah when he accompanied Zedekiah to Babylon in the fourth year of his reign. A red jasper seal from this period, with two lines of Hebrew text, may have been his official seal during the reign of Zedekiah. It reads "belonging to Seriah son of Neriah."

However, the seal was found on the antiquities market and does not give the title of Seriah, nor is the exact chronological and geographic context known, so the identification must remain tentative.

> *The message which Jeremiah the prophet commanded Seraiah the son of Neriah, the grandson of Mahseiah, when he went with Zedekiah the king of Judah to Babylon in the fourth year of his reign. (Now Seraiah was quartermaster.)* (Jeremiah 51:59).

Avigad, Nahman. *Corpus of West Semitic Stamp Seals*. Jerusalem: Hebrew University, 1997.

Schneider, Tsvi. "Six Biblical Signatures." *Biblical Archaeology Review* 17.4 (1991).

Tombs in the Kidron Valley of Jerusalem

NEBUZARADAN II

Istanbul Prism of Nebuchadnezzar II

Name: Nebuzaradan II (Nabu-zar-iddin)

Time Period: 6th century BC (Neo-Babylonian Empire)

Geographical Area: Babylon

Biblical Reference(s): 2 Kings 25:8-20; Jeremiah 39:9-13

Ancient Source(s): Istanbul Prism of Nebuchadnezzar

Identification Rating: Firm (A)

When Jerusalem was conquered and burned in 587 BC, Nebuzaradan, the "captain of the guard" (*rab tabbahim*), was the leader of the army and directly responsible for the destruction of the city, as Nebuchadnezzar was at Riblah and not present at Jerusalem. He is named in the books of Kings and Jeremiah as the commander of the Babylonian army at Jerusalem and the overseer of the final major deportation of people from Judah to Babylon.

Nebuzaradan is also named in Babylonian records as one of the leading high officials in the service of Nebuchadnezzar before Jerusalem had been destroyed. A cuneiform prism from year seven of Nebuchadnezzar or approximately 598 BC, found at Babylon, places him first in the list: "I ordered the (following) court officials in exercise of (their) duties to take up position in my (official) suite. As mašennu-officials Nebuzaradan, the chief cook, Nabuzeribni, the chief armorer" (Istanbul Prism of Nebuchadnezzar No. 7834).

This "chief cook" (*rab nuhatimmi*) was an honorific title and did not mean that his only duties were to prepare food for Nebuchadnezzar. His place of prominence in this list indicates that he would have been given important military duties, just as Nebuchadnezzar himself was made commander of the army while he was still crown prince. This Nebuzaradan also appears to be mentioned in a tablet from the temple of Nabu in Babylon: "Nebuzaradan composed a tablet and offered it for his salvation and the development of his understanding."

Although Nebuzaradan was a relatively minor character in the books of Kings and Jeremiah, he held a position of prominence in the royal administration of Nebuchadnezzar, and it is no surprise that he would be named in a list of important Babylonian officials.

> *Now on the seventh day of the fifth month, which was the nineteenth year of King Nebuchadnezzar, king of Babylon, Nebuzaradan the captain of the guard, a servant of the king of Babylon, came to Jerusalem. He burned the house of the LORD, the king's house, and all the houses of Jerusalem; even every great house he burned with fire. So all the army of the Chaldeans who were with the captain of the guard broke down the walls around Jerusalem. Then the rest of the people who were left in the city and the deserters who had deserted to the king of Babylon and the rest of the people, Nebuzaradan the captain of the guard carried away into exile* (2 Kings 25:8-11).

Da Riva, Rocio. "Nebuchadnezzar II's Prism (EŞ 7834): a new edition." *Zeitschrift für Assyriologie und Vorderasiatische Archäologie* 103.2 (2013).

Pritchard, James, ed. *The Ancient Near Eastern Texts Relating to the Old Testament.* 3rd ed. with Supplement. Princeton: Princeton University Press, 1969.

NEBO-SARSEKIM

Donation tablet of Nebo-sarsekim

Name: Nebo-sarsekim (Nabu-sharrussu-ukin)

Time Period: 6th century BC (Neo-Babylonian Empire)

Geographical Area: Babylon

Biblical Reference(s): Jeremiah 39:3

Ancient Source(s): Donation Tablet of Nebo-sarsekim

Identification Rating: Firm (A)

A Babylonian official named Nebo-sarsekim, who served during the reign of Nebuchadnezzar, was recorded in the book of Jeremiah as being present in the Middle Gate of Jerusalem after the walls were breached and the city was captured in 587 BC. Listed alongside notable people such as Nebuchadnezzar, Zedekiah, and Nergal-sar-ezer, Nebo-sarsekim is described by the title Rab-saris, meaning chief eunuch or chief officer (Jeremiah 39:1-3).

The name and title of this Babylonian official named only once in the Bible were also found on a small cuneiform donation tablet found in the Babylonian city of Sippar. The tablet came from a temple of Marduk and records his name, the amount of his contribution, and the year in reference to the reign of Nebuchadnezzar: "1.5 minas of gold, the property of Nabu-sharrussu-ukin [Nebo-sarsekim], the chief eunuch, which he sent…to [the temple] Esangila…month 11, day 18, year 10 of Nebuchadnezzar, king of Babylon." The tablet dates to late in the year of about 595 BC, which was less than eight years before Nebo-sarsekim the chief eunuch appeared in Jerusalem along with other royal officials of Babylon.

This tablet gives the name, title, and chronological context for Nebo-sarsekim, attesting to his existence and role in the administration of Nebuchadnezzar around the time of Jeremiah.

> *All the officials of the king of Babylon came in and sat down at the Middle Gate: Nergal-sar-ezer the Sim-magir, Nebu-sarsekim the chief eunuch,*

Nergal-sar-ezer the Rab-mag, and all the rest of the officials of the king of Babylon (Jeremiah 39:3).

Greenspoon, Leonard. "Recording of Gold Delivery by the Chief Eunuch of Nebuchadnezzar II." *Biblical Archaeology Review* 33.6 (2007).

NERGAL-SAR-EZER
(Neriglissar)

Name: Nergal-sar-ezer (Neriglissar)

Time Period: 6th century BC (Neo-Babylonian Empire)

Geographical Area: Babylon

Biblical Reference(s): Jeremiah 39:3-13

Ancient Source(s): Stele of Adad-guppi; Uruk King List; Basalt Stele of Nabonidus; Babylonian Chronicle; Istanbul Prism of Nebuchadnezzar

Identification Rating: Firm (A)

Neriglissar, also known as Nergal-sar-ezer, served as a high official in the court of Nebuchadnezzar II before going on to rule as the fourth king of the Neo-Babylonian Empire ca. 560–556 BC. Nergal-sar-ezer, whose name means "Nergal (god of death) protect the king," was a prominent landowner and the son of Bel-shum-ishkun. He seems to have been unrelated to the royal family, but Neriglissar became a son-in-law of Nebuchadnezzar, having married Kashshaya, who may have been the eldest child of Nebuchadnezzar and facilitated his rise to power.

Earlier in his career, Neriglissar held a title called the Rab-mag, and he is named in the book of Jeremiah as one of the officials of the king of Babylon who were present at the conquest of Jerusalem in 587 BC. Nergal-sar-ezer is listed among the royal officials at the Middle Gate, and he is also mentioned with Nebuzaradan and Nebushazban as those responsible for freeing Jeremiah from prison at the order of Nebuchadnezzar.

In the book of Jeremiah, there may be two officials named Nergal-sar-ezer, or he is mentioned with two different titles. Approximately 27 years later, after Nebuchadnezzar died and Amel-Marduk had been king for only two years, Neriglissar had Amel-Marduk assassinated and then usurped the throne of Babylon. However, after a reign of approximately three years and eight months, Neriglissar died. His son, Labashi-Marduk, ruled for only about two months before he was overthrown and assassinated in a palace coup led by Belshazzar.

According to records from the reign of Nabonidus, Neriglissar ruled for four years and was considered a legitimate king, while a later king list gives a more specific reign of three years and eight months (Stele of Adad-guppi; Uruk King List 5). Nabonidus linked himself to Neriglissar, meanwhile leaving out kings such as Nabopolassar and Amel-Marduk, who were part of the royal family. He claimed "I am the real executor of the wills of Nebuchadnezzar and Neriglissar, my royal predecessors! Their armies are entrusted to me, I shall not treat carelessly their orders and I am (anxious) to please them" (Basalt Stele of Nabonidus).

Neriglissar had one known military campaign in about 557 BC, a successful victory over the kingdom of Pirindu in Anatolia recorded in the Babylonian Chronicle: "The third year...Neriglissar mustered his army and marched to Hume to oppose him...When Neriglissar reached them he inflicted a defeat upon them and conquered the large army" (ABC 6). Cuneiform documents from Babylon during his reign also record construction projects he oversaw, including repairs on the Esagila temple, the royal palace, and possibly the Median Wall.

However, long before usurping the throne, Neriglissar appears to be mentioned in a text of Nebuchadnezzar, where he is given the title Sin-magir, matching the name and title recorded in the book of Jeremiah situated during the 587 BC conquest of Jerusalem (Istanbul Prism of Nebuchadnezzar No. 7834; Jeremiah 39:3). Most likely, this Neriglissar (Nergal-sar-ezer) is one and the same with the royal official Neriglissar who married into the family of Nebuchadnezzar and became king 27 years later. However, it is also possible that the Neriglissar Sin-magir was merely a trusted servant of Nebuchadnezzar, and the Neriglissar Rab-mag mentioned by Jeremiah was another man who became the fourth king of the Neo-Babylonian Empire.

Construction Cylinder of Neriglissar

Thus, the Neriglissar (Nergal-sar-ezer) mentioned in the book of Jeremiah is attested by Babylonian sources, but it is also possible that two different officials named Neriglissar are recorded by Jeremiah and distinguished by their titles—including one who would eventually become king.

> *Nebuzaradan the captain of the bodyguard sent word, along with Nebushazban the Rab-saris, and Nergal-sar-ezer the Rab-mag, and all the leading officers of the king of Babylon; they even sent and took Jeremiah out of the court of the guardhouse and entrusted him to Gedaliah, the son of Ahikam, the son of Shaphan, to take him home. So he stayed among the people* (Jeremiah 39:13-14).

Da Riva, Rocio. "Nebuchadnezzar II's Prism (EŞ 7834): a new edition." *Zeitschrift für Assyriologie und Vorderasiatische Archäologie* 103.2 (2013).

Glassner, Jean-Jacques. *Mesopotamian Chronicles*. Atlanta: Society of Biblical Literature, 2004.

Pritchard, James, ed. *The Ancient Near Eastern Texts Relating to the Old Testament*. 3rd ed. with Supplement. Princeton: Princeton University Press, 1969.

Weiershäuser, Frauke and Jamie Novotny. *The Royal Inscriptions of Amēl-Marduk (561–560 BC), Neriglissar (559–556 BC), and Nabonidus (555–539 BC), Kings of Babylon*. University Park: Eisenbrauns, 2020.

The Ishtar Gate of Babylon, constructed in the 6th century BC

GEDALIAH

(Son of Ahikam)

Seal of Jaazaniah, servant of the king

Name: Gedaliah (son of Ahikam)

Time Period: 6th century BC (Iron Age IIc)

Geographical Area: Babylonian Empire

Biblical Reference(s): 2 Kings 25:22-24; Jeremiah 40:7–41:10

Ancient Source(s): Bullae of Gedaliah

Identification Rating: Tentative (C)

Gedaliah, son of Ahikam, functioned as an official overseeing the land and cities of Judah after the Babylonians had destroyed Jerusalem in 587 BC and the absorption of the kingdom of Judah into their empire. This Gedaliah, son of Ahikam, interacted with the prophet Jeremiah, and he is sometimes referred to as the governor of Judah, but he is never called by that specific title. He is a different person than the Gedaliah, son of Pashhur, who served King Zedekiah of Judah and lived during the same period.

Two 6th-century BC bullae that may have been stamped by a seal inscribed with the name and position of this Gedaliah were discovered—one from Lachish and one from Tell Beit Mirsim. The bulla from Lachish reads "belonging to Gedalyahu who is over the house," while the bulla from Tell Beit Mirsim reads "belonging to Gedalyahu servant of the king." Although neither of these includes the name of his father and therefore are not definitive identifications, the bulla from Lachish is more likely to have belonged to Gedaliah, son of Ahikam, because it gives his title as "over the house," and he was called the one whom the king of Babylon had "appointed over the cities of Judah" and "appointed...over the land" (Jeremiah 40:5-7; 2 Kings 25:22). He was also obviously a servant of King Nebuchadnezzar, but Gedaliah, son of Pashhur, was a servant of King Zedekiah, so the attribution of this bulla from Tell Beit Mirsim is unclear. Another royal official contemporary with and who eventually served under Gedaliah, a man named Jaazaniah son of Hoshaiah, may also be attested by an inscribed seal

(2 Kings 25:23; Jeremiah 40:8). This onyx seal reads "belonging to Jaazaniah servant of the king" and is decorated with a rooster. As it was excavated at Tell en-Nasbeh (Mizpah), where Gedaliah met Jaazaniah, in a layer from just after the Babylonian conquest of Judah in ca. 587 BC, it is a likely identification.

The fact that the two Gedaliah bullae were not discovered in Jerusalem, which had been destroyed and was no longer the center of government for Judah, is intriguing but does not solve the problem of identity. Thus, it is possible that Gedaliah, son of Ahikam, is attested by bullae, but the evidence is inconclusive and must remain tentative unless further discoveries are made.

> *As Jeremiah was still not going back, he said, "Go on back then to Gedaliah the son of Ahikam, the son of Shaphan, whom the king of Babylon has appointed over the cities of Judah, and stay with him among the people; or else go anywhere it seems right for you to go." So the captain of the bodyguard gave him a ration and a gift and let him go* (Jeremiah 40:5).

Avigad, Nahman. *Corpus of West Semitic Stamp Seals.* Jerusalem: Hebrew University, 1997.

May, Herbert. "Three Hebrew Seals and the Status of Exiled Jehoiakin." *The American Journal of Semitic Languages and Literatures.* 56.2 (1939): 146-48.

Wright, Ernest. "Some Personal Seals of Judean Royal Officials." *The Biblical Archaeologist,* Vol. 1, No. 2 (1938).

BAALIS

Seal of Baalis

Name: Baalis (Baalisha)

Time Period: 6th century BC (Iron Age IIc)

Geographical Area: Kingdom of Ammon

Biblical Reference(s): Jeremiah 40:14

Ancient Source(s): Seal of Baalisha; Bulla of Milkom

Identification Rating: Firm (A)

Baalis was the king of Ammon during the time Gedaliah was governor of Judah, after Nebuchadnezzar had conquered and destroyed Jerusalem. According to the book of Jeremiah and later Josephus, a king of Ammon named Baalis ordered an assassin to murder Gedaliah (Josephus, *Antiquities* 10.160-172). Excavations at Tall al-Umayri (possibly the site of ancient Abel Keramim of Judges 11:33) in Jordan uncovered a clay bottle stopper dated to about 600 BC that had been impressed with an Ammonite text reading "belonging to Milkom, servant of Baalisha." It was speculated that this referred to King Baalis, who was mentioned in the book of Jeremiah.

However, more than a decade later, a brown agate royal seal originating in Jordan surfaced on the antiquities market with a three-line inscription, "Baalish, king of the sons of Ammon," and was decorated with a winged sphinx in the same style as the seal of King Pado'el of Ammon. Although the "sons of Ammon" section on the seal had to be partially reconstructed, it appears obvious and is not disputed.

As there is no other known king of Ammon named Baalis, both artifacts come from about 600 BC, and the bulla was found in excavations in the region of ancient Ammon, the chronological and geographical contexts are clear, as is the name and title of the individual. Thus, the king of Ammon named Baalis who ordered the assassination of Gedaliah appears to be attested by his own seal and possibly a bulla of someone in his royal administration.

"Are you well aware that Baalis the king of the sons of Ammon has sent Ishmael the son of Nethaniah to take your life?" But Gedaliah the son of Ahikam did not believe them (Jeremiah 40:14).

Deutsch, Robert. "Seal of Ba'alis Surfaces." *Biblical Archaeology Review* 25:2 (1999).

Mykytiuk, Lawrence. *Identifying Biblical persons in Northwest Semitic inscriptions of 1200–539 B.C.E.* Society of Biblical Literature, 2004.

HOPHRA
(Apries)

Bust of Hophra

Name: Hophra (Apries, Waphres, Wahibre Haaibre)

Time Period: 6th century BC (26th Dynasty of Egypt)

Geographical Area: Egypt

Biblical Reference(s): Jeremiah 44:30

Ancient Source(s): Stelae of Hophra; Elephantine Stele of Amasis II; bust of Hophra

Identification Rating: Firm (A)

Hophra was a pharaoh of the 26th Dynasty of Egypt, son of Psamtik II and grandson of Necho II (2 Kings 23:29), ruling about 589–570 BC until he was overthrown in a civil war by Amasis II. Hophra was king during the time that the Neo-Babylonian empire was dominant and Zedekiah was king in Judah, when Nebuchadnezzar II destroyed Jerusalem and exiled many of the people of Judah to the area of Babylon, and when Jeremiah the prophet fled to Egypt. Although Hophra attempted to come to the aid of Judah against the Babylonians around 589 BC in the hopes that Babylon could be defeated or suppressed, the army of Nebuchadnezzar only temporarily lifted the siege of Jerusalem to chase the Egyptian army, which retreated back to Egypt (Jeremiah 37:5-10; 43:6-13).

Hophra is mentioned by name only once in the Bible, but other passages in both the books of Jeremiah and Ezekiel refer to him by his title of Pharaoh (e.g., Ezekiel 29:2). A recently discovered stele of Hophra from about year one of his reign describes making his soldiers ready, which may have been in reference to preparing for the march to Jerusalem to fight the Babylonians. Another stele of Hophra from about year seven of his reign, found at Tell Defenneh (Tahpanhes), mentions Nebuchadnezzar and a defensive plan, which seems to be related to an unsuccessful attack by the Babylonians on Egypt in 582 BC. The Elephantine Stele of Amasis II also names Hophra in the context of the civil war at the end of his reign.

Pharaoh Hophra is known from many of his own monuments created during his reign, including stelae, an obelisk, one statue of him, and temples around Egypt, in addition to various inscriptions from his palace (Kom Tuman) at Memphis. The 5th-century BC Greek historian Herodotus also relays major events in the reign of Hophra, including his leading an army of mercenaries against Amasis, followed by his defeat, execution, and burial (Herodotus, *Histories* 2.161-172).

Memphis Stele of Hophra

While the details surrounding his death are disputed, Hophra was buried in the precinct of Neith at Sais, and Egyptian records have preserved his interactions with Nebuchadnezzar and possibly Judah, firmly attesting to Hophra and placing his role as Pharaoh in Egypt around the time of the destruction of Jerusalem.

> *Thus says the* L*ORD*, *"Behold, I am going to give over Pharaoh Hophra king of Egypt to the hand of his enemies, to the hand of those who seek his life, just as I gave over Zedekiah king of Judah to the hand of Nebuchadnezzar king of Babylon, who was his enemy and was seeking his life"* (Jeremiah 44:30).

Abd El-Maksoud and Valbelle. "Une stèle de l'an 7 d'Apriès découverte sur le site de Tell Défenneh." *Revue d'Égyptologie* 64 (2013).

Leahy, Anthony. "The Earliest Dated Monument of Amasis and the End of the Reign of Apries." *The Journal of Egyptian Archaeology* Vol. 74 (1988).

Nour, Mostafa Hassan et al. "The Stela of King Apries from El-Qantara Gharb: A Royal Journey to the Eastern Borders." *Studien zur Altägyptischen Kultur* 52: 221-239 (2023).

EVIL-MERODACH
(Amel-Marduk)

Prayer of Nabu-shuma-ukin from prison

Name: Evil-merodach, king of Babylon (Amel-Marduk)

Time Period: 6th century BC (Neo-Babylonian Empire)

Geographical Area: Babylon

Biblical Reference(s): 2 Kings 25:27-30; Jeremiah 52:31-34

Ancient Source(s): Lament of Nabû-šuma-ukîn; Palace of Amel-Marduk inscription; Uruk King List

Identification Rating: Firm (A)

Amel-Marduk, rendered as Evil-merodach in many Bible translations, was the king of Babylon ca. 562–560 BC, ascending to the throne after the death of his father, Nebuchadnezzar II, and reigning for two years (Uruk King List).

However, even as a prince of Babylon, he faced imprisonment and opposition. Late in the reign of Nebuchadnezzar II, when Amel-Marduk still went by the name Nabû-šuma-ukîn, he was imprisoned for an unknown reason. While in prison, he wrote a prayer of lament about being the victim of a conspiracy and appealed to the god Marduk, describing himself saying, "He weeps in his prison because his situation is so grievous…That one, has drowned his tricks against my sire, my father" (Lament of Nabû-šuma-ukîn). He was released in about 566 BC, and he may have changed his name to Amel-Marduk ("man of Marduk") after this as a way to honor Marduk, the chief god of Babylon.

When Amel-Marduk became king, one of his first acts seems to have been releasing Jehoiachin of Judah from prison, as the book of Jeremiah records Jehoiachin being freed on the 25th of Elul by Amel-Marduk in the first year of his reign, while the earliest dated tablet from the reign of Amel-Marduk was the 26th of Elul (Jeremiah 52:31). Although there is no explicit documentary evidence, it can be inferred that Amel-Marduk and Jehoiachin had become acquainted and even friends in prison.

Another tablet, discussing a time when Nebuchadnezzar was still alive, also names Amel-Marduk and appears to criticize Nebuchadnezzar for neglecting his duties and family. The text is fragmentary, but it records that "[Nebu]chadnezzar considered [.....] His life appeared of no value to [him...] And Babylonian speaks bad counsel to Amel-Marduk."

Documentation of Amel-Marduk's brief reign is sparse, and one of the few explicit records of him holding the kingship comes from an inscription on an alabaster vase found at Susa that had probably been looted from Babylon by the Elamites in ancient times. The inscription reads "Palace of Amel-Marduk, King of Babylon, son of Nebuchadrezzar, King of Babylon."

The life of Amel-Marduk was cut short after two years as king when he was assassinated by his brother-in-law Neriglissar (Nergal-sar-ezer the Rab-mag), a high official who had been present at the 587 BC destruction of Jerusalem (Jeremiah 39:3-13).

> *Now it came about in the thirty-seventh year of the exile of Jehoiachin king of Judah, in the twelfth month, on the twenty-seventh day of the month, that Evil-merodach king of Babylon, in the year that he became king, released Jehoiachin king of Judah from prison; and he spoke kindly to him and set his throne above the throne of the kings who were with him in Babylon* (2 Kings 25:27-28).

Finkel, Irving. "The Lament of Nabû-šuma-ukîn" in *Babylon: Focus mesopotamischer Geschichte, Wiege früher Gelehrsamkeit, Mythos in der Moderne: 2.* Saarbrucken, 1999.

Grayson, Albert. *Babylonian Historical-Literary Texts.* Toronto: University of Toronto Press, 1975.

BELSHAZZAR

Tablet mentioning Belshazzar, son of the king, and Nabonidus, in 545 BC

Name: Belshazzar (Bel-shar-usur)

Time Period: 539 BC (Neo-Babylonian Empire)

Geographical Area: Babylon

Biblical Reference(s): Daniel 5:1-30

Ancient Source(s): Ur Cylinder of Nabonidus; Verse Account of Nabonidus; Chronicle of Nabonidus

Identification Rating: Firm (A)

According to the book of Daniel, Belshazzar was serving as king of Babylon when the Mede and Persian alliance entered Babylon and captured the city in 539 BC. Referred to as a descendant of Nebuchadnezzar, he may have been the grandson of Nebuchadnezzar through his mother the queen, tentatively identified as Nitocris, one of the daughters of Nebuchadnezzar (Daniel 5:2, 10; Herodotus, *Histories* I.185-188).

Initially, many scholars claimed that Belshazzar was a fictional character because his name had not been found in any known records. After a significant Babylonian discovery that specified Belshazzar as the firstborn son of king Nabonidus, criticisms shifted from the existence of Belshazzar to his title "king of Babylon" and details such as his relation to Nebuchadnezzar, presence in Babylon without Nabonidus at the fall of the city, and the circumstances of his death.

Typically referred to as the last king of Babylon, his father, Nabonidus, was an odd and enigmatic figure, preferring to spend his time on religious projects and often absent from Babylon. Around 550 BC he placed four identical cuneiform cylinders at the temple of the moon god Sin in the city of Ur, south of Babylon. Found during excavations of the city and subsequently translated, part of the 62-line text revealed valuable new information, stating:

> For me, Nabonidus, king of Babylon, save me from sinning against your great godhead and grant me as a present a life long of days, and as for Belshazzar my firstborn son, my own child, let the fear of your

great divinity be in his heart, and may he commit no sin; may he enjoy happiness in life.

Thus, it was revealed that Belshazzar was not only a name used in Babylon during the reign of Nabonidus, but that he was the eldest son, heir, and crown prince—not a fictional character or mere administrator in the government. An administrative tablet from Borsippa, dating to 545 BC or year 11 of Nabonidus, also mentions "Belshazzar, son of the king." Another Babylonian tablet from the Knopf collection appears to refer to Belshazzar sharing the government with his father Nabonidus (Tablet 119). Yet the title "king of Babylon" for Belshazzar continued to be controversial among scholars who were convinced that he was merely a crown prince, since co-regency was not previously known in Babylonian history. However, Babylonian documents demonstrate that Belshazzar had been appointed co-regent with Nabonidus by approximately 549 BC. According to the Nabonidus Chronicle, the "crown prince" Belshazzar was ruling in Babylon with the officers and the army while Nabonidus was in Tayma or elsewhere for many years (ABC 7).

The circumstances are further illuminated by a cuneiform document called the Verse Account of Nabonidus, found at Babylon, which discloses that Nabonidus "entrusted the camp to his oldest son, the firstborn. The troops everywhere

Ur Cylinder of Nabonidus

in the country he ordered under his command. He let everything go, entrusted the kingship to him, and, himself, he started out for a long journey." This text makes it clear that Belshazzar was indeed granted the kingship by his father and did hold the title "king of Babylon," at least while Nabonidus was away from the capital on his journeys. This is also why Belshazzar is only able to offer Daniel third place in the kingdom, since Nabonidus and Belshazzar held the first two positions (Daniel 5:16).

In the next century, a Greek historian transmitted details about the end of the Neo-Babylonian Empire, writing that the son of a Babylonian king, also called a king, was ruling in Babylon when the city fell (Xenophon, *Cyropaedia* 4.6.3, 7.5.15-33). That Belshazzar was the grandson of Nebuchadnezzar is plausible,

Nabonidus Chronicle

although no Babylonian sources have yet been recovered that specify the details of his matrilineal lineage. However, it is now clear that Belshazzar was the name of the acting ruler in Babylon and held the position "king of Babylon" when the city was captured in 539 BC, just as the book of Daniel records.

> *Belshazzar gave orders, and they clothed Daniel with purple and put a necklace of gold around his neck, and issued a proclamation concerning him that he now had authority as the third ruler in the kingdom. That same night Belshazzar the Chaldean king was slain* (Daniel 5:29-30).

Beaulieu, Paul-Alain. *The Reign of Nabonidus, King of Babylon (556–539 BC).* New Haven: Yale University Press, 1989.

Pritchard, James, ed. *The Ancient Near Eastern Texts Relating to the Old Testament.* 3rd ed. with Supplement. Princeton: Princeton University Press, 1969.

CYRUS II

The verse account of Nabonidus

Name: Cyrus II (Cyrus the Great)

Time Period: 6th century BC (Achaemenid Empire)

Geographical Area: Persia

Biblical Reference(s): 2 Chronicles 36:22-23; Ezra 1:1-8; Isaiah 44:28–45:1; Daniel 1:21; 6:28, 10:1

Ancient Source(s): The Cyrus Cylinder; The Nabonidus Chronicle; Behistun Inscription; Xenophon, Cyropaedia; Herodotus, Histories

Identification Rating: Firm (A)

Cyrus II, son of Cambyses I and Mandane, often referred to as Cyrus the Great or Cyrus the Elder, was born around 600 BC to a father who was the king of Anshan and a mother who was a Median princess. His original name may have been Agradates according to Strabo, but this must be considered tentative due to the lack of contemporary sources on this topic.

The reign of Cyrus II is typically dated around 559–529 BC, and he is credited with establishing the Achaemenid Empire, one of the largest and most powerful in the ancient world. This empire came about as a result of combining the kingdoms of Persia and Media—perhaps made easier by his lineage—along with conquering the Babylonian Empire and other nearby nations such as Lydia.

The life of Cyrus is attested by a wide variety of inscriptions, such as the Cyrus Cylinder, three inscriptions from Pasargadae (CMa, CMb, CMc), the Babylonian Chronicles, the Verse Account of Nabonidus, and various ancient manuscripts, although a few discrepancies have been noted, especially views found in the records of Herodotus (Herodotus, *Histories*; Ctesias, *Persica*; Xenophon, *Cyropaedia*). The inscription from Gate R at Pasargadae in particular describes part of the lineage of Cyrus II, stating "Cyrus the great king, son of Cambyses the king, an Achaemenid…" It is also noteworthy that inscriptions of Cyrus II himself and the Babylonian Chronicles refer to him as the king of Anshan and not of Media, as he was the heir to Anshan but only later gained control over the Medes (e.g., the Cyrus Cylinder).

In the Bible, Cyrus II is mentioned in the books of Isaiah, Daniel, Ezra, and Chronicles. These passages primarily relate to his conquering Babylon, allowing the exiled people to return home, and issuing a decree to rebuild the temple in Jerusalem. After Babylon was captured in 539 BC, he issued a decree that captive, exiled people could return to their homelands along with their sacred religious objects that had been taken by the Babylonians. One of the original copies of this decree is preserved on the Cyrus Cylinder, found in Babylon, where it had been placed as a foundation deposit in the Esagila temple of Marduk.

This version of the decree, written for a Babylonian audience, addressed the god Marduk and stated, "Sanctuaries had been abandoned for a long time, I returned the images of the gods, who had resided there [in Babylon], to their places and I let them dwell in eternal abodes. I gathered all their inhabitants and returned to them their dwellings." The Cyrus Cylinder also characterized Nabonidus, the previous Babylonian king, as a religious heretic who had forced labor on the people of the city Babylon, but Cyrus II had come as a divinely chosen champion, liberator, and king of the world.

In the book of Ezra, the decree of 539 BC was also recorded, but it was a version written to Judah and therefore referred to Yahweh rather than Marduk.

The Behistun Inscription

It was the policy of Cyrus the Great to accommodate the subjects of his realm and their varying religious views, and this is why the names of different deities were used. However, the decree had the same essential commands and results regardless of the specific culture being addressed. This may seem inconsistent, since the kings of the Achaemenid Empire who followed him often referred to the Ahura Mazda, but there is no evidence that Cyrus II prioritized or even worshipped the Ahura Mazda, and he may have been a religious pluralist who accommodated the various belief systems represented in his empire as long as he was recognized as sovereign king.

Thus, the Cyrus the Persian mentioned in Daniel as king over Babylon, the Cyrus king of Persia mentioned in Ezra who issued an empire-wide decree allowing exiles to return to their lands with their religious objects, and Cyrus II from

The Cyrus Cylinder

The Cyrus Cylinder

ancient Achaemenid, Babylonian, and Greek records are all referring to the historical person of Cyrus the Great.

> *Now in the first year of Cyrus king of Persia—in order to fulfill the word of the* Lord *by the mouth of Jeremiah—the* Lord *stirred up the spirit of Cyrus king of Persia, so that he sent a proclamation throughout his kingdom, and also put it in writing, saying, "Thus says Cyrus king of Persia, 'The* Lord*, the God of heaven, has given me all the kingdoms of the earth, and He has appointed me to build Him a house in Jerusalem, which is in Judah. Whoever there is among you of all His people, may the* Lord *his God be with him, and let him go up!'"* (2 Chronicles 36:22-23).

Hallo, William W. and K. Lawson Younger. *Context of Scripture*. Boston: Brill, 2000.

Pritchard, James, ed. *The Ancient Near Eastern Texts Relating to the Old Testament*. 3rd ed. with Supplement. Princeton: Princeton University Press, 1969.

DARIUS I

Tablet of Darius I, year 4 from Sippar, 518 BC

Name: Darius I (Darius the Great, son of Hystaspes)

Time Period: 6th and 5th centuries BC (Achaemenid Empire)

Geographical Area: Persia

Biblical Reference(s): Ezra 4:5-24; 5:5–6:15; Haggai 1:1; Zechariah 1:1

Ancient Source(s): Behistun Inscription; Susa Royal Inscriptions; Persepolis Apadana; Foundation Tablets; Tomb of Darius I

Identification Rating: Firm (A)

Darius I, known as Darius the Great and son of Hystaspes, was king of the Achaemenid Empire ca. 522–486 BC after seizing power from either a usurper or a son of Cyrus the Great. Although Darius was part of the royal line of the Achaemenids, he was not the appointed successor by Cyrus the Great. According to his account inscribed at Mount Behistun:

> King Darius says: My father is Hystaspes; the father of Hystaspes was Arsames; the father of Arsames was Ariaramnes; the father of Ariaramnes was Teispes; the father of Teispes was Achaemenes. King Darius says: That is why we are called Achaemenids…This is Gaumata, the Magi. He lied, saying "I am Bardiya, the son of Cyrus, I am king" (Behistun Inscription).

This multilingual royal inscription makes it clear that Darius was of the royal family, but the text and accompanying images, along with other ancient sources, indicate a chaotic time between Cyrus and Darius in which sons of Cyrus—Cambyses II and Bardiya— died, and then a possible usurper and impersonator named Gaumata briefly held the throne (Herodotus, *Histories*; Ctesias, *Persica*; Xenophon, *Cyropaedia*; Aeschylus, *The Persians*). A new palace was established at Susa, one of his capital cities, and an important inscription of Darius at Susa relates that "this palace which I built at Susa, from afar its ornamentation was brought...may Ahuramazda protect me, and Hystaspes my father, and my country" ("Charter of Foundation" Darius Susa F Inscription).

At Persepolis, gold tablets of Darius placed in the foundation of the Apadana Palace preserved another important text describing him and the extent of his kingdom: "Darius the great king, king of kings, king of countries, son of Hystaspes, an Achaemenid. King Darius says: This is the kingdom which I hold, from the Sacae who are beyond Sogdia to Kush, and from Sind to Lydia" (DPh Inscription of Darius I).

Although Darius I also notably minted standardized currency in the form of a coin called the *daric*, re-dug the "Canal of the Pharaohs" connecting the Nile to the Red Sea, achieved many military victories both in and outside of his borders, and organized his kingdom into regions governed by satraps, and the empire he ruled controlled vast swaths of the ancient world, he is often known for his failed conquest of Greece that culminated in the loss at the Battle of Marathon in 490 BC. However, Darius I was also instrumental in the rebuilding of the temple of Yahweh in Jerusalem.

In the Bible, Darius I is named in the books of Ezra, Haggai, and Zechariah. A few scholars mistakenly claim that Darius I also appears in the book of Nehemiah, but in that instance it is Darius II, while the Darius son of Ahasuerus mentioned in the book of Daniel is Darius the Mede.

Relief showing Persian royal attendants at the palace of Darius I

The first returning exiles from Judah probably left Babylonia and arrived in Jerusalem around 538 BC, followed by the rebuilding of the temple under the leadership of the governor Zerubbabel, eventually completing construction during the reign of Darius I in approximately 517 BC and 70 years after it was destroyed (Ezra 2:2; 3:8; 6:15; cf. Daniel 9:2 and Jeremiah 25:11). Although this temple construction was opposed by the satrap Tattenai, who is also attested by Persian period documents, Darius I ultimately approved and endorsed the work and issued a decree to provide finances for the completion of the temple (Ezra 5:3–6:15).

Darius, son of Hystaspes, was a key figure in both ancient history and the biblical narrative, also widely attested by archaeological discoveries and ancient manuscripts.

Persepolis Foundation Apadana Tablets

The elders of the Jews were successful in building through the prophesying of Haggai the prophet and Zechariah the son of Iddo. And they finished building according to the command of the God of Israel and the decree of Cyrus, Darius, and Artaxerxes king of Persia. This temple was completed on the third day of the month Adar; it was the sixth year of the reign of King Darius (Ezra 6:14-15).

Kuhrt, Amelie. *The Persian Empire: A Corpus of Sources from the Achaemenid Period.* New York: Routledge, 2007.

Parian, Saber Amiri. "A New Edition of the Elamite Version of the Behistun Inscription (I)." *Cuneiform Digital Library Bulletin* 3 (2017).

Yamauchi, Edwin. *Persia and the Bible.* Grand Rapids: Baker Academic, 1997.

Inscribed gold bowl of Darius

TATTENAI

Name: Tattenai (Tattanu)

Time Period: 520–500 BC (Persian Period)

Geographical Area: Achaemenid Persia

Biblical Reference(s): Ezra 5:3-6; 6:6-13

Ancient Source(s): Satrap Tattanu Archive

Identification Rating: Firm (A)

Tattenai was the governor of the Persian province "Across the River" (Ebir-Nari) or Trans-Euphrates during the reign of Darius the Great and encompassing the years of approximately 520–500 BC. Initially, Tattenai inquired of Zerubbabel about who had given them permission for the rebuilding of the temple in Jerusalem and attempted to halt it, but after reading the letter from Darius I regarding his commands concerning the building project and ordering assistance from the royal treasury in funding, Tattenai and his colleagues assisted with finishing the reconstruction of the temple. The book of Nehemiah also mentions the governor of the province of Across the River, although the name of the governor is not specified, and Tattenai may have been replaced by this time (Nehemiah 3:7).

While the satrap named Ushtannu resided in Babylon around this time, his subordinate governor, Tattenai, may have been based in Damascus. The discovery and translation of numerous cuneiform tablets reveals that a governor during the reign of Darius I named Tattenai is known from an archive of the Napsanu family, who owned a vast estate outside of Borsippa, near Babylon. In this collection are 74 cuneiform tablets, and the texts primarily deal with records of transactions during the period in which the sons, grandsons, and servants of Tattenai lived.

While numerous tablets refer to Tattenai, who was head of the Napsanu family, one in particular gives details demonstrating a connection to him in the book of Ezra. This tablet, bearing the date of June 5 in the 20th year of Darius I, or 502 BC, mentions a witness who is a servant of "Tattannu, governor of Across the River." This tablet clearly attests to the person and position of Tattenai, as in addition to the name and the time period in the reign of Darius I, both the title "governor" (pahat) and province (Eber-Nari) use the identical words in the book of Ezra and the tablet.

> *At that time Tattenai, the governor of the province beyond the River, and Shethar-bozenai and their colleagues came to them and spoke to them thus, "Who issued you a decree to rebuild this temple and to finish this structure?" Then we told them accordingly what the names of the men were who were reconstructing this building. But the eye of their God was on the elders of the Jews, and they did not stop them until a report could come to Darius, and then a written reply be returned concerning it* (Ezra 5:3-5).

Olmstead, Albert. "Tattenai, Governor of 'Beyond the River.'" *Journal of Near Eastern Studies* 3 (1944).

SHELOMITH

Name: Shelomith

Time Period: 500 BC (Achaemenid Empire)

Geographical Area: Yehud Province

Biblical Reference(s): 1 Chronicles 3:19

Ancient Source(s): Seal of Shelomit

Identification Rating: Speculative (D)

Shelomith was a daughter of Zerubabbel, a governor of Yehud Province during Persian rule who oversaw the rebuilding of the temple in Jerusalem completed during the reign of Darius I around 517 BC. A seal dating to around 500 BC, found with a hoard of bullae from the beginning of the Persian Period, bears an inscription naming an important Shelomit. The text reads "belonging to Shelomit, maidservant of Elnathan the governor." Her title could indicate that she was either an official in the service of the governor or the wife of the governor. The name Elnathan is found in the book of Ezra from this period, but none of the names are associated with the position of governor (Ezra 8:16).

While it is logical that Shelomith, daughter of the governor Zerubabbel, would marry a future governor of Yehud Province, the information is insufficient to make a clear or probable identification.

> *The sons of Pedaiah were Zerubbabel and Shimei. And the sons of Zerubbabel were Meshullam and Hananiah, and Shelomith was their sister* (1 Chronicles 3:19).

Avigad, Nahman. *Corpus of West Semitic Stamp Seals*. Jerusalem: Hebrew University, 1997.

Repaired walls and tower from the Persian period in Jerusalem

XERXES I

(Ahasuerus)

Enthroned Xerxes I at Persepolis Palace

Name: Xerxes I (Ahasuerus)

Time Period: 5th century BC (Persian Period)

Geographical Area: Achaemenid Persia

Biblical Reference(s): Esther 1:1–10:3; Ezra 4:6

Ancient Source(s): Susa and Persepolis Inscriptions; Herodotus; Aeschylus; Ctesias

Identification Rating: Firm (A)

Ahasuerus, more commonly known as Xerxes I, was king of the Achaemenid Persian Empire ca. 486–465 BC, succeeding his father, Darius the Great, and following in the footsteps of his maternal grandfather Cyrus the Great. After the death of his father, Xerxes I suppressed revolts in Egypt and Babylon, then prepared for a renewed invasion of Greece that he would lead himself in order to ensure Persian victory.

Departing for Greece in 480 BC, Xerxes I led a massive army and navy that made the Persian conquest seem inevitable. However, after a pyrrhic victory at Thermopylae and capture of Athens, Xerxes I and his fleet were defeated by the Greek coalition at the Battle of Salamis, and he retreated back into his empire. Following this surprising loss, Xerxes I focused the rest of his reign on construction projects, including Susa, Persepolis, and the Royal Road. The Greeks recorded select aspects of his reign, found in the writings of authors such as Herodotus, Ctesias, and Aeschylus.

In the Bible, Ahasuerus (Xerxes I) is mentioned in the book of Ezra along with the Persian kings who came before and after him, and throughout the book of Esther, which is set in the capital city of Susa. Xerxes is the Greek rendering of the Persian Xšayārša, while Ahasuerus is the Babylonian and Hebrew rendition of the name.

Xerxes I and attendants at Persepolis

Xerxes I is widely attested as king of Persia, successor to Darius I, predecessor to Artaxerxes I, and a monarch who spent much time in Susa during the 5th century BC, as demonstrated by his own inscriptions and ancient historical records of the Greeks. In the book of Ezra, the lineage of these Persian kings is mentioned over four generations—Cyrus I, Darius I, Xerxes I, and Artaxerxes I (Ezra 4:5-7). The family connections and succession of these kings is confirmed by numerous archaeological sources, including a set of four silver bowls bearing an inscription naming Artaxerxes I, son of Ahasuerus (Xerxes I), son of Darius I.

Another aspect of his lineage, tracing the patrilineal line, is found on an inscription of Xerxes from Persepolis: "King Xerxes says: My father was Darius. Darius' father was named Hystaspes. Hystaspes' father was named Arsames. Both Hystaspes and Arsames were living at the time. Thus was Ahuramazda's desire when my father Darius was made king of this earth" (Harem Inscription XPf).

That Xerxes ruled a massive empire stretching from India to Ethiopia from his palaces at Susa and Persepolis is known from his official inscriptions, mentioned in the book of Esther, and recorded by Herodotus:

> King Xerxes says: By the grace of Ahuramazda these are the countries of which I was king apart from Persia. I had lordship over them. They bore me tribute. What was said to them by me, that they did. My law, that held them: Media, Elam, Arachosia, Armenia, Drangiana, Parthia, Aria, Bactria, Sogdia, Chorasmia, Babylonia, Assyria, Sattagydia, Lydia, Egypt, Yauna, those who dwell on this side of the sea and those who dwell across the sea, men of Maka, Arabia, Gandara, India, Cappadocia, the Dahae, the haoma-drinking Sacae, the

Sacae wearing pointed caps, Thrace, men of Akaufaciya, Libyans, Carians, and the Nubians (Daiva Inscription XPh; cf. Esther 1:1-2).

Across the Persian Empire, where excavations have uncovered architecture and numerous inscriptions from the time of Xerxes I, this king is named in his monuments, the monuments of his son, Artaxerxes I, and depicted on stone reliefs. When Xerxes I returned home in 479 BC after the failed invasion of Greece, he began monumental construction projects in the capital cities of Susa and Persepolis, sought consolation in his harem, and selected a new queen (Esther 2:1-17; Herodotus, *Histories* 9.108-113). His building projects are broadly discussed in an inscription from Persepolis naming himself: "I am Xerxes, the great king, the king of all countries…When I became king, I built much excellent [construction]. What had been built by my father, that I protected, and other building I added" (Xerxes Persepolis F Inscription; cf. Gate of All Nations Inscription).

Esther, who held the position of queen for at least six years and seems to have resided in Susa, does not appear to be named in any known inscriptions or the ancient Greek texts that record information about Xerxes, although it may be significant that Herodotus does not discuss details of the later reign of Xerxes beginning in year seven when Esther first encountered the king (Esther 2:16). Further, Xerxes I had multiple queens, and yet the names of most remain unknown. Inscriptions at Susa do, however, identify Xerxes I as king and the person responsible for completing the palace there: "Xerxes the King says: I built

Harem Inscription of Xerxes from Persepolis

this palace after I became king. This I ask as a boon from Ahuramazda" (Xerxes Susa C inscription).

The King's Gate at Susa also bears a significant trilingual inscription in Old Persian, Elamite, and Babylonian: "King Xerxes says: By the grace of Ahuramazda, king Darius, my father, built this portico" (Xerxes Susa D inscription; cf. Esther 2:19). Elsewhere in the empire, Xerxes had monumental inscriptions carved at Van and near Ecbatana in which he names himself, his father, his accomplishments, and his dedication to the god Ahuramazda (Xerxes Van Inscription; Gandj Nameh Inscription).

Xerxes I is attested by his own seals and also depicted on stone reliefs at Persepolis along with his father, Darius I, and his figure is carved into the monument of his presumed tomb at Naqsh-e Rostam. Xerxes I was assassinated by the commander of his royal bodyguard, Artabanus, who was eventually executed by the next king, Artaxerxes I. Thus, not only is Ahasuerus (Xerxes I) attested through numerous inscriptions, manuscripts, and reliefs, but details of his lineage and reign as presented in the books of Ezra and Esther are also in agreement with the archaeological discoveries.

> *Now it took place in the days of Ahasuerus, the Ahasuerus who reigned from India to Ethiopia over 127 provinces, in those days as King Ahasuerus sat on his royal throne which was at the citadel in Susa, in the third year of his reign he gave a banquet for all his princes and attendants, the army officers of Persia and Media, the nobles and the princes of his provinces being in his presence* (Esther 1:1-3).

Lecoq, Pierre. *Les inscriptions de la Perse achéménide*. Paris: Gallimard, 1997.

Yamauchi, Edwin. *Persia and the Bible*. Grand Rapids: Baker Academic, 1997.

MORDECAI

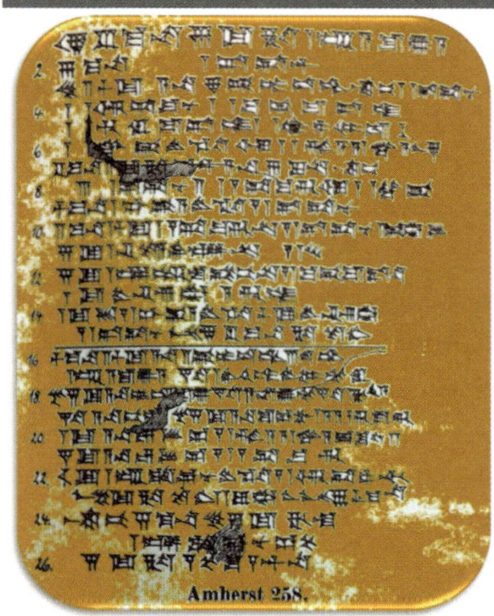

Marduka the sipir tablet

Name: Mordecai (Marduka)

Time Period: 5th century BC (Achaemenid Persian Period)

Geographical Area: Persia

Biblical Reference(s): Esther 2:5–3:3

Ancient Source(s): Amherst Tablets

Identification Rating: Probable (B)

Mordecai, son of Jair, was the older cousin of Esther (Hadassah), who functioned as her guardian while also serving as an official in the royal court of Persia. The book of Esther refers to the third year of Ahasuerus (Xerxes I), which places the events and his service to the king from at least 483 BC (Esther 1:3). However, Mordecai had presumably started his career prior to the third year of Xerxes I, since he was at that time already serving in the capital city of Susa.

This Mordecai cousin of Esther, or Marduka as his name was rendered in its Babylonian original, might be named in Persian records of the time. While numerous tablets from the period of Darius and Xerxes have been discovered in the Persepolis Administrative Archives, and 66 of the tablets date to the reign of Xerxes, which mention officials in the government named Marduka, there might be up to four different officials with the name Mordecai or Marduka. It is possible that the Mordecai of Esther is named among these officials, but this cannot be substantiated based on the currently available information.

However, another tablet, thought to be found at Borsippa south of Babylon but mentioning the "land of Susa" near the end of the text, may refer specifically to the Mordecai known from the book of Esther. This cuneiform tablet dates to the period around the end of the reign of Darius I or the beginning of the reign of Xerxes I, approximately 490–480 BC, which situates it during the time when Mordecai would have been in the service of the Persian government. The tablet contains a list of payments made to Persian officials and their retainers and names Marduka as a scribe and translator under the authority of Ushtannu, the satrap of the province of Babylon and Across the River (Amherst 258).

This province, with Babylon as the capital, was one of the most important administrative districts in the Persian Empire. The text of Esther indicates that Mordecai was living in Babylon prior to moving to Susa, and since he was in a high government position in Susa, it is likely that he also previously served in the Persian government in Babylon while living there. The position this Marduka held was "sipir," whose duties included scribe, translator, and administrator. The duties of this Marduka mentioned in the tablet would have involved interaction with people of various linguistic groups that lived in the Babylon region, including the Judeans who had previously been settled in the area due to the Babylonian exile in the time of Nebuchadnezzar. Because Mordecai probably spoke and wrote Hebrew, Aramaic, Persian, and possibly even other languages, he would have been a perfect candidate for this position.

The identification of this official named Marduka with the Mordecai (Marduka) cousin of Esther has been both supported and opposed by scholars, with acknowledged difficulties such as a lack of lineage mentioned and that this Marduka may have been living or working far from Susa. However, since the names are the same, the time period is the same, both were multilingual government officials, and Mordecai was probably living in Babylon prior to moving to the

Persian royal attendants at the palace

capital city Susa as he advanced to higher positions within the royal administration, eventually sitting in the gate of the king at the Susa palace complex, it is plausible that this particular tablet contains an official Persian reference to Mordecai, son of Jair, named in the book of Esther.

> *In those days, while Mordecai was sitting at the king's gate, Bigthan and Teresh, two of the king's officials from those who guarded the door, became angry and sought to lay hands on King Ahasuerus. But the plot became known to Mordecai and he told Queen Esther, and Esther informed the king in Mordecai's name* (Esther 2:21-22).

Clines, David. "In Quest of the Historical Mordecai." *Vetus Testamentum* 41 (1991).

Yamauchi, Edwin. "Mordecai, the Persepolis Tablets, and the Susa Excavations." *Vetus Testamentum* 42 (1992).

Decorative wall from the palace of Darius and Ahasuerus at Susa

ARTAXERXES I

Inscribed silver bowl of Artaxerxes with his lineage

Name: Artaxerxes I (son of Xerxes I)

Time Period: 5th century BC (Achaemenid Persian Period)

Geographical Area: Persia

Biblical Reference(s): Ezra 4:7-23; 7:7-26; Nehemiah 2:1-8

Ancient Source(s): Silver Bowls of Artaxerxes I; Aswan Sandstone Stele

Identification Rating: Firm (A)

Artaxerxes I, or Artaxshasa, was the son of Xerxes I and a queen named Amestris, reigning over the Achaemenid Persian Empire ca. 465–424 BC. According to the 1st-century Greek historian and philosopher Plutarch, Artaxerxes I was also called "Longimanus" or "long-handed" because his right hand was supposedly longer than his left (Plutarch, *Life of Artaxerxes* 1.1). Artaxerxes I was probably buried northwest of Persepolis at Naqsh-e Rostam, where a rock-carved mural appears to depict this king standing and is located near the tombs of Darius I, Xerxes I, and Darius II.

The book of Nehemiah mentions Artaxerxes I multiple times beginning in year 20 of his reign, while the book of Ezra also refers to Artaxerxes I but much earlier in year seven of his reign. According to the book of Nehemiah, while Artaxerxes I was sitting on his throne at the capital of Susa with his queen beside him, Nehemiah, his cupbearer, asked and was granted the request that the walls of Jerusalem be rebuilt. This decree was made in approximately 444 BC.

Artaxerxes I is attested by many inscriptions from his reign, including multilingual inscriptions and decorative wine bowls, in addition to images of the king such as the relief at his probable tomb and a 5th-century BC chalcedony seal that appears to show Artaxerxes I defeating the Egyptian Inaros II. A famous Old Persian inscription on silver bowls for drinking wine, four of which were found at Hamdan (Ecbatana) in Persia, translates as "Artaxerxes the great king, king of kings, king of lands, son of Xerxes the king, Xerxes son of Darius the king, the Achaemenid, in whose house this silver bowl was made." It is possible that Artaxerxes I himself used these bowls for his wine and Nehemiah handled them as his cupbearer.

Far away, at Aswan in southern Egypt, a building inscription called the Aswan Sandstone Stele has a 5th century-BC Aramaic text noting that "the Troop Commander of Syene made in the month of Sivan, that is Meḥir, year seven of Artaxerxes the king." This inscription not only mentions Artaxerxes I, but includes year seven of his reign, the same year of Artaxerxes I specified in the book of Ezra concerning his decree for a return to Jerusalem and funds for the temple.

Although Artaxerxes I is one of the more poorly attested Achaemenid Persian monarchs, the known archaeological materials are clear enough to substantiate numerous facts about him and that he was the powerful king mentioned in the books of Nehemiah and Ezra.

> *It came about in the month Nisan, in the twentieth year of King Artaxerxes, that wine was before him, and I took up the wine and gave it to the king. Now I had not been sad in his presence* (Nehemiah 2:1).

Curtis, John et al. "A Silver Bowl of Artaxerxes I." *Iran* 33 (1995).

De Vogue, C.J.M. "Inscription araméenne trouvée en Égypte" in *Comptes rendus des séances de l'Académie des Inscriptions & Belles-Lettres* 47.4 (1903).

Seal depicting Artaxerxes defeating Inaros II

SANBALLAT

Bulla of son of Sanballat, governor of Samaria

Name: Sanballat

Time Period: 5th century BC (Achaemenid Persian Period)

Geographical Area: Samaria

Biblical Reference(s): Nehemiah 2:10-19; 6:1-14

Ancient Source(s): Elephantine Papyri; Bulla of Sanballat

Identification Rating: Firm (A)

Sanballat the Horonite was a local official in the service of Artaxerxes I and Darius II around the time when Nehemiah was governor of Yehud in the 5th century BC. Sanballat, associated with the location Horon (Huwara) or Beth-horon at the foot of Mount Gerizim in Samaria, was probably a Samaritan who allied himself with Tobiah of Ammon and Geshem of Qedar against Nehemiah—and in particular against the rebuilding of the walls of Jerusalem by the returning exiles.

Although Sanballat opposed Nehemiah and the rebuilding project in Jerusalem, his daughter married the son of Joiada, the son of Eliashib the high priest (Nehemiah 13:27-28). This marriage, however, was apparently to a foreign woman and a violation of the Mosaic Law. And according to Josephus, Sanballat was a foreigner sent to Samaria and involved in building the Samaritan temple on Mount Gerizim during the reign of Darius (Josephus, *Antiquities* 11.302-346).

Mentioned in the Elephantine Papyri, Sanballat was the governor of Samaria during the reign of Darius II. He also had at least two sons named in a letter from Egypt that dates to 407 BC. The letter is concerned with the rebuilding of the temple of Yahu in Elephantine, but near the end it refers to Sanballat in the context of his sons, who were involved in the political appeal: "Because of this we have written to inform you. We have also set the whole matter forth in a letter in our name to Delaiah and Shelemiah, the sons of Sanballat the governor of Samaria… year 17 of King Darius" (Petition to Bagoas).

The island fortress of Elephantine

Byzantine ruins over the Samaritan temple on Gerizim

Sanballat may also be mentioned on a bulla found attached to an Aramaic papyrus that was a deed of sale for a vineyard, discovered at Wadi Daliyeh near Jericho. The bulla might date to either the 5th or 4th century BC, and it belonged to a son of Sanballat—perhaps Delaiah or Shelemiah, both of whom were likely still alive decades later. The seal impression translates as "belonging to...iah son of Sanballat, Governor of Samaria." While a few scholars suggest that this bulla could be from about 50 years after the time of Sanballat and question the connection, the inscription may indeed refer back to when Sanballat held the position of governor.

Regardless of whether this bulla refers to the Sanballat who was in conflict with Nehemiah, the letter from Elephantine does clearly attest to him in a position of authority in Samaria during the late 5th century BC.

> *Now it came about that when Sanballat heard that we were rebuilding the wall, he became furious and very angry and mocked the Jews. He spoke in the presence of his brothers and the wealthy men of Samaria and said, "What are these feeble Jews doing? Are they going to restore it for themselves? Can they offer sacrifices? Can they finish in a day? Can they revive the stones from the dusty rubble even the burned ones?"* (Nehemiah 4:1-2).

Cowley, Arthur. *Aramaic Papyri of the Fifth Century B.C.* Eugene: Wipf & Stock, 2005.

GESHEM

Bowl of Qaynu, son of Geshem, king of Qedar

Name: Geshem

Time Period: 5th century BC (Achaemenid Persian Period)

Geographical Area: Kingdom of Qedar

Biblical Reference(s): Nehemiah 2:19; 6:1-6

Ancient Source(s): Bowl of Qaynu and Geshem; Inscription of Nuran

Identification Rating: Firm (A)

Geshem was the king of Qedar around 450–430 BC, while his son and successor, Qaynu, reigned about 430–410 BC. According to the book of Nehemiah, Geshem the Arab was a local ruler aligned with Sanballat and Tobiah against Nehemiah during the reign of Artaxerxes I when they were all subjects of the Achaemenid Empire. Qedar was an Arab kingdom attested as early as the 9th century BC by the Assyrians and Shalmaneser III, and thus Geshem of Qedar in the 5th century BC would equate to Geshem the Arab. Since Nehemiah arrived in Jerusalem around 444 BC or soon after, the known reign of Geshem of Qedar would have overlapped with the time that Nehemiah was rebuilding the city wall.

Geshem, king or ruler of Qedar, is known from two inscriptions of the period that appear to substantiate him as a local Arab ruler named Geshem during the time of Nehemiah. An Aramaic inscription on a silver bowl found at a shrine in Tell-el Maskhuta near the Sinai from the period about 430–410 BC, dedicated by his son, reads "that which Qaynu son of Geshem, king of Qedar, brought in offering to Han-'ilat." This Geshem is also attested on an inscription from their capital city of Dedan (al-Ula), Arabia that reads "In the time of Geshem son of Shahru and Abd the governor of Dedan." This Abd was apparently the Persian governor of the province, while Geshem was the local king, and both exerted authority in Qedar.

Since these inscriptions contain his name, lineage, title, and nation, an identification with the ruler named Geshem the Arab mentioned in the book of Nehemiah appears obvious.

> *When Sanballat the Horonite and Tobiah the Ammonite official, and Geshem the Arab heard it, they mocked us and despised us and said, "What is this thing you are doing? Are you rebelling against the king?"* (Nehemiah 2:19).

Cross, Frank Moore. "Geshem the Arabian, Enemy of Nehemiah." *The Biblical Archaeologist* 18 (1955).

Rabinowitz, Isaac. "Aramaic Inscriptions of the Fifth Century B.C.E. from a North-Arab Shrine in Egypt." *Journal of Near Eastern Studies* Vol. 15, No. 1 (1956).

DARIUS II

Elephantine Papyrus version of the Behistun Inscription from 417 BC

Name: Darius II (Ochus, Nothus, Darius the Persian)

Time Period: 5th century BC (Achaemenid Persian Empire)

Geographical Area: Persia

Biblical Reference(s): Nehemiah 12:22

Ancient Source(s): Tomb of Darius II; Elephantine Papyri

Identification Rating: Firm (A)

Darius II, originally named Ochus, was king of the Achaemenid Empire ca. 423–404 BC, gaining power after a struggle for the throne following the death of his father, Artaxerxes I. He was the son of Artaxerxes I and Cosmartidene of Babylon—a woman who was not the official queen—thus the nickname Nothus (meaning "bastard") used in Greek sources. Darius II married his half-sister Parysatis by another secondary wife of Artaxerxes I, and she became both influential and powerful in the royal court.

During his reign, Darius II dealt with numerous rebellions and power struggles, and he is more poorly attested by archaeological remains than many of the other kings in his dynasty (Ctesias, *Persica*). However, inscriptions of his from Susa have been found on column bases (D2Sb), a gold tablet from Ecbatana names him and his lineage (D2Ha), the Murashu archives from Nippur mention him as king in relation to building activity and administration during his reign, and the Elephantine Papyri reference him. He was presumably buried at Naqsh-e Rostam in a monumental tomb with a depiction of him on a stone relief, alongside the tombs of Artaxerxes I, Darius I, and Xerxes I.

Darius II appears only once in the Bible, connected to the time when Nehemiah was governor and Johanan was high priest (Nehemiah 12:22-23). Many of the Elephantine Papyri were produced during the reign of Darius II, including an Aramaic copy of the Behistun Inscription written around 417 BC in year seven of Darius II (DB Aram, Pap. Berlin P. 13447). In the Passover Papyrus from Elephantine, year five of Darius II or about 429 BC is noted, and in the Petition to Bagoas, a letter about the request to rebuild the temple of Yahweh at Elephantine, year 17 of Darius II is given as the date along with mention of "the high priest Johanan and his colleagues, the priests in Jerusalem." This connects Johanan the high priest to the time of Darius II around 407 BC and makes it clear that the Darius the Persian named in the book of Nehemiah is Darius II.

> *As for the Levites, the heads of fathers' households were registered in the days of Eliashib, Joiada, and Johanan and Jaddua; so were the priests in the reign of Darius the Persian* (Nehemiah 12:22).

Kuhrt, Amelie. *The Persian Empire: A Corpus of Sources from the Achaemenid Period.* New York: Routledge, 2007.

Mitchell, Christine. "Berlin Papyrus P. 13447 and the Library of the Yehudite Colony at Elephantine." *Journal of Near Eastern Studies* 76.1 (2017): 139-47.

JOHANAN

Letter mentioning the high priest Johanan

Name: Johanan (grandson of Eliashib)

Time Period: 5th century BC (Achaemenid Persian Period)

Geographical Area: Yehud Province

Biblical Reference(s): Ezra 10:6; Nehemiah 12:22-26

Ancient Source(s): Elephantine Papyri

Identification Rating: Firm (A)

Johanan, son of Eliashib, was a priest in Jerusalem beginning in the reign of Darius II of Persia near the end of the 5th century BC, after the period of the rebuilding of the wall and the tenure of Nehemiah as governor of Yehud Province (Nehemiah 12:11-23). He held the office of high priest from about 410 BC, spanning the time of Darius II and perhaps Artaxerxes II (Josephus, *Antiquities* 11.297).

Among the Elephantine Papyri, Aramaic texts found in Egypt at Elephantine Island, a letter to Bagoas the governor of Yehud sent from Yedoniah at Elephantine mentions the high priest Johanan in Jerusalem. The letter gives the date as the 17th year of Darius II, or 407 BC:

> To our lord Bagoas, governor of Judah, your servants Yedoniah and his colleagues, the priests who are in the fortress of Elephantine...We have also sent a letter before now, when this evil was done to us, to our lord and to the high priest Johanan and his colleagues the priests in Jerusalem and to Ostanes the brother of Anani and the nobles of the Jews...On the 20th of Marshewan, year 17 of king Darius (Petition to Bagoas).

Since Johanan is recorded in the book of Nehemiah as priest during the reign of Darius II, and Josephus notes that Bagoas was governor when Johanan, son of Eliashib, was priest, then the priest Johanan in the Elephantine Papyri must be the same Johanan, son of Eliashib.

Another official mentioned in the Elephantine Papyri might also be one of the prominent people named in the book of Nehemiah, although the connection is more speculative than Johanan the high priest. At the beginning and end of the Passover Papyrus from ca. 419 BC, an official in Judah named Hananiah identifies himself as the sender of the letter to Yedaniah at the garrison in Elephantine. Since this appears to be military correspondence, and probably from Jerusalem based on information from other letters, the sender could have been the leader known as "Hananiah the commander of the fortress in charge of Jerusalem," whom Nehemiah appointed in the late 5th century BC (Nehemiah 7:2).

Further evidence for Johanan might be found on a coin. A few scholars have suggested that a Yehud coin with the inscription "Johanan the priest" attests to the Johanan mentioned in the book of Nehemiah and the Elephantine Papyri, but others argue that the date of the coin may be several decades after his time and could refer to another person. Regardless, the letter from Elephantine provides a clear reference to Johanan the high priest in the 5th century BC.

> *As for the Levites, the heads of fathers' households were registered in the days of Eliashib, Joiada, and Johanan and Jaddua; so were the priests in the reign of Darius the Persian. The sons of Levi, the heads of fathers' households, were registered in the Book of the Chronicles up to the days of Johanan the son of Eliashib* (Nehemiah 12:22-23).

Cowley, Arthur. *Aramaic Papyri of the Fifth Century B.C.* Eugene: Wipf & Stock, 2005.

Porten, Bezalel, et al. *The Elephantine Papyri in English: Three Millennia of Cross-Cultural Continuity and Change.* Leiden: Brill, 1996.

BAGOAS

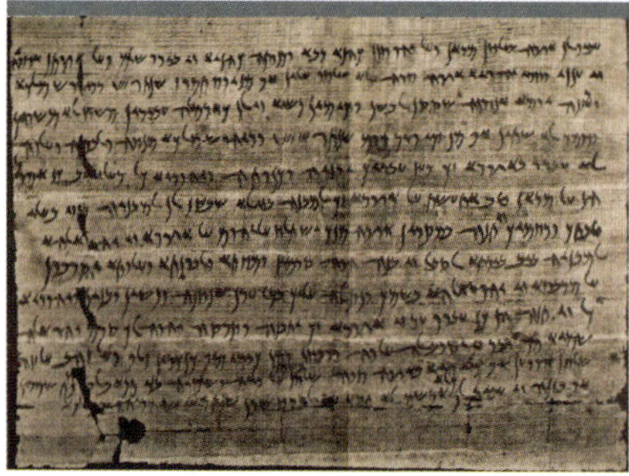

Petition to Bagoas from the Elephantine Papyri

Name: Bagoas (Bigvai)

Time Period: 5th century BC (Persian Period)

Geographical Area: Yehud Province

Biblical Reference(s): Nehemiah 10:16

Ancient Source(s): Elephantine Papyri

Identification Rating: Probable (B)

Bagoas, also known as Bagohi or Bigvai, held the position of governor of the Persian province of Yehud in the late 5th century BC, probably immediately following Nehemiah as governor. Bagoas is the Greek rendering of the name Bagohi or Bigvai, which is probably Persian in origin.

Mentioned once in the book of Nehemiah, a Bagoas was named as a leader of the people who was among the witnesses that signed the sealed document agreeing to keep the Law of Moses, along with Nehemiah the governor. About two decades later, Bagoas is named as the governor of Yehud in letters from Elephantine dated to 407 BC that concern the destruction of the Yahweh temple and a request to rebuilt it: "To our lord Bagoas, governor of Judah, your servants Yedoniah and his colleagues, the priests who are in the fortress of Elephantine... from then to now, in the year 17 of King Darius" (*Petition to Bagoas*, Elephatine Papyri). A copy of the response about the temple was also found among the letters, once more naming Bagoas:

> Memorandum of what Bagoas and Delaiah said to me: Let this be an instruction to you in Egypt to say before Arsames about the house of offering of the God of Heaven which had been in existence in the fortress of Elephantine...was destroyed by that wretch Vidaranag in the year 14 of King Darius: to rebuild it on its site as it was before (*Advice of the Governors of Judah and Samaria*, Elephantine Papyri).

These two letters from Elephantine, dated to approximately 407 BC in the reign of Darius II, establish that a prominent leader in Yehud Province had become governor near the end of the 5th century BC, after the term of Nehemiah. Unfortunately, there can be confusion about this individual because of other officials named Bagoas known from different periods and sources, including Bagoas the Elder, who was vizier of Artaxerxes III in the 4th century BC; Bagoas the eunuch, who served Alexander the Great; and a Bagoas who is mentioned in the book of Judith.However, based on the match in time period and location, the prominent Bagoas living in Judah at the time of Nehemiah can be identified with the Bagoas named in the Elephantine correspondence.

> *Now on the sealed document were the names of: Nehemiah the governor, the son of Hacaliah, and Zedekiah... The leaders of the people: Parosh, Pahath-moab, Elam, Zattu, Bani, Bunni, Azgad, Bebai, Adonijah, Bigvai, Adin* (Nehemiah 10:1, 14-16).

Cowley, Arthur. *Aramaic Papyri of the Fifth Century B.C.* Eugene: Wipf & Stock, 2005.

Yamauchi, Edwin. *Persia and the Bible.* Grand Rapids: Baker Academic, 1997.

PART 2

NEW TESTAMENT PEOPLE

(CHRONOLOGICAL ORDER)

HEROD I

Coin of King Herod the Great

Name: Herod I (Herod the Great)

Time Period: 1st century BC (Roman Period)

Geographical Area: Herodian Kingdom

Biblical Reference(s): Matthew 2:1-22; Luke 1:5

Ancient Source(s): Josephus; Monumental inscriptions; coins

Identification Rating: Firm (A)

Herod, usually described as Herod the Great, was the second son of Antipater, an ethnarch of Idumea, and Cypros, a princess of Nabatea from their capital city of Petra. Thus, although the family of Herod had converted to Judaism during the Hasmonean period, Herod was descended from the Edomites to the south and the Nabateans to the east.

Born around 72 BC, Herod rose through the political ranks quickly, first as the governor of Galilee in about 47 BC, then a tetrarch around 41 BC, and then declared client king of Judea by the Roman Senate in 40 BC. However, Herod was not able to effectively rule his kingdom until he conquered Jerusalem by force in 37 BC.

Throughout his reign, Herod often consolidated or protected his power through executions and assassinations, including the remaining members of the Hasmonean dynasty, his wife Mariamne I, and his sons Aristobulus IV, Alexander, and Antipater II. His family was extremely large, as he had ten wives, eight of whose names are currently known, and at least 15 children, although many did not survive past the death of Herod.

While paranoid and violent, Herod was also an accomplished architect, with the highlight of his construction projects being a complete rebuild of the temple in Jerusalem. According to the writings of Josephus, who recorded extensive biographic sections on the life of Herod the Great and is the main source of information on this controversial figure, Herod had every stone of the previous temple replaced, employing 1,000 priests as masons and carpenters inside the actual sanctuary that supposedly took only 18 months, while about 18,000 skilled laborers worked on the entire project (Josephus, *Antiquities* 15.380-425). The initiation of the temple rebuild is typically dated to around 19 BC, but continued work on the temple complex spanned decades.

This magnificent building, however, lasted only briefly, as it was destroyed when the Romans conquered Jerusalem in AD 70. Other significant building projects of Herod included the harbor and palace at Caesarea Maritima, Herodium, and the fortress of Masada.

Herod the Great appears in the Gospels of Matthew and Luke as king of Judea leading up to and for a few years after the birth of Jesus, and his depiction as a ruler willing to resort to egregious violence in order to retain his power and prestige is consistent with how he is described by Josephus (e.g., Matthew 2:1-22). The death of Herod is briefly mentioned in the Gospel of Matthew without specific chronological information, but the more detailed account of his death by Josephus is usually dated to about 4 BC, after which his son Archelaus became ethnarch of Judea, his son Antipas became tetrarch of Galilee, and his son Philip became tetrarch of Ituraea and Trachonitis (Josephus, *Antiquities* 17.167-191; Luke 3:1).

After Herod died, his corpse was transported to Herodium, near Bethlehem, where it was placed in a sarcophagus and buried in a mausoleum. This mausoleum of Herod the Great, and probably his sarcophagus, were rediscovered during archaeological excavations at Herodium after being lost to history for centuries. The mausoleum had been constructed using white limestone and in a Hellenistic style. The sarcophagus found had been partially destroyed, probably in antiquity, but its restoration shows that it was made of a red limestone and carved with rosette designs. However, since no inscription was found on or in the sarcophagus identifying it as belonging to Herod the Great, a few scholars have questioned if it was his sarcophagus or that of another member of his family.

In addition to the detailed information about the life of Herod in the writings of Josephus and his monumental building projects, Herod is attested by numerous inscriptions from all around his kingdom and beyond, and thousands of coins from his reign. His coins, which feature many sizes and designs, were minted with the name and title "King Herod" in Greek. Notable inscriptions naming Herod the Great include wine jars from his Masada palace reading "King Herod of Judea" and inscribed statue bases naming Herod that were erected in Athens, Kos, and Sia. Despite the many monuments and inscriptions

Sarcophagus of Herod the Great

that Herod commissioned over his long reign, no image of him from antiquity has yet been discovered.

This local king who ruled at the time of the birth of Jesus Christ, Herod the Great, has become one of the most famous and studied rulers of antiquity, and knowledge about him and his life from archaeological discoveries and ancient historical accounts far surpasses that of most monarchs.

> *Now after Jesus was born in Bethlehem of Judea in the days of Herod the king, magi from the east arrived in Jerusalem, saying, "Where is He who has been born King of the Jews? For we saw His star in the east and have come to worship Him." When Herod the king heard this, he was troubled, and all Jerusalem with him* (Matthew 2:1-3).

Krumeich, Ralf and Achim Lichtenberger. "Searching for Portraits of King Herod." *Biblical Archaeology Review* 45.6 (2019).

AUGUSTUS

Bronze statue of Augustus

Name: Augustus (Octavian)

Time Period: 27 BC–AD 14 (Roman Period)

Geographical Area: Rome

Biblical Reference(s): Luke 2:1

Ancient Source(s): Josephus; Suetonius; Tacitus; inscriptions; coins; statues

Identification Rating: Firm (A)

Caesar Augustus, the first emperor of Rome, is one of the most famous and powerful figures in all of history, ruling for over four decades during a transformational period in civilization. Although he was the Roman emperor so long, he is only mentioned by name once in the Bible because the only period in which his reign overlapped with a segment of the New Testament was the birth of Jesus.

Born Gauis Octavius into the equites class, he was adopted by Julius Caesar as his heir. Thus, when Julius Caesar was assassinated in 44 BC at the theatre of Pompey in Rome, Octavian (Augustus) became the leader of Caesar's legions and soon allied with Marc Antony and Marcus Lepidus in the Second Triumvirate. The three eventually turned on one another, and in 31 BC Octavian emerged victorious at the Battle of Actium. Then, on October 16 of 27 BC, the Senate conferred upon him the title "augustus," and his time as emperor began.

Augustus is, of course, thoroughly documented by numerous Roman authors and historians from antiquity, in addition to the many coins bearing his name and likeness, statues, monuments, inscriptions, and other artwork. Highlights of his life are also found in his autobiography, *Res Gestae Divi Augustus* (*Deeds of the Divine Augustus*), which is partially preserved by Latin and Greek versions carved onto stone monuments that have survived in a fragmentary state. The most complete text of *Res Gestae* is found at the Monumentum Ancyranum temple in Ankara.

The birth of Jesus occurred around the middle of the reign of Augustus, prior to the death of Herod the Great, and the Gospel of Luke states that in the time leading up to the nativity, Caesar Augustus had issued a decree for a census of the Roman world. According to *Res Gestae*, Augustus himself declared that he ordered censuses of the empire and recorded the number of citizens. One of these, carried out during the consulship of Gaius Censorinus and Gaius Asinius, or 8 BC, coincides with the time prior to the birth of Jesus Christ.

> *Now in those days a decree went out from Caesar Augustus, that a census be taken of all the inhabited earth* (Luke 2:1).

Cooley, Alison. *Res Gestae divi Augusti: Text, Translation and Commentary*. Cambridge: Cambridge University, 2009.

Emperor Augustus as Pontifex Maximus

The biography of Augustus, *Res Gestae Divi Augustus*

QUIRINIUS

Funerary inscription from Syria mentioning the legate Quirinius and a census

Name: Quirinius (Publius Sulpicius Quirinius)

Time Period: 1st century BC and AD (Roman Period)

Geographical Area: Rome and Syria

Biblical Reference(s): Luke 2:2

Ancient Source(s): Lapis Venetus; *Res Gestae;* Josephus; Tacitus; Pliny the Elder; Suetonius

Identification Rating: Firm (A)

Quirinius, or Publius Sulpicius Quirinius, was a Roman citizen and patrician who held the rank of consul in 12 BC, commanded legions as a legate, served as a governor, and was elected as a duumvir. Born around 51 BC in Lanuvium near Rome, his rise to power coincided with Caesar Augustus, and during the reign of Emperor Tiberius, he continued to hold a favorable position until his death in AD 21.

Quirinius is mentioned by name only once in the New Testament, where he is recorded as being the Roman official responsible for carrying out the census around the time Jesus was born (Luke 2:2). In the ancient Roman historical sources, various details about the career of Quirinius are discussed by numerous authors, including his becoming a consul, a tax assessment in Judea after the exile of Archelaus, battles against enemy tribes and rebels, family tragedies, and his state funeral (e.g., Josephus, *Antiquities* 17.354-20.102; Tacitus, *Annals* 3.22-48; Pliny the Elder, *Natural History* 5.23; Suetonius, *Tiberius* 49).

From an archaeological perspective, Quirinius is attested by at least four official inscriptions that supplement the historical sources. The earliest of these inscriptions, and the one most relevant to the mention of Quirinius in the Gospel of Luke, is a funerary monument of a Roman military officer holding the rank of prefect named Quintus Aemilius Secundus. Discovered in Beirut, which was part of Syria Province in Roman times, the Latin text gives a brief biography of this officer, including that he was

> decorated with honors in the service of the deified Augustus under Publius Sulpicius Quirinius, legate of Caesar in Syria...At the command of Quirinius, I carried out a census of the district of Apamea involving 117,000 citizens. Likewise when sent by Quirinius against the Itureans, I captured their fort on the Mount Lebanon (CIL III.6687).

Apamea was a major city in western Syria on the Orontes River, and Mount Lebanon was an area north of the Sea of Galilee and part of the kingdom of Herod the Great. Not only does this inscription name Quirinius and demonstrate his high rank with the title of legate, but it discusses a census being overseen by Quirinius in Syria Province during the reign of Augustus (cf. Luke 2:1-2). Because it was Roman protocol for the military to carry out a census, it is consistent with Roman practice that as a military commander, Quirinius would be responsible for its administration.

Augustus himself also mentioned Quirinius as a consul in his biographical inscriptions, referring back to 12 BC when Quirinius and Gaius Valgius were consuls (Res Gestae Divi Augusti). Two minor inscriptions from Pisidian Antioch in the province of Asia, dating to AD 3, name Quirinius and that he served in the position of duumvir, a title that describes a pair of joint magistrates (ILS 9502-3).

Another inscription occasionally connected to Quirinius, the Lapis Tiburtinus, may instead refer to a different Roman official. Found near the villa of Quintilius Varus at Tivoli, east of Rome, it records the career of a distinguished Roman, but the name is unfortunately damaged. The inscription states that this official was once proconsul of Asia and then of Syria, which does not match

Lapis Tiburtinus mentioning a governor of Syria

what is known of Quirinius. As the Lapis Tiburtinus was found near the villa of Quintilius Varus and he served as governor of Syria, it could be honoring his career, but similarities have also been noted with the life of L. Calpurnius Piso.

Information about the life of Quirinius is scattered but vast, yet his attestation as a Roman legate in Syria Province at the time of a census in the reign of Augustus enables a definitive identification.

> *Now in those days a decree went out from Caesar Augustus, that a census be taken of all the inhabited earth. This was the first census taken while Quirinius was governor of Syria* (Luke 2:1-2).

Ehrenberg, Victor and A.H.M. Jones. *Documents Illustrating the Reigns of Augustus and Tiberius*. Oxford: Oxford University Press, 1976.

Huebner, Sabine. *Papyri and the Social World of the New Testament*. Cambridge: Cambridge University Press, 2019.

Kennedy, Titus. *Excavating the Evidence for Jesus*. Eugene: Harvest House, 2022.

The Forum of Augustus in Rome

JESUS OF NAZARETH

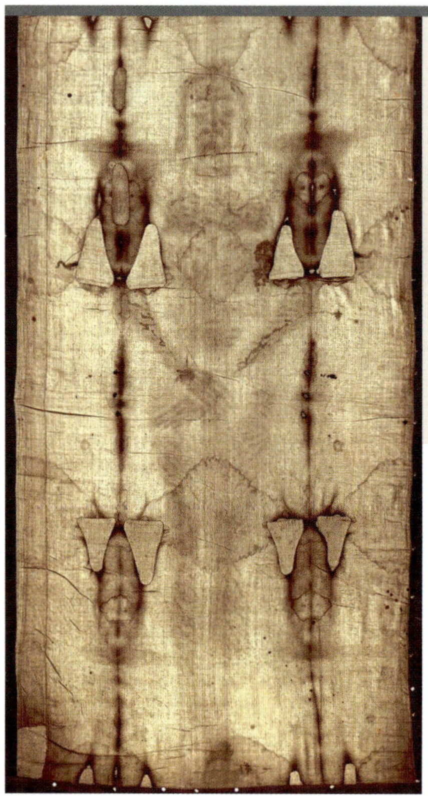
The Shroud of Turin

Name: Jesus of Nazareth (Jesus Christ)

Time Period: 1st century (Roman Period)

Geographical Area: Galilee and Judea

Biblical Reference(s): Matthew 26:71; Mark 1:24; Luke 4:34; 18:37; John 1:45; Acts 10:38; 26:9

Ancient Source(s): James Ossuary; Christ Magician Cup; Josephus; Tacitus; Pliny the Younger

Identification Rating: Firm (A)

Jesus of Nazareth, or Jesus Christ, is almost certainly the most famous person in all of history. And yet many think Jesus is not attested by any contemporary sources of the 1st century AD. For some this has no bearing on the Jesus of Nazareth being a historical person, while for others it indicates that Jesus may have been a type of mythical character if nothing has been discovered to confirm his existence in the 1st century.

Yet Jesus Christ is indeed named in the writings of historians and philosophers who lived in the 1st century AD, and various ancient manuscripts of these works still exist today. The historians and philosophers who lived in the 1st century AD and mention Jesus Christ as an historical person in their known writings include Flavius Josephus (ca. AD 37–100), Mara Bar Serapion (around AD 73), Tacitus (ca. AD 56–117), Pliny the Younger (ca. AD 61–113), and Suetonius (ca. AD 69–130). Josephus, a native of Judea, used both the name Jesus and the title Messiah (Christ), recording that "there was a wise man called Jesus...Many people among the Jews and the other nations became his disciples...Accordingly, he was perhaps the Messiah...And the tribe of the Christians, so named after him, has not disappeared to this day" (Josephus, *Antiquities* 18.63-64).

Serapion referred to Jesus similarly as the "wise King" and teacher who was executed (Serapion, *Letter to His Son*). The renowned chronicler Tacitus used the title "Christus" and noted his death in Judea (Tacitus, *Annals* 15.44). Pliny the Younger also used the title "Christ" in his mention of Jesus (Pliny, *Letter to Trajan*). The Roman historian Suetonius, who wrote biographies of the emperors, once more used the title for Jesus, calling him "Chrestus" (Suetonius, *Divus Claudius* 25). Of these references, the clearest is Josephus, who also happens to be the only one of the authors who lived in Judea and may be the oldest of the five writers. He mentions Jesus in two separate passages of his *Antiquities*. Thus, based on the ancient historical writings alone, Jesus Christ was clearly recorded as an historical person by people who lived in the 1st century AD.

In addition to references mentioning Jesus or Christ by multiple authors from antiquity, two archaeological inscriptions of the 1st century also appear to attest to his existence as an important historical person. One Aramaic inscription, found on the side of the James ossuary and situated in Jerusalem around AD 62, identifies James, the son of Joseph, as "the brother of Jesus." This James was almost certainly James the Just, who is labeled as the brother of Jesus Christ in both the 1st-century writings of Josephus and the New Testament. Thus, this ossuary inscription appears to be naming Jesus of Nazareth or Jesus Christ, identified in this case by his familial relationships rather than his common titles.

Another inscription, found on a ceramic cup dated to the 1st century and discovered in the harbor of Alexandria, Egypt, seems to mention Jesus using his title Christ. The Greek phrase translates as "through Christ the magician" and may reflect a belief in Egypt that Jesus was a powerful magician who performed miracles and cast out demons. These two inscriptions and their interpretation, while disputed by various scholars, could be the only currently known archaeological corroboration of Jesus Christ from the 1st century. Perhaps the earliest artistic rendering of Jesus, found on the Alexamenos graffito from AD 100 or so in Rome, depicts Jesus on the cross but with the head of a donkey, while the famous and debated Shroud

The Alexamenos graffito, mocking Jesus being crucified

James son of Joseph, brother of Jesus inscription

The James Ossuary

of Turin bears what is believed by many to be an image of the entombed Jesus. Thus, it is probable that Jesus of Nazareth or Jesus Christ is attested by archaeological artifacts contemporary with the era in which he lived.

Even if these are set aside, however, the ancient manuscripts preserving writings of historians and philosophers who lived during the 1st century AD demonstrate that Jesus Christ was a historical person.

> *Pilate said to them, "Then what shall I do with Jesus who is called Christ?" They all said, "Crucify Him!"* (Matthew 27:22).

Kennedy, Titus. *Excavating the Evidence for Jesus*. Eugene: Harvest House, 2022.

TIBERIUS

Head and name of Tiberius on a denarius

Name: Tiberius (Tiberius Julius Caesar Augustus)

Time Period: 1st century AD (Roman Period)

Geographical Area: Rome

Biblical Reference(s): Luke 3:1

Ancient Source(s): Roman historians; coins; statues; monumental inscriptions

Identification Rating: Firm (A)

Tiberius was born to a patrician family in Rome during the tumultuous period of the Second Triumvirate in 42 BC. When he was a young boy, he joined an even more powerful family when his mother, Livia Drusilla, divorced his father and married Octavian, the future Caesar Augustus. Not until AD 4, however, when Gaius, the grandson of Augustus, died in battle, was Tiberius adopted as the heir to Augustus. Then in AD 12, after returning to Rome from a campaign in Germania, Tiberius was given joint governing powers with Augustus (Suetonius, *Tiberius* 21).

Two years later Augustus died, and Tiberius became the second emperor of Rome on September 17 of AD 14. A few years later in Galilee, Herod Antipas the Tetrarch built a new capital in about AD 19 and named it Tiberias in honor of the emperor, and the Sea of Galilee was also called the Sea of Tiberias for a short period (John 6:1, 23).

Although he had been a competent commander and leader, leading successful military campaigns and overseeing notable construction projects such as his palace in Rome on the Palatine Hill, a temple in Rome dedicated to his stepfather and predecessor, Augustus, and restorations to the famous theatre of Pompey in Rome, Tiberius appears to have had little interest in directly ruling the empire. In AD 26 he moved to a villa on the island of Capri and isolated himself, allegedly engaging in numerous immoral acts and allowing his various administrators to manage many of the duties of the emperor (Suetonius, *Tiberius* 43–45). At this point in time, Lucius Aelius Sejanus, the commander of the Praetorian Guard, began to exercise immense power in Rome, and Pontius Pilatus was selected as the new prefect of Judea Province.

The sole mention of Tiberius by name in the New Testament, in reference

Coin bearing the names of Sejanus and Tiberius as joint consuls

Bust of young Tiberius after adoption by Augustus

to his fifteenth year, comes in the context of the period when Tiberius had already isolated himself on Capri and left the administration of the empire to others, such as Sejanus. He is, however, referred to by the name and title Caesar multiple times elsewhere in the Gospels (Luke 3:1). The denarius coin with the image of Tiberius is also mentioned in reference to rendering that which is Caesar's to Caesar (e.g., Matthew 22:17-21; Mark 12:13-17; Luke 20:22-25). In AD 29, Livia, the mother of Tiberius and one of the "august lords," died, and Sejanus became even more powerful.

Eventually, in AD 31, Tiberius was informed that Sejanus was plotting to overthrow him and become emperor. Tiberius then issued a letter ordering the execution of Sejanus, and a violent purge ensued in which not only Sejanus but many of his family members and associates were executed. Tiberius lived out his final years in paranoia and interfered little in the administration of the empire. He died in AD 37 at age 77, probably due to assassination, and Caligula became the next emperor after a brief power struggle (Suetonius, *Tiberius* 73; Tacitus, *Annals* 6.50-51; Cassius Dio, Roman History 58.28). Tiberius was only the first of many Roman emperors to be assassinated.

> *Now in the fifteenth year of the reign of Tiberius Caesar, when Pontius Pilate was governor of Judea, and Herod was tetrarch of Galilee, and his brother Philip was tetrarch of the region of Ituraea and Trachonitis, and Lysanias was tetrarch of Abilene...* (Luke 3:1).

LYSANIAS

Name: Lysanias

Time Period: 1st century (Roman Period)

Geographical Area: Abilene

Biblical Reference(s): Luke 3:1

Ancient Source(s): Lysanias inscriptions; Josephus

Identification Rating: Firm (A)

According to the book of Luke, Lysanias was the name of a tetrarch who ruled over Abilene during the ministry of Jesus in approximately AD 28, probably encompassing at least several years around this time. Abila was the capital city of the region of Abilene. In the context of the death of Tiberius and succession of Caligula in AD 37, Herod Agrippa I was promised various lands, and Caligula "put a diadem upon his head, and appointed him to be king of the tetrarchy of Philip. He also gave him the tetrarchy of Lysanias" (Josephus, *Antiquities* 18.237). The area of this tetrarchy was specified as "Abila of Lysanias, and all that lay at Mount Libanus" (Josephus, *Antiquities* 19.275; cf. 20.138).

Bust of Livia, mother of Tiberius

Confusion has come about due to other people named Lysanias from different times and places. For example, the Lysanias who was tetrarch of Abilene in the early 1st century AD may have been the son of the tetrarch Zenodorus and grandson of the Lysanias executed by Cleopatra. However, the tetrarchy of Lysanias in Abila, referred to by Josephus in the context of AD 37 and following, is obviously the Lysanias whom Luke mentions.

However, not only is this Lysanias who

ruled in the 20s and 30s AD noted in the 1st-century AD records of Josephus, but archaeological discoveries have confirmed his existence, title, location, and time. While Lysanias the tetrarch may have never issued coins with his name and title, two nearly identical inscriptions of the early 1st century AD discovered at Abila document this Lysanias who Luke stated was a tetrarch during the time of Tiberius and Pontius Pilate. The Greek inscriptions, one carved into rock along a road and another on the wall of a temple, were made to honor Lysanias for building projects he had carried out at Abila. The most intact of the two inscriptions translates as "For the salvation of the August lords and of all their household, Nymphaeus, freedman of Eagle. Lysanias the tetrarch established this street and other things."

The name and title on the inscription are an obvious match, and the location of Abila also corresponds, but the time period requires explanation. The use of the honorific title "August lords" refers to Emperor Tiberius and his mother, Livia, and means the inscription would date to no later than AD 29 when Livia died, in agreement with the time mentioned in the Gospel of Luke for Lysanias to be tetrarch of Abilene.

Thus, the name, title, location, and date all match for this Lysanias who is attested in both ancient manuscripts and by inscriptions from the city where he ruled.

> *Now in the fifteenth year of the reign of Tiberius Caesar, when Pontius Pilate was governor of Judea, and Herod was tetrarch of Galilee, and his brother Philip was tetrarch of the region of Ituraea and Trachonitis, and Lysanias was tetrarch of Abilene...* (Luke 3:1).

Savignac, Raphaël. "Texte complet de l'inscription d'Abila relative a Lysanias." *Revue Biblique* 9.4 (1912).

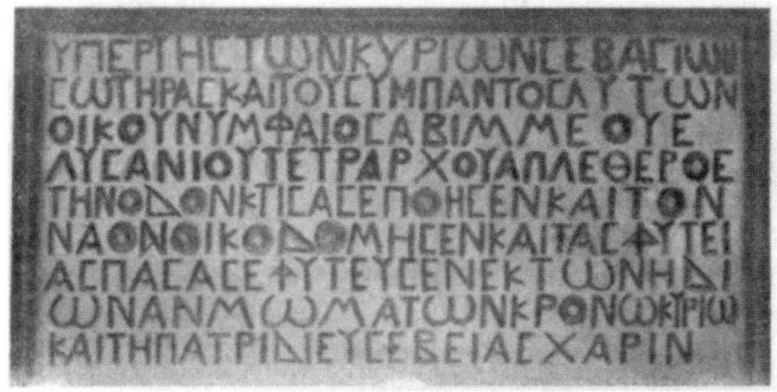

Lysanias the tetrarch inscription from Abila

JOHN THE BAPTIST

Machaerus, where John the Baptist was imprisoned by Antipas

Name: John the Baptist (John the Forerunner)

Time Period: 1st century AD (Roman Period)

Geographical Area: Judea

Biblical Reference(s): Matthew 3:1; 14:2-8; Mark 1:4; 6:14-25; Luke 1:13-36; 3:1-20; John 1:6-36

Ancient Source(s): Josephus

Identification Rating: Firm (A)

John the Baptist, also called John the Forerunner, was the son of Zacharias the priest and Elizabeth. According to the Gospel of Luke, he was born about six months before Jesus of Nazareth. As his name suggests, John was known for baptizing people in the Jordan River, and particularly at the sites of Bethany beyond the Jordan and Aenon of Salim (John 1:28; 3:23).

John was an enigmatic figure, described as living in the wilderness, wearing a garment of camel hair, and eating locusts and honey, yet he also had disciples and even interacted with the political elite such as Herod Antipas the Tetrarch. Besides the baptism of Jesus, John is most known for his criticism of Antipas and Herodias that ultimately resulted in his imprisonment and death. In fact, these events involving John were seen as so significant that many people believed it led to a shift of political power in the region and was worthy of being recorded by the historian Flavius Josephus.

The backstory of the interaction between John the Baptist, Antipas, Herodias, and Salome began with an affair between Antipas and Herodias before they were married. While visiting Rome, Antipas stayed with his brother Philip (Herod II) and fell in love with his brother's wife Herodias. Antipas then divorced Phasaelis, Herodias left Philip, and Antipas married Herodias. Princess Phasaelis fled to her father Aretas IV of Nabatea, war eventually broke out, and Antipas was soundly defeated (Josephus, *Antiquities* 18.109-115). In the midst of the scandal, John the Baptist proclaimed that the marriage between Antipas and Herodias was against the Law of Moses (cf. Leviticus 20:21). His exhortation was not appreciated, and he was locked up in prison by Antipas at the fortress palace of Machaerus, located on top of a high hill east of the Dead Sea.

The synoptic Gospels refer to the proclamation, imprisonment, and execution of John the Baptist, but the writings of Josephus give additional details of the events, even specifically naming him as "John, that was called the Baptist" (Josephus, *Antiquities* 18.116). This John that Josephus refers to was certainly the same John the Baptist discussed in the New Testament, as Josephus described him as "a good man, and commanded the Jews to exercise virtue, both as to righteousness towards one another, and piety towards God, and so to come to baptism" and that he was executed at Machaerus by order of Antipas after the problems involving Herodias (Josephus, *Antiquities* 18.116-119). Although Josephus viewed the events from a perspective different from that of the Gospel writers, the events and people are undoubtedly the same. Based on a compilation of the difference sources, it is likely that John had been in prison at Machaerus for a while before his head was requested at the birthday banquet, then he was beheaded and his remains brought to Salome and Herodias.

Although John was beheaded, his disciples were able to recover his body and bury him in a tomb (Matthew 14:12; Mark 6:29). The location of this tomb is uncertain, but in the 4th century a Byzantine church was built in Sebaste to commemorate the death of John the Baptist and his tomb. The church had three apses and a crypt, but the origin of the burial tradition is unknown. John the Baptist also appears to be memorialized by a carved illustration depicting him, probably made around the 4th to 6th century AD during the Byzantine period and found on the wall of a monastic cave alongside a baptismal installation, near his hometown of Ein Kerem.

Considering that John the Baptist held no political or religious office, was not wealthy, apparently had no children, and lived a short life, from a historical perspective it is astonishing that his legacy survives in the records of Josephus and that an ancient church was erected in his honor.

Further, not only is John the Baptist attested in ancient manuscripts, but most of the other people involved and mentioned in the incident of his arrest and death—Herod Antipas, Herodias, Philip, Phasaelis, Aretas IV, and Salome—have all been confirmed by archaeological sources and ancient historical writings.

> *Now in those days John the Baptist came, preaching in the wilderness of Judea...Now John himself had a garment of camel's hair and a leather belt around his waist; and his food was locusts and wild honey. Then*

Jerusalem was going out to him, and all Judea and all the district around the Jordan; and they were being baptized by him in the Jordan River, as they confessed their sins (Matthew 3:1-6).

Conder, C.R. and H.H. Kitchener. *The Survey of Western Palestine: Memoirs of the Topography, Orography, Hydrography, and Archaeology*, Vol. 2. London: Palestine Exploration Fund, 1882.

The Judean Wilderness

ARETAS IV

Name: Aretas IV Philopatris (Haritat)

Time Period: 1st century AD (Roman Period)

Geographical Area: Nabatea

Biblical Reference(s): 2 Corinthians 11:32

Ancient Source(s): Josephus; coins; royal tomb; Inscription of Itaybel

Identification Rating: Firm (A)

Coins of Aretas IV bearing his image and name

King Aretas IV Philopatris, also known by his Aramaic name Haritat, came to power as the king of Nabatea after the assassination of his predecessor, Obodas III, and enjoyed a long reign from about 9 BC to AD 40 (Josephus, *Antiquities* 16.294-355). Originally named Aeneas, Aretas was selected as his throne name, and his official inscriptions usually read "Aretas, king of the Nabataeans, friend of his people." Emperor Augustus recognized Aretas IV as a client king of the Roman Empire, and this kingdom status for Nabatea lasted until Trajan transformed the region into the senatorial province of Arabia Petraea in AD 106.

Aretas IV is named in the second letter of Paul to the Corinthians in a section narrating an event from AD 35 just after the conversion of Paul. However, long before this, Aretas IV was involved in a family dispute mentioned in the Gospels. His daughter, Phasaelis, had married Herod Antipas the Tetrarch and son of Herod the Great, but in about AD 26, when Herod Antipas divorced her and married Herodias, Phasaelis fled to her father, Aretas IV. Phasaelis is also named on certain coins of Aretas IV.

Although Phasaelis is not specifically named in the Gospels, nor is her father, the situation is briefly mentioned by Matthew, Mark, and Luke, and the writings of Josephus give details about the events (cf. Matthew 14:3-4; Mark 6:17-19; Luke 3:19). Not only did this divorce and remarriage face bold criticism from John the Baptizer, but combined with a previous border dispute, it prompted Aretas IV to launch a retaliatory military campaign against Herod Antipas. With a much larger force and treacherous assistance from Philip the Tetrarch, Aretas IV was able to destroy the army of Herod Antipas and annexed part of his lands. Aretas IV was probably a distant relative of the Herods, as his ancestor Malichus I of Nabatea seems to have been a cousin of Herod the Great. But the family ties and allegiance to Rome apparently did nothing to prevent the intrigue and wars.

The city of Damascus, which had been a Decapolis city for many years, may have been part of the territory gained by Aretas IV during his reign—and perhaps as a result of his campaign against Herod Antipas. Around AD 35, after his conversion, the apostle Paul began preaching in Damascus, and this caused an uproar in the city. A plot was then made to catch and murder

Nabatean inscription of Itaybel mentioning King Aretas IV

Paul, and an ethnarch in the administration of Aretas IV was collaborating with this plan, searching Damascus and planning to seize Paul. According to the second letter to the Corinthian church, the Christians in Damascus helped Paul evade the Nabatean official attempting to arrest him by lowering Paul down the outside of the city wall at night in a basket (2 Corinthians 11:32-33; cf. Acts 19:23-25).

Numerous coins issued by Aretas IV bear his name, many Nabatean inscriptions also state his title as king of the Nabateans, and his royal tomb may be the most iconic monument at Petra—the Treasury. Connecting to the time of Paul, however, a Nabatean funerary inscription found near Madaba, south of Damascus, dates to AD 37, only two years after Paul narrowly escaped death in Damascus at the hands of an ethnarch under Aretas IV. The Nabatean inscription mentions King Aretas IV and two of his officials (strategos), a father named Itaybel and his son. Although the ethnarch pursuing Paul in Damascus was probably a different person, the inscription does attest to Aretas IV as king only two years later and in the same region.

The probable tomb of King Aretas IV at Petra

In Damascus the ethnarch under Aretas the king was guarding the city of the Damascenes in order to seize me, and I was let down in a basket through a window in the wall, and so escaped his hands (2 Corinthians 11:32-33).

Hendin, David. *Guide to Biblical Coins*, 5th ed. New York: Amphora, 2010.

Taylor, Justin. "The Ethnarch of King Aretas at Damascus: A Note on 2 Cor 11, 32-33." *Revue Biblique* 99.4 (1992).

HEROD ARCHELAUS

Coin of Herod Archelaus with his name Herod and title ethnarch

Name: Herod Archelaus (Herod the Ethnarch)

Time Period: 1st century BC–1st century AD (Roman Period)

Geographical Area: Judea

Biblical Reference(s): Matthew 2:22

Ancient Source(s): Josephus; Cassius Dio; coins

Identification Rating: Firm (A)

Archelaus was a son of Herod the Great by Malthace and the oldest surviving son by the time Herod died. As such, he could have expected to inherit the kingdom from his father, but Herod the Great had altered his will multiple times. When Archelaus and Antipas traveled to Rome to sort out the details of their father's plans, no one was proclaimed king of Judea. Instead, the kingdom was divided up amongst four heirs. Archelaus, however, did receive the largest area, including Judea, Idumea to the south, and Samaria to the north, along with the title of ethnarch, or ruler of a people.

Archelaus ruled from only 4 BC to AD 6, but during this time he angered the people under his authority, and by extension, the Roman government. His acts that offended and enraged the locals included replacing multiple high priests in Jerusalem (Josephus, *Antiquities* 17.339-341), diverting water from Neara to his new palace at Jericho (Josephus, *Antiquities* 17.340), and marrying Glaphyra, the former wife of his brother Alexander and current wife of the king of Mauritania (Josephus, *Antiquities* 17.341).

Numerous passages in the writings of Josephus describe how cruel and violent Archelaus was, with the most egregious example being a retaliation against an angry crowd of Pharisees during Passover that resulted in the execution of 3,000 people before Archelaus had even been designated ethnarch (Josephus, *Antiquities* 17.213-218). Due to these tyrannical and blasphemous acts, a delegation of Judeans and Samaritans traveled to Rome to make a formal complaint to the Senate and the emperor in hopes that Rome would remove him from power (Josephus, *Antiquities* 17.342-344). His brothers and co-rulers of the region, Philip and Antipas, even directly brought accusations against Archelaus to Emperor Augustus (Cassius Dio, *Historia* LV 27.6).

In the 10th year of his reign, Archelaus was summoned to Rome, and the decision of August was to take his money and banish him to Vienna, resulting in the former lands of Archelaus becoming the Roman province of Judea, ruled by a prefect named Coponius (Josephus, *Antiquities* 17.342-354; cf. Strabo, Geography 16.2.46).

Archelaus is named only once in the New Testament, in the book of Matthew. This mention is at the beginning of his reign, and the impression given is that Joseph already knew, as apparently so many people did, how horrible and violent Archelaus was. So he avoided Judea completely and went back to the region of Galilee where Antipas ruled as the tetrarch.

In addition to ancient historical manuscripts, Archelaus is attested archaeologically by the coins he issued. These coins were small and simple, made out of bronze, with basic designs such as a galley or an anchor or cornucopia. But their distinguishing feature was the name and title "Herod ethnarch" stamped in Greek letters.

> *When he heard that Archelaus was reigning over Judea in place of his father Herod, he was afraid to go there. Then after being warned by God in a dream, he left for the regions of Galilee* (Matthew 2:22).

Hendin, David. *Guide to Biblical Coins*, 5th ed. New York: Amphora, 2010.

HEROD ANTIPAS

Coin of Herod Antipas the tetrarch, bearing his name and title

Name: Herod Antipas (Herod the Tetrarch)

Time Period: 1st century AD (Roman Period)

Geographical Area: Galilee and Peraea

Biblical Reference(s): Matthew 14:1-6; Mark 6:14-22; Luke 3:1, 19-20; 23:7-15; Acts 13:1

Ancient Source(s): Josephus; Philo of Alexandria; inscriptions; coins

Identification Rating: Firm (A)

Herod Antipas, also called Herod the Tetrarch, was one of the primary sons and heirs of Herod the Great, presiding over the Galilee region after the death of his father from about 4 BC to AD 39. He is often designated as Antipas or Herod Antipas to prevent confusion among the many Herodian rulers, although the Gospels refer to him as Herod the Tetrarch, which he began using in AD 6 (Matthew 14:1; Luke 3:1; cf. Mark 6:14).

When Herod Antipas's father died, a power struggle ensued between him and his brother Archelaus over who would inherit their father's throne resulted in a trip to Rome for Augustus to adjudicate the situation. The result, following the final will Herod left behind, split the kingdom so that no one became king. Antipas was instead made the tetrarch of Galilee and Peraea, while two of his brothers and his aunt Salome I also received portions of the kingdom. The Herodian Tetrarchy form of the kingdom was short-lived since Rome made Judea an imperial province in AD 6, but Antipas retained his lands and title.

Herod Antipas married the princess Phasaelis, the daughter of Aretas IV, king of Nabatea, in what was assuredly a wise political move. However, while visiting Rome, Antipas stayed with his brother Philip and fell in love with Herodias, who was married to Philip at the time. The resulting scandal has gone down in history, as Antipas divorced Phasaelis and married Herodias, causing strife between brothers, the imprisonment and death of John the Baptist, and a war between Antipas and Aretas IV (Josephus, *Antiquities* 18.111-115).

Usually, Antipas generally lived according to the laws and customs of Judaism, never building pagan temples, never putting a face on his coins, and never placing statues in the Jerusalem temple area. However, in the case of marrying Herodias, John the Baptizer rebuked him for clear violation of the Mosaic Law (Mark 6:14-18).

Ruins of the capital city of Antipas at Tiberius

With a long reign stretching to AD 39, Antipas was still in power during the trial of Jesus, whom he finally encountered for the first time (Luke 23:8-12). In his year 43, Antipas was suddenly removed from power and exiled to Lugdunum by Emperor Caligula at the behest of his nephew Herod Agrippa I, who accused him of treason and then became king of Judea (Josephus, *Antiquities* 18.240-252 and *Wars* 2.181-183).

Antipas is discussed at length in the writings of Josephus, referred to indirectly by Philo of Alexandria, and attested on his own coins and inscriptions. Antipas also carried out construction at Sepphoris, then moved his capital and built the new city of Tiberius on the western coast of the Sea of Galilee in AD 19 (cf. John 6:23). Similar to his father, Antipas had inscribed statue bases that named him, including those found at Kos and Delos giving his lineage and title as "Herod, son of king Herod, tetrarch." The coins of Antipas featured plant designs such as palms, with some naming the city Tiberias that he founded, but all stamped with his name and title "Herod the Tetrarch."

Thus, Herod Antipas the Tetrarch is attested by ancient historical manuscripts, honorific inscriptions, coins he issued, and through his building projects.

> *At that time Herod the tetrarch heard the news about Jesus, and said to his servants, "This is John the Baptist; he has risen from the dead, and that is why miraculous powers are at work in him"* (Matthew 14:1-2).

Hendin, David. *Guide to Biblical Coins*, 5th ed. New York: Amphora, 2010.

Hoehner, Harold. *Herod Antipas: A Contemporary of Jesus Christ.* Grand Rapids: Zondervan, 1980.

PHILIP THE TETRARCH

Coin of Philip the tetrarch, bearing his name and title

Name: Philip the Tetrarch (Herod Philip II)

Time Period: 1st century AD (Roman Period)

Geographical Area: Gaulanitis

Biblical Reference(s): Luke 3:1

Ancient Source(s): Josephus; coins

Identification Rating: Firm (A)

Philip the Tetrarch was one of the three sons of Herod the Great who inherited a portion of the kingdom after their father's death, along with his half-brothers Antipas and Archelaus, and by far the least influential of the rulers. Philip the Tetrarch was given the regions of Gaulanitis, Trachonitis, Batanaea, and Panias in the northeast. Beginning his reign soon after the death of Herod the Great, he ruled until about AD 34, basing his kingdom at Panias, which he expanded and renamed Caesarea Philippi in honor of the emperor and himself (Josephus, *Antiquities* 18.28).

Scholars often note that Philip the Tetrarch should not be confused with another Philip (Herod II) in his family, who was the son of Herod the Great and Mariamne, and the first husband of Herodias before Antipas took her as his wife (Matthew 14:3; Mark 6:17; Luke 3:19). In the writings of Josephus, it is recorded that Philip the Tetrarch eventually married Salome, the daughter of Herodias, and the family tree can become confusing due to similar names, intermarriage, divorce, and remarriage (Josephus, *Antiquities* 18.136-137).

If this is correct, then the New Testament mentions both Philip the Tetrarch and another Herodian Philip (Herod II), who are also attested in the writings of Josephus. This Philip, husband of Herodias, had no political position, probably due to his mother, Mariamne II, being disowned, and he is not attested by any known inscriptions or coins. However, it may also be a possibility that Herodias was married first to Philip (Herod II), then to Philip the Tetrarch, and finally to Herod Antipas, although this cannot be substantiated by the ancient sources.

Although mentioned only once in the New Testament, not counting the references to his namesake city Caesarea Philippi, the son of Herod the Great identified as Philip the Tetrarch is clearly attested in the archaeological record in addition to the ancient writings of Josephus. The coins he issued were stamped with his name and title, "Philip tetrarch," and feature portraits of himself and emperors Augustus and Tiberius, along with images of pagan temples. Based on the area in which he ruled and the people who inhabited that region, this is to be expected.

During his 37 years as a tetrarch, Philip erected temples, named places after the emperors and the imperial family, and remained on good terms with the Romans. Compared to his brothers and heirs, Philip seems to have had a tranquil reign, was never deposed and exiled, and apparently died peacefully.

> *Now in the fifteenth year of the reign of Tiberius Caesar, when Pontius Pilate was governor of Judea, and Herod was tetrarch of Galilee, and his brother Philip was tetrarch of the region of Ituraea and Trachonitis, and Lysanias was tetrarch of Abilene...* (Luke 3:1).

Hendin, David. *Guide to Biblical Coins*, 5th ed. New York: Amphora, 2010.

PETER

The Basilica of Saint Peter, above the tomb

Name: Peter (Simon)

Time Period: 1st century AD (Roman Period)

Geographical Area: Galilee, Judea, and Rome

Biblical Reference(s): Matthew 4:18; Mark 3:16; Luke 6:14; John 1:40-44; Acts 15:7; Galatians 2:7-8; 1 Peter 1:1; 2 Peter 1:1

Ancient Source(s): House of Peter; Tomb of Peter; Clement; Ignatius; Papias; Polycarp

Identification Rating: Firm (A)

Simon Peter the apostle, also known as Cephas, was born around the beginning of the 1st century AD, became one of the most prominent disciples of Jesus, and was martyred in Rome. From the town of Bethsaida in Galilee, Peter had moved to Capernaum on the northwestern shore of the lake where he worked as a fisherman and eventually met Jesus. Peter had a brother named Andrew who was also a disciple of Jesus, he was married, he had a house in Capernaum, and the name of his father was John (Matthew 4:18; Mark 1:30; Luke 4:38; John 1:42). Two epistles in the New Testament are attributed to Peter, and besides the four Gospels, Peter also appears throughout the book of Acts and he is mentioned in letters of the apostle Paul (1 Peter 1:1; 2 Peter 1:1; Acts 1:13-15; 1 Corinthians 15:5; Galatians 1:18–2:8).

Outside of the Bible, Peter is also named by four Christian writers who lived during the 1st century AD, giving substantial historical confirmation for Peter and his life from authors who lived within decades of this disciple. Clement of Rome, Ignatius of Antioch, Papias of Hierapolis, and Polycarp of Smyrna give brief biographic information about Peter, including that he was an apostle, that Mark wrote down information about Jesus that Peter dictated to him, references to the epistle of 1 Peter, and that he was persecuted and killed in Rome (Clement, *1 Clement* and *2 Clement*; Ignatius, *To the Romans* and *To the Smyrnaeans*; Papias, *Exposition of the Sayings of the Lord*; Polycarp, *Epistle to the Philippians*).

However, due to the age of the existing manuscripts and the way in which these sources were preserved by later writings, there may be objections about the measure of their historical worth.

Yet Peter is unique among the disciples of Jesus in that he is also known from archaeological discoveries. Although James the Just appears to be attested by an inscribed ossuary bearing his name, and the tomb of Paul was arguably found in Rome, neither of these men were part of the original 12 disciples of Jesus. Investigating the archaeology related to this disciple reveals inscriptions, a house, and a tomb that are connected to Peter.

According to the Gospels, the house of Peter in the village of Capernaum was often used by Jesus and was extremely close to the synagogue (Matthew 8:5-17; Mark 1:21-33; Luke 4:38). The ancient synagogue, which has been excavated, is located along the main north-south street of Capernaum and only about 90 feet to the north of a Byzantine-period church that was built over an earlier church and a 1st-century house. Excavations at this site discovered that the house, originally built in the 1st century BC, had been converted into a building used by a community of Christians around AD 50, continued to be used as a house church with slight modifications, was expanded in the 4th century AD, and then an octagonal church was built in the 5th century AD. The building and its uses are both significant and interesting, but the most important findings related to the existence of Peter and his connection to Capernaum were found carved on the walls. Around AD 200, Christian pilgrims had begun to carve graffiti into the plaster in Aramaic, Greek, Syriac, and Latin, including inscriptions mentioning "Peter" and affirming not only that he was considered an important historical person, but also the idea that this church had once been his home in Capernaum. Although there has been debate about the legibility of the inscriptions reading "Peter," one of the three inscriptions appearing to mention Peter is clear.

Perhaps the most important of the archaeological discoveries related to Peter, however, is the tomb of Peter and the accompanying inscription, found underneath the Basilica of Saint Peter. Numerous sources from antiquity situate Peter in Rome near the end of his life, and relate that three months after the Great Fire of Rome in AD 64 he was executed

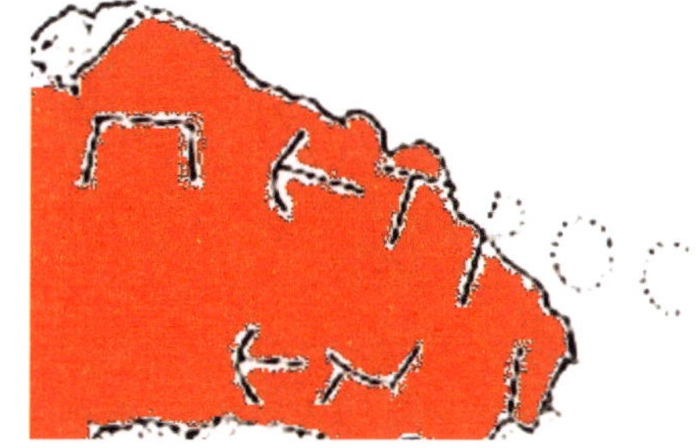

Inscription mentioning Peter from his burial monument in Rome

by crucifixion, perhaps upside down, at the Circus of Nero, which was located inside what is now the Vatican (Clement, *1 Clement* 5:4; *Acts of Peter* 36-40; Tertullian, *Scorpiace* 15; John 21:18-19; cf. 1 Peter 5:13). Peter was then buried nearby, and in the 4th-century Emperor Constantine had a church built to commemorate the martyrdom of Peter at the location of the "trophy" tomb monument mentioned by Gaius around AD 200 (Eusebius, *Church History* 2.25).

Excavations seem to have rediscovered this monument and a reburial of the apostle Peter, along with an inscription that may have identified the person associated with the monument tomb. In AD 64, Peter had been buried in a cemetery near the north wall of the Circus of Nero, and archaeological investigations underneath the Basilica of Saint Peter found that indeed the area had been a cemetery in the 2nd and 1st centuries AD, including during the reign of Vespasian (AD 69–79), who came to power after Nero. A tomb monument built around AD 160 was constructed over a grave, which was open when rediscovered. This monument, or funerary aedicula, was set into a plastered wall called the "Red Wall" on which Christian graffiti was found, including a Greek inscription reading "Peter is within" dated to approximately the 2nd century AD. Excavations also found human skeletal remains in a niche in the monument, while the grave below was empty. It is thought that when Constantine had the church built that the bones from the grave were relocated into the monument.

Subsequent analysis of the bones determined the remains to be of a man between about 60 and 70 years of age. Another curiosity of the skeleton is that the bones of the feet below the ankles were missing, suggesting that the deceased may have been cut down from a cross before his burial. Although the monument dedicated to Peter was not constructed soon after Peter died, it appears that it was built over the grave of Peter in order to commemorate his martyrdom and preserve the location of his burial.

The house of Peter at Capernaum

Regardless of whether or not the bones discovered were those of Peter, the monument and the inscription mentioning Peter demonstrate his regard as an historically important figure in early Christianity and his presence in Rome prior to his death. Two other apostles, Philip of Bethsaida and Paul of Tarsus, are also mentioned in numerous sources from antiquity and have archaeological remains associated with them, although the discoveries are not as clear or numerous as those connected to Peter (John 1:44; Acts 21:39). In Hierapolis, where, according to early tradition, Philip died a 1st-century tomb thought to be the tomb of Philip was found at the center of a Byzantine church built to commemorate the martyrdom of Philip. In Rome, an ancient marble sarcophagus with a Latin inscription translating "Paul the apostle and martyr" was found in excavations along the Via Ostiensis at the Church of Saint Paul Outside the Walls, where, according to early church history, he was buried.

Although the inscriptions mentioning Peter and the ancient authors who discuss his life and letters date to decades after his death, and perhaps even into the period around AD 200, the wide variety of surviving sources from antiquity for a fisherman from Galilee who became a disciple of Jesus is astonishing. The specific context and content of these inscriptions, archaeological finds, and historical writings allow a certain identification with Simon Peter and attest to his existence and role as a prominent apostle in the 1st century AD.

> *He brought him to Jesus. Jesus looked at him and said, "You are Simon the son of John; you shall be called Cephas" (which is translated Peter). The next day He purposed to go into Galilee, and He found Philip. And Jesus said to him, "Follow Me." Now Philip was from Bethsaida, of the city of Andrew and Peter* (John 1:42-44).

Chadwick, Henry. "St. Peter and St. Paul in Rome: The Problem of the Memoria Apostolorum ad Catacumbas." *The Journal of Theological Studies* 8.1 (1957).

Finegan, Jack. "The Death and Burial of St. Peter." *Biblical Archaeology Review* 2.4 (1976).

Guarducci, Margherita. *The Tomb of St. Peter: The New Discoveries in the Sacred Grottoes of the Vatican*. New York: Hawthorn, 1960.

Tzaferis, Vassilios. "New Archaeological Evidence on Ancient Capernaum." *The Biblical Archaeologist* 46.4 (1983).

Tzaferis, Vassilios et al. *Excavations at Capernaum*. University Park: Eisenbrauns, 1989.

JAMES
(Son of Joseph)

Aramaic inscription naming James, son of Joseph, brother of Jesus

Name: James, the son of Joseph (James the Just)

Time Period: 1st century AD (Roman Period)

Geographical Area: Jerusalem

Biblical Reference(s): Matthew 13:55; Mark 6:3; Acts 12:17; 1 Corinthians 15:7; Galatians 1:19; Jude 1:1

Ancient Source(s): James Ossuary; Josephus

Identification Rating: Firm (A)

James, or Jacob, also known as James the Just, was a brother of Jesus Christ, son of Joseph, and the leader of the early church in Jerusalem. In the New Testament he is referred to as the brother of Jesus in three sources—Matthew, Mark, and Galatians. His identification as the brother of Jesus appears to be his primary association in order to distinguish him from others named James or Jakob. This status as the brother of Jesus is also reflected in ancient sources such as Hegesippus, who wrote around AD 130–180 and distinguished him as "James, the brother of the Lord…He has been called the Just" (Hegesippus, *Memoirs* 5 via Eusebius, *Church History*).

More importantly, the 1st-century AD historian Josephus, who had lived in Judea, also identifies this James as the brother of Jesus Christ when narrating the trial and death of James the Just: "He assembled the Sanhedrin of judges, and brought before them the brother of Jesus, who was called Christ, whose name was James" (Josephus, *Antiquities* 20.200). Not only does this confirm the existence and position of James as a leader in the Jerusalem church during the 1st century AD, but the established connection between James and his brother Jesus, and the use of this as an identifier is significant for evaluating an archaeological attestation of this James.

An ossuary, or bone box, with a unique inscription came to light on the antiquities market in Jerusalem and immediately caught the interest of many scholars. This ossuary had been looted from a tomb, and therefore skepticism and claims of forgery began to circulate because of the names inscribed on the side. The Aramaic inscription, which would have been identifying the deceased, reads "James, son of Joseph, brother of Jesus." Since this type of ossuary was commonly used for only a brief time in Jerusalem, from the late 1st century BC until the siege and destruction of the city ending AD 70, this limits the lifetime of the people mentioned in the inscription to a specific period.

While this ossuary and its accompanying inscription were carefully scrutinized by scholars in different specialties over a period of years, important facts were established. First, geologic analysis showed that the ossuary was carved from limestone local to the Jerusalem area. Second, the style of the ossuary was of the type made in Jerusalem from the 1st century BC to AD 70. Third, the Aramaic letters, according to epigraphic comparisons, match the 1st century AD. Forth, microscopic inspection of the patina (ancient residue) inside the inscribed letters demonstrated that all three of the names and relationships had been inscribed prior to the ossuary being placed in a tomb in Jerusalem, as the

The ossuary of James from Jerusalem

residue was present in all sections of the inscription and had formed over the centuries. Therefore, the ossuary and accompanying inscription appear to have been verified as originating in 1st-century AD Jerusalem.

The content of the inscription itself seems to identify the deceased as James the Just, son of Joseph and brother of Jesus, based on the unique combination of names and the emphasis on the identity of the brother, as seen in writings of the 1st and 2nd centuries that refer to James the Just. The ossuary inscription is also significant in that it seems to name his father, Joseph the carpenter (Matthew 13:55). Although Joseph is referred to in later writings from antiquity, such as the Protoevangelium of James, church fathers, and Eusebius, this inscription would be the only 1st-century source mentioning him. It was also exceptionally rare to mention the name of a brother on an ossuary, as out of all known ossuary inscriptions only one other does. Based on name statistics and population, it is unlikely that there could have been more than two people called James, son of Joseph, brother of Jesus in 1st-century AD Jerusalem, but the historical precedent of identifying James as the brother of Jesus and the prominence of James the Just make it improbable that the inscription could be referring to anyone else. Therefore, the inscription corroborates the ancient records about the existence and family of James, and the bone box itself was probably used for the remains of James the Just after his martyrdom in about AD 62.

Regardless of whether one accepts the James ossuary inscription, James the Just is still attested by the 1st-century writings of Josephus.

> *Is not this the carpenter's son? Is not His mother called Mary, and His brothers, James and Joseph and Simon and Judas?* (Matthew 13:55).

Lemaire, André. "Burial Box of James the Brother of Jesus: Earliest Archaeological Evidence of Jesus found in Jerusalem." *Biblical Archaeology Review* 28:6 (2002).

Shanks, Hershel. "Predilections—Is the 'Brother of Jesus' Inscription a Forgery?" *Biblical Archaeology Review* 41.5 (2015).

HERODIAS

Name: Herodias

Time Period: 1st century AD (Roman Period)

Geographical Area: Galilee and Perea

Biblical Reference(s): Matthew 14:3-6; Mark 6:17-19; Luke 3:19

Ancient Source(s): Josephus

Identification Rating: Firm (A)

Herodias was the daughter of Aristobulus IV, a granddaughter of Herod the Great through Berenice, and a sister of Herod of Chalcis and Herod Agrippa I. She was originally married to Philip (aka Herod II) and had a daughter named Salome. However, she divorced her first husband and married his half-brother Herod Antipas, who had in turn divorced his wife the princess Phasaelis, daughter of Aretas IV. The resulting scandal was criticized by John the Baptist as unlawful, it caused international strife between the tetrarchy of Antipas and the kingdom of Aretas IV leading to a disastrous war that was convincingly won by the Nabateans, and eventually Antipas fell out of favor and was banished by Caligula.

Josephus interpreted it as divine judgment, and Herodias was at the center of everything. Out of spite, she requested the execution of John the Baptist, then years later convinced her husband to overplay his political hand, causing division between Antipas and her brother Agrippa I and sealing their fate when Agrippa I convinced the emperor to turn on them (Josephus, *Antiquities* 18.109-256; Mark 6:17-24). In the end, Herodias was loyal to Antipas, choosing to be banished with him to Gaul rather than keep her money and stay with her brother Agrippa I.

Unlike her daughter Salome, Herodias is not known to be represented on any coins, but she is extensively documented in the ancient records of Josephus.

> *Herod himself had sent and had John arrested and bound in prison on account of Herodias, the wife of his brother Philip, because he had married her. For John had been saying to Herod, "It is not lawful for you to have your brother's wife." Herodias had a grudge against him and wanted to put him to death and could not do so* (Mark 6:17-19).

SALOME

Coin of Chalcis bearing the image and name of Salome

Name: Salome (Salome III, daughter of Herodias)

Time Period: 1st century AD (Roman Period)

Geographical Area: Galilee

Biblical Reference(s): Matthew 14:6-11; Mark 6:22-28

Ancient Source(s): Josephus; Coins

Identification Rating: Firm (A)

Salome, or Shlomit, was the daughter of Herodias and Philip (Herod II) who became the stepdaughter of Herod Antipas the Tetrarch when her mother remarried, and in an odd and complicated web of familial relationships, Salome was also both a granddaughter and great-granddaughter of Herod the Great. Salome eventually married one of her uncles, Philip the Tetrarch, and subsequently one of her cousins, Aristobulus V.

A few ancient manuscripts of Mark read "his daughter Herodias" rather than "the daughter of Herodias," causing a few scholars to suggest that she may have also had the name Herodias, like her mother, but was typically called by her other name, Salome, to avoid confusion. A different Salome was a witness to the crucifixion of Jesus and one of the first visitors to the empty tomb (Mark 15:40; 16:1).

Attested briefly in the writings of Flavius Josephus, Salome was involved in the execution of John the Baptist and later became a queen. Probably born around AD 15, she lived until at least AD 67 based on the coins she shared with her second husband. At the prompting of her mother, Herodias, Salome requested the head of John the Baptizer on a platter as a favor from Herod Antipas for her dance at his birthday celebration around AD 31.

Perhaps soon after these events, Salome first married Philip the Tetrarch, her uncle, and then after his death in AD 34, she married her cousin Aristobulus V of Chalcis, becoming queen of Chalcis and Armenia Minor (Josephus, *Antiquities* 18.136-137). Outside of the manuscripts of Josephus, Salome is named on an extremely rare coin of Chalcis, the latest of which dates to about AD 56. The obverse shows the head of Aristobulus with the Greek inscription "King Aristobulus V," and the reverse shows a portrait of Salome with the Greek inscription "Queen Salome."

> *When the daughter of Herodias herself came in and danced, she pleased Herod and his dinner guests; and the king said to the girl, "Ask me for whatever you want and I will give it to you." And he swore to her, "Whatever you ask of me, I will give it to you; up to half of my kingdom." And she went out and said to her mother, "What shall I ask for?" And she said, "The head of John the Baptist." Immediately she came in a hurry to the king and asked, saying, "I want you to give me at once the head of John the Baptist on a platter"* (Mark 6:22-25).

Hendin, David. *Guide to Biblical Coins*, 5th ed. New York: Amphora, 2010.

ANNAS

Tomb of Annas

Name: Annas (son of Seth)

Time Period: 1st century BC and 1st century AD (Roman Period)

Geographical Area: Judea

Biblical Reference(s): Luke 3:2; John 18:24; Acts 4:6

Ancient Source(s): Josephus; Tomb of Annas

Identification Rating: Firm (A)

Annas, son of Seth, was appointed as the high priest of Judaism in AD 6 when Judea became a Roman province, serving in that role until he was removed in AD 15, although he continued to be an influential person in the religion and politics of Judea for many years. Annas was the acting high priest of Judaism about AD 6–15, appointed when Judea became a Roman province and the prefect Coponius began his tenure as governor. His role as high priest lasted until the later prefect Valerius Gratus removed him from office.

Annas is documented as the son of Seth who was appointed as high priest by the Romans following Joazar (Josephus, *Antiquities* 18.26-27). At some point, one of his daughters married a man named Joseph Caiaphas, who served as high priest from AD 18–36, which allowed Annas and his family to continue wielding power for decades. A former high priest and father-in-law of the acting high priest Caiaphas, Annas was still considered a high priest according to the lifetime appointment system of the Mosaic Law, and he continued to retain significant influence even after being deposed. This is evident in that his family members and descendants later served as high priest, including his son Eleazar and son-in-law Caiaphas, the most notable among them.

The discovery of an incredible 1st-century AD tomb in the Hinnom Valley south of ancient Jerusalem, certainly the burial place of one of the most wealthy and powerful families around the time of Jesus and the apostles, has also been tentatively identified as the tomb of Annas and his high priestly family through a comparison of descriptions in Josephus to the geographic location and archaeology of the tomb.

Thus, Annas the high priest in Jerusalem during the time of Jesus is attested by ancient manuscripts of Josephus and probably also by his majestic tomb at Akeldama.

> *When He had said this, one of the officers standing nearby struck Jesus, saying, "Is that the way You answer the high priest?" Jesus answered him, "If I have spoken wrongly, testify of the wrong; but if rightly, why do you strike Me?" So Annas sent Him bound to Caiaphas the high priest* (John 18:22-24).

Ritmeyer, Leen and Kathleen. "Potter's Field or High Priest's Tomb?" *Biblical Archaeology Review* 20.6 (1994).

Akeldama area of Jerusalem

CAIAPHAS

Elaborate ossuary of Joseph Caiaphas, bearing his name

Name: Caiaphas (Joseph son of Caiaphas)

Time Period: 1st century AD (Roman Period)

Geographical Area: Judea Province

Biblical Reference(s): Matthew 26:3-57; Luke 3:2; John 11:49; Acts 4:6

Ancient Source(s): Josephus; Caiaphas ossuary; Miriam ossuary

Identification Rating: Firm (A)

Caiaphas the high priest, whose full name was Joseph son of Caiaphas, lived in Jerusalem during the 1st century and served as the high priest ca. AD 18–36 (Josephus, *Antiquities* 18.34-95). Not only was Caiaphas a prominent member of the priests and the Sanhedrin, but he was a member of the sect of the Sadducees. This period in which Joseph Caiaphas held the position of high priest and leader of the Sanhedrin coincided with the ministry of Jesus Christ, and the two interacted during the trial of Jesus (Matthew 26:3; Luke 3:2; John 11:49). The Gospels and the book of Acts refer to him using his family name and title, Caiaphas the high priest, while Josephus recorded additional information about his name being Joseph from the Caiaphas family.

Around AD 18, the Roman prefect of Judea, Valerius Gratus, removed Eleazar as high priest and appointed Joseph Caiaphas, whose tenure lasted through the time of Pontius Pilatus. After Pilate was recalled to Rome and Marcellus became the new prefect, Jonathan, son of Ananus, replaced Caiaphas. However, since Caiaphas had held the position previously, was the father-in-law of Annas, and had come from a priestly family, he likely still retained immense influence until his death, and his family was perhaps the most prominent in all of Jerusalem.

While Caiaphas is probably referred to in the Mishnah and the Babylonian Talmud, he is certainly attested in two ossuary inscriptions of the 1st century AD from Judea. One ossuary of the Caiaphas family came from a tomb in the Elah Valley in southwestern Judea and probably dates to after AD 70. This Miriam ossuary, designated because of the name of the deceased, has an Aramaic inscription reading "Miriam, daughter of Yeshua, son of Caiaphas, Priest of Ma'aziah from Beth 'Imri." This was the ossuary of a granddaughter of Caiaphas, and he is identified as a priest from the lineage of Ma'aziah tracing back to the time of David (cf. 1 Chronicles 24:18; Nehemiah 10:8). The association between this Caiaphas the priest and Joseph Caiaphas the high priest is highly probable.

High priest's mansion in Jerusalem

A second ossuary inscription, however, is definitive in its identification of the high priest who presided over the trial of Jesus in Jerusalem. Inside a 1st-century AD tomb located outside the walls of Jerusalem, in the area of the Jerusalem Peace Forest, 12 ossuaries were discovered and excavated. It was a family tomb with four niches, and two of the ossuaries were inscribed in Aramaic. Both of these inscribed ossuaries had the family name Caiaphas. One was inscribed "Miriam, daughter of Simeon," and a coin of Herod Agrippa I issued in AD 42–43 was found, demonstrating that the tomb was used from this period until AD 70, when Jerusalem was destroyed.

The placement of the coin in the mouth shows that the Greek tradition of payment for Charon the boatman to cross the River Styx in the underworld was being followed and indicates the adoption of Hellenistic and Roman practices reflective of the Sadducees. The other inscribed ossuary was the most ornate of all and had an inscription reading "Joseph son of Caiaphas," belonging to and attesting to the infamous high priest.

Thus, Caiaphas the high priest is attested by the writings of Josephus, an ossuary inscription of his granddaughter, and by his own ossuary.

> *Those who had seized Jesus led Him away to Caiaphas, the high priest, where the scribes and the elders were gathered together* (Matthew 26:57).

Zissu, Boaz and Yuval Goren. "The Ossuary of 'Miriam Daughter of Yeshua Son of Caiaphas, Priests [of] Ma'aziah from Beth 'Imri.'" *IEJ* 61.1 (2011).

PILATE

The Pilato ring from Herodium

Name: Pontinus Pilatus (Pilate the Prefect)

Time Period: 1st century AD (Roman Period)

Geographical Area: Judea Province

Biblical Reference(s): Matthew 27:2; Mark 15:1-44; Luke 3:1; John 18:33; Acts 4:27; 1 Timothy 6:13

Ancient Source(s): Pilate Stone; Pilato Ring; Ameria inscription; coins; Josephus; Philo; Tacitus

Identification Rating: Firm (A)

Pontius Pilatus was a Roman of the equestrian rank who served as prefect of Judea Province and probably in other governmental roles in the 1st century AD. Pilate was born in the Roman Empire, possibly in the village of Bisenti in the region of Samnium, Italy, that his family name, (nomen) Pontius, is connected to (Eusebius, *Historia Ecclesiae*).

Pilate was married, and according to one source from late antiquity, his wife's name was Procula (Matthew 27:19; Gospel of Nicodemus; cf. Origen, Homilies on Matthew). As a Roman citizen of the equites class, Pilate was eligible to be appointed to governmental positions such as prefect, which was his role as the fifth prefect or governor of Judea during the time of Jesus in AD 26–36 (Luke 3:1). As prefect, Pilate commanded more than a thousand Roman auxiliary soldiers, could appoint and depose high priests, and could impose the death penalty. His authority over life and death is why he had the final decision to either grant or deny permission to crucify Jesus (John 19:4-6).

Pontius Pilatus is more thoroughly documented in ancient historical and archaeological sources than most prefects of the 1st century AD. Discussed in the writings of Josephus, Philo of Alexandria, and Tacitus, in addition to numerous early Christian sources, Pilate is also attested by definitive archaeological discoveries. According to Josephus, Pontius Pilatus was appointed as governor of Judea in AD 26 and served in this capacity until he was recalled to Rome in AD 36 (Josephus, *Antiquities* 19.35-89; Josephus, *Wars* 2.160-177). His time in office was tumultuous, exhibiting the clash between Judaism and Roman worldviews. One of these conflicts is described by Philo, another 1st-century AD source, who also names Pilate as the governor of Judea during the reign of Tiberius and casts the Roman official in a negative light (Philo of Alexandria, Embassy to Gaius 299-305). The Roman historian Tacitus, writing in the 2nd century AD, also briefly mentions Pontius Pilate as the governor of Judea and in connection with the trial of Jesus (Tacitus, *Annals* 15.44).

The archeological sources for Pilate are significant, and in addition to corroborating basic facts, they fill in details not known from the ancient manuscripts. Similar to other governors of Judea, Pilate had coins minted for the province that featured Roman symbols, such as the lituus staff, the sipulum, and the patera libation bowl, all stamped with the names of Tiberius Caesar and Julia in Greek. The inscriptions mentioning Pilate by name, however, are the most definitive. A Latin dedicatory inscription found at Caesarea Maritima, the Roman capital for Judea Province, gives the name and title of Pilate along with mention of the emperor, and was almost certainly commissioned by Pilate himself.

The stone slab was discovered in secondary use in the theatre, but it had previously been displayed where it could be read. The text translates as "Tiberium... Pontius Pilatus, Prefect of Judea...dedicated" with the Tiberium being a building that was built to honor the emperor Tiberius. Although Pilate was incorrectly referred to as a procurator in later Roman historical sources due to the change in title for governors of Judea beginning in AD 44, the inscription demonstrates that Pilate held the position of prefect, which is also more consistent with the Greek title used for him in the Gospels (Matthew 27:2; Luke 3:1).

A second artifact naming Pilate and found in Judea Province is a copper alloy ring discovered in a 1st-century AD context at the palace fortress of Herodium near Bethlehem. The ring was decorated with an amphora encircled by the name Pilate, or "Pilato" in Greek letters. Pilato

Coin of Pilate with the name Tiberius Caesar

Inscribed stone from Caesarea reading "Pontius Pilatus, prefect of Judea"

is the Greek spelling of his name found in the New Testament and equivalent to the Latin name Pilatus. The ring seal was probably used by an administrator who served under Pilate, not Pilate himself, to stamp official documents. The name Pilatus is of Italian origin, and the ring cannot plausibly be associated with anyone else in 1st-century Judea other than Pontius Pilate.

Another inscription mentioning a Roman official named Pilatus, found in Italy, can only be tentatively identified with the Pontius Pilatus who served as the prefect of Judea. Known as the America Inscription, it was discovered outside the Church of San Secondo in Amelia, located northwest of the possible birthplace of Pilate at Bisenti and northeast of Rome. The inscribed stone named a Pilatus as a city official called a quattuorvir, who was part of a board of four men that would have served in a local government capacity (CIL XI.2.1.4396).

The fate of Pontius Pilate is uncertain after he returned to Rome, with conflicting sources from antiquity suggesting that he was either exiled to Vienna and committed suicide or cleared of charges and he and his wife became Christians (Eusebius, *Historia Ecclesiae* 2.7; Celsus, *The True Word*; Tertullian, *Apology*). No matter what happened in his final years, Pontius Pilate is definitively attested in the archaeological record as the governor of Judea during the time of Jesus.

> *Now in the fifteenth year of the reign of Tiberius Caesar, when Pontius Pilate was governor of Judea, and Herod was tetrarch of Galilee, and his brother Philip was tetrarch of the region of Ituraea and Trachonitis, and Lysanias was tetrarch of Abilene, in the high priesthood of Annas and Caiaphas, the word of God came to John, the son of Zacharias, in the wilderness* (Luke 3:1-2).

Amorai-Stark, Shua et al. "An Inscribed Copper-Alloy Finger Ring from Herodium Depicting a Krater," *IEJ* 68:2 (2018).

Vardaman, Jerry. "A New Inscription Which Mentions Pilate as "Prefect." *Journal of Biblical Literature* 81.1 (1962).

SIMON OF CYRENE

Name: Simon of Cyrene

Time Period: 1st century AD (Roman Period)

Geographical Area: Jerusalem

Biblical Reference(s): Matthew 27:32; Mark 15:21; Luke 23:26

Ancient Source(s): Ossuary

Identification Rating: Tentative (C)

Following the trial of Jesus but prior to his crucifixion, the Roman soldiers picked a bystander out of the crowd named Simon of Cyrene and forced him to carry the wooden crossbeam for Jesus up to Golgotha. According to the Gospel of Mark, this Simon from Cyrene had sons named Alexander and Rufus.

Although not mentioned in any other historical narrative, Simon of Cyrene appears to be attested by inscriptions found on one or possibly two 1st-century AD ossuaries discovered inside a tomb in the Kidron Valley of Jerusalem. These inscribed ossuaries may have belonged to his children, as both specify that their father was named Simon.

Ossuary 9 is particularly important, as it has two inscriptions in Greek and Aramaic that give details about names, family relationships, and their place of origin. The Greek inscription on this ossuary reads "Alexander son of Simon," while the Aramaic inscription reads "Alexander QRNYT [Cyrenean]." Ossuary 5 has a Greek inscription that translates as "Sara, daughter of Simon, of Ptolemais."

Alexander, son of Simon of Cyrene ossuary

Not only was Sara a common name in Cyrene, but Ptolemais was the name of one of the five major cities (Pentapolis) in Cyrene, demonstrating that the geographic connection to Cyrene is present on both ossuaries.

Thus, there is a match between the names of the father and son, the country of origin, and the time period. Since it is highly unlikely that there were numerous Cyrenean people named Alexander son of Simon in 1st-century AD Jerusalem, the identification is plausible but tentative.

> *They pressed into service a passer-by coming from the country, Simon of Cyrene (the father of Alexander and Rufus), to bear His cross* (Mark 15:21).

Powers, Tom. "Treasures in the Storeroom: Family Tomb of Simon of Cyrene." *Biblical Archaeology Review* 29.4 (2003).

THEOPHILUS

The Ephesus agora

Name: Theophilus

Time Period: 1st century AD (Roman Period)

Geographical Area: Unknown

Biblical Reference(s): Luke 1:3; Acts 1:1

Ancient Source(s): Ossuary of Johanna; Ephesus inscriptions; Josephus

Identification Rating: Speculative (D)

Theophilus was the person to whom the two-volume work of Luke and Acts was addressed, but the details of his identity and existence are unknown. Since so little information about the Theophilus mentioned in the books of Luke and Acts is given, it is difficult to determine if he was a Roman official, in addition to his geographic origin, family lineage, or occupation.

Theophilus is addressed as "most excellent," suggesting that he may have been a Roman who held a significant political position or was from the patrician class. However, numerous suggestions have been made, since Origen in the 3rd century AD, that Theophilus was a title or a symbolic term and not his given name, and he might be identified with more famous figures such as Titus Flavius Clemens, the nephew of Vespasian or Herod Agrippa II. But these connections are speculative, and Luke elsewhere uses the personal names of numerous people rather than merely titles or monickers. Further, because Theophilus is attested as a Greek name beginning in the 3rd century BC and found in numerous inscriptions of the 1st century AD, this indicates that Luke specified the actual name of an individual rather than masking him as a mysterious benefactor.

Approaching the issue from the perspective that Theophilus was the name of a person, suggested identifications with known persons who might have been acquainted with or encountered the apostle Paul include Theophilus ben Ananus, who held the position of high priest in Jerusalem ca. AD 37–41, and Mattathias ben Theophilus, who also served as high priest ca. AD 65–66 (Josephus, *Antiquities* 18.123, 19.297, 20.223). Theophilus ben Ananus is attested by a three-line Aramaic inscription on the ossuary of his granddaughter, reading "Johanna daughter of Yehohanan son of Theophilus the High Priest."

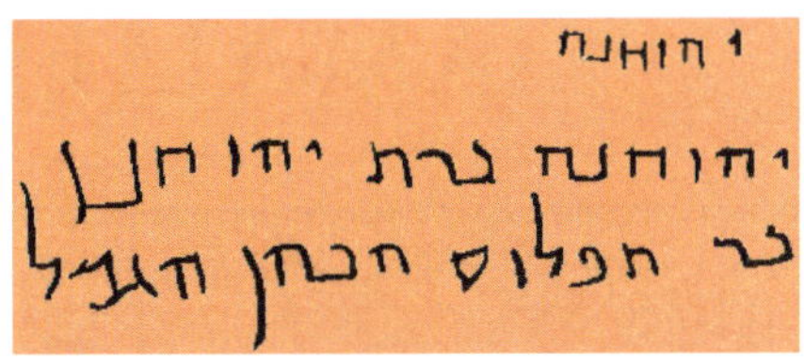

Aramaic inscription from the ossuary of Johanna, daughter of Theophilus

However, another possible identification appeals to a Theophilus named in an inscription from Ephesus dating to the middle of the 1st century AD. The mention of a Theophilus on an inscription from a column in the prytenion of Ephesus that also names Tyrannus and Trophimus presents an intriguing idea connecting two people that would have known both Luke and Paul (cf. Acts 19:9; 20:4). Yet it should be noted that the name Theophilus is found elsewhere on inscriptions from 1st-century Ephesus and also on a few inscriptions from Italy and numerous from Attica.

Thus, without details such as his city of residence or his family lineage, these mentions of Theophilus cannot be conclusively linked to the person Luke addressed. Although it is possible that Theophilus is attested by ancient manuscripts or an inscription of the 1st century AD, the data at present is insufficient, and the connection must remain speculative unless more information is discovered in the future.

> *It seemed fitting for me as well, having investigated everything carefully from the beginning, to write it out for you in consecutive order, most excellent Theophilus; so that you may know the exact truth about the things you have been taught* (Luke 1:3-4).

Barag, Dan and David Flusser. "The Ossuary of Yehohanah Granddaughter of the High Priest Theophilus." *Israel Exploration Journal* 36 (1986).

Cooper, Michael. *Mind the Gap: Filling a Void in Missiology with the Archaeological Record of Asia Minor.* Eugene: Wipf & Stock, forthcoming.

GAMALIEL THE ELDER

Name: Gamaliel the Elder

Time Period: 1st century AD (Roman Period)

Geographical Area: Judea Province

Biblical Reference(s): Acts 5:34; 22:3

Ancient Source(s): Josephus

Identification Rating: Firm (A)

Gamaliel the Elder was a prominent Pharisee who lived and taught in Jerusalem during the 1st century AD. As the son of Simeon and the grandson of Hillel the Elder, Gamaliel continued a long line of influential rabbis during the Roman period in Judea. His son, Simeon, became the leader of the Sanhedrin and participated in the revolt against the Romans, but he was apparently overthrown by the Zealot faction and killed in AD 70 (Josephus, *Life* 189, 309).

Gamaliel himself, who probably lived until about AD 50, is also referenced in the Mishnah and the Talmud. According to the book of Acts, the apostle Paul, prior to his conversion, had been educated by Gamaliel, a respected Pharisee and teacher of the Mosaic Law who participated in the Sanhedrin.

The 1st-century AD attestation for this Gamaliel the Elder, former teacher of Paul, is limited to the brief reference in the writings of Josephus but unquestioned.

> *I am a Jew, born in Tarsus of Cilicia, but brought up in this city, educated under Gamaliel, strictly according to the law of our fathers, being zealous for God just as you all are today* (Acts 22:3).

JUDAS OF GALILEE

Name: Judas of Galilee

Time Period: 1st century BC (Roman Period)

Geographical Area: Galilee

Biblical Reference(s): Acts 5:37

Ancient Source(s): Josephus

Identification Rating: Firm (A)

Judas of Galilee was a Zealot who led a small revolt against the Romans after Herod Archelaus was exiled in AD 6, during the following period in which the new prefect of Judea, Coponius, was working with Quirinius on a tax assessment of Judea. Further details and backstory about this Judas of Galilee and his revolt are mentioned in writings of Josephus.

The timing of the revolt is specified as the beginning of the time of Coponius, who was governor from AD 6–9, along with their reasoning being Roman tax demands (Josephus, *Wars* 2.117-119). Josephus also recorded that the sons of Judas—James and Simon—had been crucified by order of the procurator Tiberius Julius Alexander in about AD 46, perhaps also as rebels (Josephus, *Antiquities* 20.102). According to the book of Acts, Judas of Galilee started a revolt in the days of the census, which would be reference to the AD 6 tax assessment census, but Judas was killed and his followers were scattered.

Although Judas of Galilee led a brief and unsuccessful revolt against Rome, he was significant enough to be remembered and mentioned in both the book of Acts and two works of Josephus. On the other hand, the identification of the rebel Theudas, who prior to Judas of Galilee led 400 men in a failed uprising to the magician Theudas, does not seem possible based on an apparent four-decade separation of time and differing descriptions of the person (Acts 5:36; Josephus, *Antiquities* 20.97-99).

> *After this man, Judas of Galilee rose up in the days of the census and drew away some people after him; he too perished, and all those who followed him were scattered* (Acts 5:37).

CANDACE

Kandake Amanitore depicted and named at the Apedemak temple in Naqa

Name: Candace (Kandake)

Time Period: 1st century AD (Roman Period)

Geographical Area: Kingdom of Meroe

Biblical Reference(s): Acts 8:27

Ancient Source(s): Meroitic Inscriptions

Identification Rating: Probable (B)

Candace, referencing a queen in the book of Acts, is often mistaken as a personal name. However, Kandake was the Meroitic term for queen or royal woman, rather than the name of a particular monarch, and it was used as the title for the women who ruled the Kingdom of Meroe in Kush.

Around AD 35, on the road between Gaza and Jerusalem, the deacon Philip encountered the Ethiopian eunuch who was in the service of the Kandake as her official court treasurer (Acts 8:26-40). During the Classical period, Roman and Greek texts used the term Aethiopia to refer to the region of Kush, which at that time was the Kingdom of Meroe, named for its capital city. As the chief financial officer of a wealthy kingdom, the eunuch held a position of great power and influence, and his return to Meroe with Christianity likely had a significant impact.

Based on the time period, the Kandake referred to in the book of Acts would have been the famous Queen Amanitore Merkare, who ruled the Kingdom of Meroe about AD 1–41. Those who held the rank of Kandake were often fully independent rulers and also known to be warriors. Although Amanitore ruled alongside her husband or son Natakamani initially, she was the sole monarch of Kush for the last half of her reign.

Extensive building projects around the kingdom, including many temples and a palace, also indicate a reign of prosperity. Depicted in many scenes on temples and stelae as a powerful warrior smiting her enemies with a sword, such as in the relief on the front of the temple of Apedemak at Naqa, Amanitore seems to have been one of the most successful queens of Meroe. Her pyramid at Meroe is also known and was her final resting place. While only her title is given and the general time period, it is likely that the Kandake can be identified with Amanitore Merkare, a powerful queen who is attested by numerous monuments and inscriptions.

> *He got up and went; and there was an Ethiopian eunuch, a court official of Candace, queen of the Ethiopians, who was in charge of all her treasure; and he had come to Jerusalem to worship* (Acts 8:27).

Yamauchi, Edwin. *Africa and the Bible*. Grand Rapids: Baker Academic, 2004.

The pyramid tomb of Amanitore in Meroe

CLAUDIUS

Bust of Emperor Nero

Name: Claudius (Germanicus)

Time Period: 1st century AD (Roman Period)

Geographical Area: Rome

Biblical Reference(s): Acts 11:28; 18:2

Ancient Source(s): Coins; inscriptions; statues; Josephus; Seneca the Younger; Pliny the Elder

Identification Rating: Firm (A)

Claudius, or Tiberius Claudius Caesar Augustus Germanicus, was the fourth emperor of Rome and a member of the Julio-Claudian dynasty. Born to Drusus and Antonia Minor in Gaul, he became emperor in AD 41 after the assassination of Caligula and was in power until AD 54, when he himself was assassinated. While ideas vary about the exact details of his death, it was apparently due to poisoning by his fourth and final wife, Agrippina, and her son Nero became the next emperor (Suetonius, *Claudius* 43; Josephus, *Antiquities* 19.164–20.151).

Claudius was regarded as an apt administrator who made changes to the Senate, oversaw building projects, hosted games, and issued an edict declaring that the rights and privileges of Jews to practice Judaism would be preserved (Josephus, *Antiquities* 19.279-285). This edict came about as a result of his friendship with Herod Agrippa I and his brother Herod of Chalcis, who appear together on a coin of AD 43 with Claudius showing the emperor being crowned by them. Just after this time, a famine occurred in the Roman Empire, and in the book of Acts this event is mentioned in reference to the reign of Claudius (Acts 11:28; Josephus, *Antiquities* 20.101).

The only other mention of Claudius in the New Testament is set in the time when Paul arrived at Corinth around AD 50, when it is stated that the emperor commanded all the Jews to leave Rome (Acts 18:2). This expulsion by Claudius was recorded by Roman historians, with the reason seemingly due to disputes about Christus or Christ (Suetonius, *Claudius* 25). It is also possible that Claudius was the Caesar who issued the edict known as the Nazareth Inscription, which proscribes the death penalty for anyone who steals a body out of a stone-sealed, rock-carved tomb (cf. Matthew 28:11-15).

Archaeological attestation for Claudius as emperor can be clearly seen on his coins, official inscriptions, and statues, in addition to the Roman historical writings. Emperor Nero succeeded his stepfather Claudius and ruled AD 54–68, becoming infamous for cruel and insane actions, including setting fire to Rome in order to build himself a new palace, and was eventually declared a public enemy (Suetonius, *Nero* 33-49; Tacitus, *Annals* 15.38-44; Cassius Dio, *Roman History* 62.11-18; Plutarch, *Life of Galba* 4-7). Nero, who blamed Christians for the Great Fire of Rome and ordered the martyrdoms of Peter and Paul, was mentioned by Paul using his dynastic name Caesar around AD 60, before many of the most horrific actions of Nero (Philippians 4:22). This emperor, the last of the Julio-Claudian dynasty, is also thoroughly documented by ancient Roman historians, coins bearing his name and image, statues, and monumental inscriptions.

> *After these things he left Athens and went to Corinth. And he found a Jew named Aquila, a native of Pontus, having recently come from Italy with his wife Priscilla, because Claudius had commanded all the Jews to leave Rome. He came to them* (Acts 18:1-2).

Sestersius of Claudius, with his name and image

Statue of Emperor Claudius

HEROD AGRIPPA I

Coin of Herod Agrippa I, bearing his name and title

Name: Herod Agrippa I (Marcus Julius Agrippa)

Time Period: 1st century AD (Roman Period)

Geographical Area: Judea

Biblical Reference(s): Acts 12:1-23

Ancient Source(s): Inscriptions; coins; Josephus; Philo of Alexandria; Cassius Dio

Identification Rating: Firm (A)

Herod Agrippa I was a grandson of Herod the Great who ruled as king of Judea in AD 41–44 when Judea Province briefly ceased to exist. Agrippa I was closely connected with the Roman emperors Caligula and Claudius, and this political influence ultimately gained him the kingship over the realm previously ruled by his grandfather as a client king of Rome. His brother, Herod of Chalcis, ruled nearby lands, while his son, Agrippa II, would also become a local king.

Before benefiting from the favor of Caligula and Claudius, however, Agrippa I was arrested by Tiberius for supporting Caligula and spent six months in prison until the new emperor was declared (Josephus, *Antiquities* 18.204-236). About three years following the death of Philip the Tetrarch, just after his release from prison, Agrippa I received those territories in the northeastern area of what had previously been the Herodian kingdom in AD 37. At the same time, while his uncle Antipas was still tetrarch, Agrippa I began maneuvering to also take over the region where Antipas was ruler. Eventually, Agrippa I was able to accuse Antipas of treason, convince Caligula to exile Antipas, and as a result gain additional lands in AD 39.

Following this, Agrippa I went back to Rome where he discovered that Caligula had planned to erect a statue of himself in the form of Jupiter inside the Jerusalem temple—an act that probably would have started a rebellion. However, through much reasoning and discussion, Agrippa I was able to convince Caligula to discard this plan, and the disaster was thwarted (Josephus, *Antiquities* 18.296-301 and *Wars* 2.184-203; Philo, Embassy to Gaius 261-334). Agrippa I then continued his quest for the kingship, and after Caligula's death and the ascension of Claudius, Agrippa I was declared king of Judea by the Roman Senate. A coin of Herod of Chalcis shows the close relationship between Agrippa I and Claudius, depicting both Agrippa I and Herod of Chalcis crowning Claudius. This connection to the emperor allowed Agrippa I to not only become a regional king, but may have influenced early Roman policy toward Christians.

Back in Judea, Herod Agrippa I seems to have been concerned with pleasing the religious leaders of Judaism, persecuting the early Christians, and prior to this taking a substantial risk in begging Caligula not to place a statue of himself in the temple. According to the book of Acts, King Agrippa I not only harassed the church and arrested Peter but had James, the son of Zebedee, beheaded (Acts 12:1-4). This behavior is consistent with his apparent zeal for Judaism, and it may have been a factor in the issuing of the Nazareth Inscription by Claudius, attempting to stamp out rumors of the resurrection.

Coin showing Agrippa I and Herod of Chalcis crowning Claudius

During a festival at Caesarea Maritima in AD 44, however, the reign of Agrippa I was cut short. The book of Acts relates how he put on his royal garment, went to the bema (judgment seat), and began giving a speech, and the people praised him as one with the voice of a god. Because he accepted this praise and did not give glory to God, an angel struck him with an ailment, and "he was eaten by worms and died" (Acts 12:21-23).

Incredibly, the writings of Josephus also record this, but from another perspective that gives additional details. This version notes that Agrippa I had come to Caesarea Maritima for a festival, and on the second day he came into the theatre wearing a silver garment that reflected the sun. People then began to say he was a god, and yet he did not reject this flattery. After he looked up and saw an ominous sign of an owl, he was immediately struck with violent pains in his abdomen, and after five days he died (Josephus, *Antiquities* 19.343-350). After his death, the kingdom reverted back to direct control by the Romans, with Judea Province then being ruled by procurators.

In addition to narratives about his life found in the ancient manuscripts of Josephus, Philo, and Cassius Dio, Herod Agrippa I is attested by the coins he issued. Coins of Agrippa I are stamped with his name and title, reading "King Agrippa," but their designs vary based on the beliefs of the people where they were used. Some of his coins merely show objects, while others have the head and name of the emperor along with Roman symbols, demonstrating how he attempted to live in both worlds of adhering to the Mosaic Law and following Roman conventions.

> *Now about that time Herod the king laid hands on some who belonged to the church in order to mistreat them. And he had James the brother of John put to death with a sword. When he saw that it pleased the Jews, he proceeded to arrest Peter also. Now it was during the days of Unleavened Bread* (Acts 12:1-3).

Kokkinos, Nikos. *The Herodian Dynasty: Origins, Role in Society and Eclipse*. London: Spink & Son, 2010.

Ruins of the Herodian palace at Caesarea Maritima

SERGIUS PAULUS

Sergius Paulus as curator of the Tiber River in Rome

Name: Sergius Paulus (Lucius Sergius Paulus)

Time Period: 1st century AD (Roman Period)

Geographical Area: Cyprus

Biblical Reference(s): Acts 13:7

Ancient Source(s): Soloi Inscription; Tiber Inscription; Pisidian Antioch inscriptions

Identification Rating: Firm (A)

Sergius Paulus was a Roman patrician of the powerful Sergia family, holding multiple influential offices in the Roman Empire during the 1st century AD. Roman archaeological sources make it clear that this family had a long and storied history and for a time was prominent in the region of Pisidian Antioch, based at a large estate northeast of the city in Vetissus, although the family held distinguished roles all over the Republic and Empire.

Elsewhere, the Arch of the Sergii in Pula commemorates a relative named Lucius Sergius Lepidus for his role in the battle of Actium in 31 BC. According to the book of Acts, when Paul and Barnabas visited Paphos, they met Sergius Paulus, who was the proconsul of the Roman province of Cyprus at the time. Although he is only once named by a Roman author, specifically as a person who was a source for Pliny the Elder around AD 77, Sergius Paulus appears to be attested archaeologically by four inscriptions of the 1st century AD (Pliny, *Natural History* 18.90).

Around AD 45, Paul and Barnabas landed at Salamis on the coast of Cyprus, journeyed over to the other side of the island to the Roman capital city of Paphos, and met the governor or proconsul named Sergius Paulus. At the time, Cyprus was a Roman senatorial province, and the title for the governor was proconsul. Perhaps the most important inscription connecting to this Sergius Paulus was found on Cyprus, north of Paphos, at Soloi. Inscribed in Greek, the text names the "proconsul Paulus" while placing his tenure as governor of the island before the 13th year of Claudius, or prior to AD 53 (IGR III, 930).

However, another detail on the inscription notes how Claudius "also altered the senate by means of assessors during the time of the proconsul Paulus." From Roman historical records, it is known that Claudius made modifications to the Senate in approximately AD 46–47, indicating that Sergius Paulus was still serving as proconsul of Cyprus until AD 46–47, placing him chronologically as governor in Paphos during the period Paul visited (Tacitus, *Annals* 11.25). Note that Luke also correctly used the Greek word *anthupatos*, the equivalent of Latin proconsul and the Greek term found on the inscription, to describe the position of Sergius Paulus, while *hegemon* is used for Pontius Pilatus, who was a prefect (Acts 13:7; Luke 20:20).

From the city of Rome, another inscription also attests to Sergius Paulus and his prominence in the Roman political system. An official boundary stone discovered in Rome and dated to AD 47 based on the names and the use of the title princeps rather than censor for Claudius bears a Latin inscription that records curators of the banks and channel of the Tiber River, among them Sergius Paulus. It reads "L. Sergius Paulus...The commissioners of the banks and beds of the Tiber, by the authority of Tiberius Claudius Caesar Augustus Germanicus, leader of the Senate..." (CIL VI, 31545).

A curator of this type was supposed to manage the water supply and was appointed either by the Senate or the emperor himself. Because only the most influential and successful politicians in the empire, usually restricted to the patricians, could govern provinces and receive prestigious appointments in Rome, it is likely that during the 1st century AD there was only one Sergius Paulus of this

Paulus the proconsul inscription from Cyprus

high rank and prominence, and therefore implausible that this Sergius Paulus who was appointed a curator in Rome around AD 47 was a different person than the Sergius Paulus who had served as proconsul of Cyprus about a year before.

Shifting to Pisidian Antioch, where the Sergia family had an estate and Paul and Barnabas traveled to immediately after meeting Sergius Paulus on Cyprus, two other inscriptions appear to mention this proconsul and curator (Acts 13:4-14). Carved in large Latin letters on a stone found at Pisidian Antioch in the Roman province of Galatia, a fragmentary text mentions a notable person with the name L. Sergius Paulus. While this could be the same L. Sergius Paulus found on the boundary inscription from Rome, it is difficult to make a definitive connection.

However, an honorific inscription with more detail, once again referring to a Lucius Sergius Paulus, was also found near Pisidian Antioch. This text mentions a father and son both named Lucius, and notes that L. Sergius Paulus was a quaestor with Legio VI Ferrata (AE 2002, 01457). Because Legio VI Ferrata was involved in battles to the east of Pisidian Antioch, such as at Tigranocerta between AD 54 and AD 68, prior to the legion being deployed to Judea Province and staying in what would become Syria Palaestina, this inscription refers to a prominent L. Sergius Paulus in the area of Pisidian Antioch around the middle of the 1st century AD. This would likely be none other than the Sergius Paulus who served as proconsul of Cyprus and a curator in Rome during the 40s AD.

Beyond these mentions of Sergius Paulus, in an inscription from Kythraia, Cyprus is also occasionally suggested as possibly attesting to the Sergius Paulus

Quintus Sergius from Kythraia

L Sergius Paulus inscription from Pisidian Antioch

the proconsul mentioned in the book of Acts. However, this text refers to a person named Quintus Sergius, and the Caesar mentioned in the text is unknown (IGR III, 935). The primary problem of associating this inscription with Sergius Paulus the proconsul of Cyprus is that the "Paulus" section of the inscription is completely missing and thus purely speculative, in addition to Quintus Paulus instead of Lucius Paulus, no title present, and the time period unknown. It is possible that this member of the Sergii family was a relative of Sergius Paulus named Quintus Sergius, but not the proconsul who encountered the apostle Paul.

Although named only once in the book of Acts during a brief encounter with Paul, the proconsul Sergius Paulus is attested archaeologically by multiple Roman inscriptions, including one on Cyprus featuring the title proconsul from the reign of Claudius and in the writings of an ancient historian.

> *When they had gone through the whole island as far as Paphos, they found a magician, a Jewish false prophet whose name was Bar-Jesus, who was with the proconsul, Sergius Paulus, a man of intelligence. This man summoned Barnabas and Saul and sought to hear the word of God* (Acts 13:6-7).

Kennedy, Titus. "Finding Sergius." *Salvo* 70 (2024).

Windle, Bryan. "The Roman Tiber River Inscription and the Cypriote Proconsul Sergius Paulus." *Near East Archaeological Society Bulletin* 67 (2022).

GALLIO

Closeup of Gallio segment

Name: Gallio (Junius Gallio)

Time Period: 1st century AD (Roman Period)

Geographical Area: Corinth

Biblical Reference(s): Acts 18:12-17

Ancient Source(s): Delphi Inscription; Seneca; Cassius Dio; Tacitus; Pliny the Elder

Identification Rating: Firm (A)

Gallio, or Junius Gallio, was the son of Seneca the Elder and a prominent Roman who served as a governor, senator, and consul, living about 5 BC–AD 65. Both he and his more famous brother, Seneca the Younger, held official positions under both Claudius and Nero, and Seneca was even a close advisor to Nero until he fell out of favor with the emperor. The entire family eventually suffered from the terror of Nero around AD 65, as Seneca was executed after being accused of an assassination attempt in the Piso conspiracy, his other brother Annaeus Mela committed suicide, and himself Gallio was denounced in the Senate as a public enemy, which may have led to his death either by execution or forced suicide (Tacitus, *Annals* 15.73–16.17).

During calmer days in the reign of Claudius, Gallio had been assigned to the role of proconsul of Achaia Province in Greece. It was here that he met the apostle Paul around AD 51, not long after Paul had moved to Corinth. According to the book of Acts, Gallio presided over a brief legal hearing involving Paul at the bema (judgment seat), located in the agora of Corinth. Many of the members of the synagogue had opposed Paul and his teaching, hoping to have him punished, so he was brought to the proconsul to be accused. Gallio, however, considered it an internal religious dispute and had no interest in adjudicating, probably declining the accusation as *cognitio extra ordinem*, extraordinary or irrelevant. Paul was therefore free to continue his teaching in Corinth, according to Roman law.

Seneca the Younger, brother of Gallio, seems to give insight into the indifferent attitude of Gallio while in Achaia, remarking that Gallio disliked the place and wanted to return to Rome (Seneca the Younger, *Moral Epistles* 104; cf. Pliny the Elder, *Natural History* 31.33). Although a fairly minor episode that resulted in no punishment or expulsion, this interaction with Gallio is a chronological and historical anchor for events in the book of Acts and the life of Paul thanks to an inscription of Emperor Claudius internally dated AD 52 that names Gallio as proconsul in Achaia.

Clear archaeological attestation for Gallio, as proconsul of Achaia, and at the time in which Paul was residing in Corinth, is found on a Roman edict of Emperor Claudius in his twelfth year, discovered in the ruins of Delphi, located north of Corinth in Achaia. Excavations around the temple of Apollo discovered this edict inscribed into a limestone block, although it is now broken into nine known fragments. The edict concerns bringing citizens to the depopulated city of Delphi, and states "Tiber[ius Claudius C]aes[ar...invested with tribunician auth]ority [for the twelfth time, acclaimed Imperator for t]he twenty-sixth time, F[ather of the Fa]therland, [Consul for the fifth time...[L. Ju]nius Gallio, my fr[iend] an[d procon]sul."

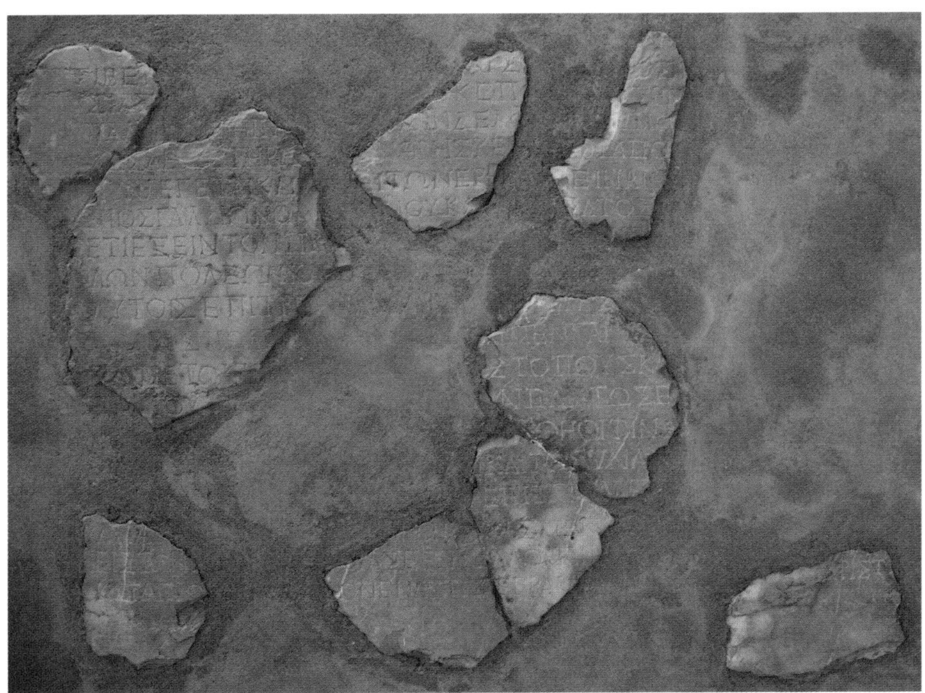

The Gallio inscription from Delphi, mentioning Claudius in AD 52

Since Delphi was in the senatorial province of Achaia, proconsuls had short terms of office, and details about the specific year are given, the inscription demonstrates that Gallio was the proconsul of Achaia Province, of which Corinth was the capital city, from about AD 51–52. This inscription definitively identifies the Gallio mentioned in Acts, with whom Paul interacted as Junius Gallio, the prominent Roman politician.

Thus, not only is Gallio known from the ancient manuscripts of the Roman authors Cassius Dio, Seneca, and Tacitus, but the Delphi inscription names him and places him as proconsul of Achaia when Paul was living at Corinth.

> *While Gallio was proconsul of Achaia, the Jews with one accord rose up against Paul and brought him before the judgment seat, saying, "This man persuades men to worship God contrary to the law." But when Paul was about to open his mouth, Gallio said to the Jews, "If it were a matter of wrong or of vicious crime, O Jews, it would be reasonable for me to put up with you; but if there are questions about words and names and your own law, look after it yourselves; I am unwilling to be a judge of these matters." And he drove them away from the judgment seat* (Acts 18:12-16).

Murphy-O'Connor, Jerome. *St. Paul's Corinth: Text and Archaeology*. Liturgical Press, 2002.

Winter, Bruce. "Rehabilitating Gallio and his Judgement in Acts 18:14-15." *Tyndale Bulletin* 57.2 (2006).

The bema in Corinth, where Gallio rendered judgment

TYRANNUS

Possible location of the lecture hall of Tyrannus at Ephesus

Name: Tyrannus

Time Period: 1st century AD (Roman Period)

Geographical Area: Ephesus

Biblical Reference(s): Acts 19:9

Ancient Source(s): Ephesus Inscriptions

Identification Rating: Speculative (D)

Tyrannus of Ephesus was the owner or primary teacher of a lecture hall, auditorium, or school where the apostle Paul taught in Ephesus around AD 53–55, perhaps similar to but much less famous than the Lyceum of Aristotle. The name Tyrannus is known from 1st-century AD inscriptions found at Ephesus, dating from approximately AD 54–93 and overlapping with the period during which Paul was living and teaching in the city.

Paul may have taught in this school or lecture hall from the fifth hour to the tenth hour, as other scholars and teachers of the period did, beginning their educational endeavors at the conclusion of the normal Roman business day that typically encompassed the first four to five hours of the morning (Codex Bezae; Martial, *Epigrams*). As for the location of the lecture hall, two known buildings have been suggested. Adjacent to the Library of Celsus, a building designated as an "auditorium" by a 3rd-century AD inscription could be a possibility, although some scholars argue that it was used as a courtroom for the proconsul.

Multiple people with the name Tyrannus have been discovered in inscriptions from Ephesus, including at least three from the 1st century AD who could have owned a school or lecture hall: Tyrannus, son of Apollonius, the priest of Ares (I. Eph. 3417); M. Pacuvius, Tyrannus the Curator (I. Eph. 1001); and L. Tarutilius, Tyrannus the Curator (I. Eph. 1012, 1029). Although the New Testament does not elaborate on the identity of Tyrannus, it was probably the name of the man who owned the school or lecture hall rather than a title. However, due to insufficient data, this individual in the book of Acts cannot be definitively identified at this time.

When some were becoming hardened and disobedient, speaking evil of the Way before the people, he withdrew from them and took away the disciples, reasoning daily in the school of Tyrannus (Acts 19:9).

Wilson, Mark. *Biblical Turkey: A Guide to the Jewish and Christian Sites of Asia Minor*. Istanbul: Ege Yayınları, 2010.

ERASTUS

Name: Erastus

Time Period: AD 50–67 (Roman Period)

Geographical Area: Corinth

Biblical Reference(s): Acts 19:22; Romans 16:23; 2 Timothy 4:20

Ancient Source(s): Erastus Inscription

Identification Rating: Firm (A)

Erastus was a local official who lived in Corinth at the time Paul arrived in the city around AD 50, and at one point he held the position of "manager of the city" or "city treasurer." According to the books of Acts, Romans, and 2 Timothy, the persuasive preaching of Paul in Corinth led to numerous people becoming Christians, including Erastus. This friend of Paul's traveled with him for a time, but eventually he ended up back in Corinth by about AD 57, when he held the position of city treasurer (Romans 16:23). Erastus is also referred to as having stayed at Corinth in a letter of Paul's probably written around AD 66 (2 Timothy 4:20).

Excavations at Corinth uncovered at least two inscriptions of the Roman period that mention a person named Erastus. An inscription written in Greek and appearing to be mentioning prominent people in Corinth does include an Erastus, but it is both fragmentary and lacks additional information that could link it specifically to the Erastus of the New Testament. However, an almost completely intact inscription found during excavation of a stone pavement near

Erastus the aedile, inscription at Corinth

the theatre from the middle of the 1st century AD revealed details about a certain individual.

One of the rectangular paving stones had a Latin inscription honoring a city official who managed public works and commercial affairs named Erastus. The inscription, which is still in place, reads ERASTVS. PRO. AED. S. P. STRAVIT or "Erastus in return for his aedileship paved it at his own expense." The office of aedile was a city official who managed public works and commercial affairs, and in the book of Romans, Paul used a Greek phrase equivalent to the Latin term aedile to describe the position that Erastus held. The inscription from Corinth was dated to the middle of the 1st century and the name Erastus was quite rare, showing a match of name, date, location, and official title.

This connection has been disputed by a few scholars, but it is extremely unlikely that there was another Erastus in Corinth around AD 57 who also held the office of city treasurer, and even more unlikely since Paul chose to identify Erastus by his city and occupation. Thus, Erastus the friend of Paul and city treasurer of Corinth appears to be attested by an inscription that he himself commissioned while he held public office in the city.

> *Gaius, host to me and to the whole church, greets you. Erastus, the city treasurer greets you, and Quartus, the brother* (Romans 16:23).

Clarke, Andrew. "Another Corinthian Erastus Inscription." *Tyndale Bulletin* 42.1 (1991).

Gill, David. "Erastus The Aedile." *Tyndale Bulletin* 40.2 (1989).

DEMETRIUS

Name: Demetrius

Time Period: AD 52–55 (Roman Period)

Geographical Area: Ephesus

Biblical Reference(s): Acts 19:24-38

Ancient Source(s): Ephesus temple warden inscription

Identification Rating: Tentative (C)

Demetrius the silversmith was an influential resident of Ephesus who fiercely opposed the apostle Paul and Christianity due to their impact on the cult of Artemis and the local economy connected to Artemis, including his silversmith business. At the end of Paul's lengthy stay in Ephesus, around AD 55, Demetrius gathered the artisans to address this problem. Enraged at the thought of their trade being damaged and their goddess losing followers, they stirred up a crowd, two Christians were dragged into the theatre, and an impromptu city meeting commenced. Although the town clerk was able to prevent a riot by affirming the greatness of Artemis and her temple, the incident ultimately led to Paul leaving Ephesus (Acts 19:23–20:1).

The leader and instigator of this opposition, a silversmith named Demetrius, probably encountered Paul on a regular basis in the agora and was witness to the change that Christianity was bringing to the city of Ephesus and the province of Asia. Archaeological investigations at Ephesus have uncovered silversmith shops in the commercial agora along Arkadiane Street, running east-west from the theater to the harbor (e.g., I. Eph. 547). Other inscriptions of the Roman period at Ephesus also mention silversmiths, including a leader of the silversmith guild and a silversmith named M. Antonias Hermeias, who served as the warden for the temple of Artemis (I. Eph. 425.10; I. Eph. 2212.a.6-7; I Ephes. 636.9-10). In the book of Acts, Demetrius appears to be a notable citizen and leader who also has great dedication and zeal for the cult of Artemis, perhaps holding an official position in Ephesus at some point.

This Demetrius of Ephesus, silversmith and dedicated follower of Artemis, might be named in an official list of notable Ephesian citizens, arranged according to their tribes, on a marble monument pillar found in 19th-century excavations at Ephesus. The inscription dates to the second half of the 1st century AD, or roughly in the timeframe of AD 50–100. A section of the text reads: "The senate and people do public honor to those who served as temple wardens...in the year of Demetrius...Of the Ephesian tribe: Demetrius, son of Menophilus, son of Tryphon, of the Thousand Borei..." (I. Eph. 1578a). Twelve of these temple wardens were appointed every year, and their role was to act as supervisors for temple maintenance and offerings, including idols and religious objects made out of silver, gold, or bronze.

The information from the inscription makes it clear that around AD 50–100, an important citizen of Ephesus named Demetrius served as a temple warden for Artemis, which would have also given him a connection to artisans that crafted offerings for the goddess. Although the position of silversmith is not mentioned, the close connection with the cult of Artemis is obvious, and as Demetrius is placed first in the list, his prominence in Ephesus is demonstrated. Thus, there is a match in name, location, chronological period, prominence, and association.

In the books of Luke and Acts, local people who hold political office and prominent positions are often mentioned, including Sergius Paulus, Gallio, Erastus, and numerous others, suggesting that Demetrius may have been more than a mere artisan. However, information about the family lineage of Demetrius the silversmith is missing in the book of Acts, as is specific mention of his profession in the inscription from Ephesus. Therefore, the attestation is possible, but due to a lack of data, the identification of Demetrius the silversmith must remain tentative unless further discoveries reveal a more definitive connection.

Hicks, E.L. "Demetrius the Silversmith." *Expositor* Ser. IV, Vol. I (1890).

Keener, Craig. *Acts: An Exegetical Commentary*. Grand Rapids: Baker, 2014.

THE EGYPTIAN

Name: The Egyptian (Personal Name Unknown)

Time Period: 1st century AD (Roman Period)

Geographical Area: Judea

Biblical Reference(s): Acts 21:38

Ancient Source(s): Josephus

Identification Rating: Firm (A)

An enigmatic revolutionary known only as "the Egyptian" operated in Judea during the period that Antonius Felix was governor of the province, around AD 52–59. Though little is known about him, he seems to have originated in Egypt and moved to Judea to amass more followers, posing as a prophet and inciting rebellion against the Romans. He led a revolt consisting of at least 4,000 of the Sicarii—rebels, thieves, and assassins who used curved daggers—although more people were probably involved.

The Egyptian and his followers emerged out of the wilderness and attempted to attack the Roman garrison in Jerusalem by way of the Mount of Olives. But they were thwarted by Felix, and he fled back into the wilderness (Josephus, *Wars* 2.261-263; Acts 21:38). The procurator Felix had found out about the insurrection and led his Roman soldiers against them, killing 400 and capturing 200, but the rest escaped, including their leader, the Egyptian (Josephus, *Antiquities* 20.169-172).

The exact date of these events is unknown, but it seems to have occurred prior to AD 57, when Paul was arrested and initially misidentified by the tribune Claudius Lysias as the Egyptian, who was still unaccounted for and being pursued by the Romans. Apparently, either the apostle Paul had been falsely accused of being the Egyptian or the Roman commander Lysias mistakenly thought he was this rebel until he began to speak with him in Greek. The personal name of this rebel is unknown, but "the Egyptian" mentioned in the book of Acts is undoubtedly "the Egyptian" attested in the ancient historical manuscripts of Josephus.

> *As Paul was about to be brought into the barracks, he said to the commander, "May I say something to you?" And he said, "Do you know*

Greek? Then you are not the Egyptian who some time ago stirred up a revolt and led the four thousand men of the Assassins out into the wilderness?" (Acts 21:37-38).

View from the Mount of Olives, east of Jerusalem, where the Egyptian assembled his army

ANANIAS

The ruins of Masada

Name: Ananias, son of Nedebeus

Time Period: 1st century AD (Roman Period)

Geographical Area: Judea

Biblical Reference(s): Acts 23:1-5; 24:1

Ancient Source(s): Josephus; Hananiah Ostracon

Identification Rating: Firm (A)

Ananias, son of Nedebeus, was appointed to the position of high priest in Jerusalem by Herod Agrippa II and held the office about AD 47–58 (Josephus, *Antiquities* 20.103-137; Acts 23:2; 24:1). At the beginning of the First Judean Revolt against Rome in AD 66, the palace of Ananias the high priest was burnt together with the palace of Agrippa and Berenice, and while hiding in an aqueduct, the high priest and his brother were killed by other Jews for collaborating with the Romans (Josephus, *Wars* 2.426-443).

The apostle Paul encountered Ananias at Caesarea Maritima around AD 57, and he said he was unaware Ananias was the high priest (Acts 23:1-5). This occurred when Felix was the governor of Judea Province, and while it has been suggested that this could have been after Ananias had been removed from office and a new priest appointed, such as Joshua ben Gamla, Paul may have simply not accepted the Roman political appointment of a high priest or was not personally acquainted with Ananias (Acts 23:24).

In addition to this high priest Ananias being described in the writings of Josephus, preserved in numerous ancient manuscripts, he might also be attested on a 1st-century AD ostracon discovered in a room at the fortress of Masada. The ostracon is written in Aramaic, and reads "Hananiah the high priest, Aqavya his son." Ananias in Greek is the equivalent of Hananiah in Aramaic, and because the fortress was taken over by the Sicarii in AD 66, and fell to the Romans in AD 73 only a few years after the death of Ananias, it is likely that this ostracon refers to the Ananias mentioned in Acts rather than to another priest with a similar name, even though the name of this son Aqvya is not currently known from other sources.

Paul, looking intently at the Council, said, "Brethren, I have lived my life with a perfectly good conscience before God up to this day." The high priest Ananias commanded those standing beside him to strike him on the mouth (Acts 23:1-2).

Mykytiuk, Lawrence. "New Testament Religious Figures Confirmed." *Biblical Archaeology Review* 47.2 (2021).

FELIX

Antonius Felix named on an inscription from the theatre of Balbus in Rome

Name: Felix the Procurator (Marcus Antonius Felix)

Time Period: 1st century AD (Roman Period)

Geographical Area: Judea Province

Biblical Reference(s): Acts 23:24–24:27

Ancient Source(s): Josephus; Suetonius; Tacitus; Antonius Felix Inscription; coins

Identification Rating: Firm (A)

Marcus Antonius Felix, also known as Tiberius Claudius Felix, was the fourth procurator of Judaea Province from ca. 52–59 AD. His interactions with the apostle Paul are found in the book of Acts, while details about his life and career were recorded by Josephus, Suetonius, and Tacitus. Felix is additionally attested through coins he issued in Judea and by at least one inscription of the Roman period. Debate exists over which was his real name, but it is possible that he was given the names Marcus Antonius after being freed by Antonia, then later added more names or replaced names when he was adopted by Emperor Claudius.

Felix has a rather unique story, as he was born a slave and yet rose to the position of a Roman procurator, first being freed by his master and rising to positions above his rank because of his association with Emperor Claudius, commanding cohorts, becoming a procurator of a province, and marrying three queens, including the granddaughter of Marc Antony and Cleopatra (Seutonius, Claudius 28; Tacitus, *Annals* 12.54; Josephus, *Wars* 2.252). One of his wives, Drusilla, died along with his son Marcus Antonius Agrippa at the eruption of Mount Vesuvius in AD 79.

Felix also had a brother named Pallas, who was also born a slave, then freed and became secretary of the treasury under Emperor Claudius, proving to be an important political asset. Supposedly, Felix and Pallas were descended from the kings of Arcadia in Greece. Felix was known to the Romans as rather barbarous and power hungry (Tacitus, *Histories* 5.9). The previous procurator of Judea Province, Ventidius Cumanus, dealt with violent uprisings very harshly and had formal complaints made against him by the high priest Jonathan, leading to Claudius appointing Felix in AD 52. Felix inherited these problems and attempted to deal with them by ruling brutally, even manipulating the Sicarii to assassinate the high priest Jonathan, who had tried to undermine Felix.

However, Felix also fought the Sicarii, caught a famous bandit named Eleazar, stopped a rebellion attempt incited by "the Egyptian" and pursued this mysterious figure (cf. Acts 24:2). After the apostle Paul was arrested in Jerusalem in AD 57 and taken to Caesarea Maritima, he appeared before the Roman procurator Felix, who was very familiar with Christianity, probably as a result of its spread throughout the Empire and because of his time in Judea Province (Acts 24:22).

Coins of the procurator Antonius Felix

Paul was imprisoned for about two years while Felix was procurator, as Felix was both interested in conversing with Paul and hoped to receive a bribe from him for his release from prison. Ultimately, however, Felix left Paul imprisoned as a favor to the religious establishment of Judaism, and the next procurator, Festus, inherited this famous prisoner.

As procurator of Judea Province, Felix had official Roman coinage issued, although these coins bore only the names of the emperors Claudius and Nero rather than the name Felix. Inscriptions mentioning Felix use both his Antonius name (in Latin and from the theatre of Balbus in Rome) and his Claudius name (in Greek and from Judaea a bit north of Caesarea), suggesting that both were used. The inscription from Judaea names him as the procurator of Judaea and Agrippa II as the local king.

Thus, Felix is not only attested by the ancient manuscripts of three Roman historians and inscriptions, but the information from antiquity is vast about his unconventional life and context behind his interactions with the apostle Paul.

> *He called to him two of the centurions and said, "Get two hundred soldiers ready by the third hour of the night to proceed to Caesarea, with seventy horsemen and two hundred spearmen." They were also to provide mounts to put Paul on and bring him safely to Felix the governor* (Acts 23:23-24).

Kokkinos, Nikos. "A Fresh Look at the gentilicium of Felix Procurator of Judaea." *Latomus* 49.1 (1990): 126-41.

Weaver, Paul. "Indicating Status in the Dedication by L. Aufidius Aprilis." *Zeitschrift für Papyrologie und Epigraphik* 122 (1998).

DRUSILLA

Name: Drusilla (Julia Drusilla)

Time Period: 1st century AD (Roman Period)

Geographical Area: Judea

Biblical Reference(s): Acts 24:24

Ancient Source(s): Josephus

Identification Rating: Firm (A)

Drusilla was the youngest daughter of Herod Agrippa I and the sister of Herod Agrippa II and Bernice (Josephus, *Antiquities* 19.354). Born around AD 38, she was probably named after the wife of Augustus or the sister of Claudius, and her name reflected the deep ties her family had to Rome and the Julio-Claudian dynasty. When she was initially married to Azizus, the king of Emesa, at about 15 years of age, Antonius Felix fell in love with her and sent a friend of his named Simon, who was a Jew from Cyprus and allegedly a sorcerer, to convince her to leave her husband (Josephus, *Antiquities* 20.139). In the first year of Nero ca. AD 54, Azizus died, and Drusilla married Felix, who was the Roman procurator of Judea Province.

About three years later Drusilla met the apostle Paul while he was in custody at Caesarea Maritima (Acts 24:24). Drusilla was the second wife of Felix the procurator, and the couple had one known son named Agrippa. During the eruption of Mount Vesuvius in AD 79, her son Agrippa died along with either his wife or more likely his mother, Drusilla, as Felix is known to have taken a third wife (Josephus, *Antiquities* 20.141-44).

Although the evidence from antiquity for Drusilla, the wife of Felix, is limited, she is attested in ancient manuscripts of Josephus.

> *Some days later Felix arrived with Drusilla, his wife who was a Jewess, and sent for Paul and heard him speak about faith in Christ Jesus* (Acts 24:24).

FESTUS

Coins of the procurator Festus, inscribed for the emperor

Name: Festus (Porcius Festus)

Time Period: 1st century AD (Roman Period)

Geographical Area: Judea Province

Biblical Reference(s): Acts 24:27; 25:1–26:32

Ancient Source(s): Josephus; coins

Identification Rating: Firm (A)

Porcius Festus was appointed by Nero as the procurator of Judea, replacing Felix in about AD 59 and interacting with the apostle Paul while he was imprisoned at Caesarea Maritima. During his time in office, Festus appears to have avoided grievances from the local populace better than his predecessor, tried to bring law and order by destroying the sicarii robbers and rebels, and also dealt with a dispute between Herod Agrippa II and the priests (Josephus, *Antiquities* 20.182-200 and *Wars* 2.271).

Similar to many other governors of Judea, Festus was concerned with pleasing the Judean religious and political establishment so that no complaints would be brought against him, often leading to punishment or loss of favor with Rome, which was the reason his predecessor Felix was relieved of duty (Acts 25:9). Although Festus recognized that Paul had broken no Roman law and that the dispute was about religious beliefs, he would not give Paul a fair trial and thus essentially forced Paul to employ his right as a Roman citizen to appeal his case before Caesar, who at the time was Nero. Paul was therefore sent off to Rome by ship, and Festus continued as procurator in Judea until he died in about AD 62 and was succeeded by Albinus.

Beyond the brief accounts about his time as procurator of Judea in the

1st-century writings of Josephus, Festus is not named, and the few details known about his life are restricted to those years. Festus did have coins minted during his time as governor, probably in his first year, but these name only Caesar Nero and not Porcius Festus.

Coin of procurator Porcius Festus

> *Festus then, having arrived in the province, three days later went up to Jerusalem from Caesarea. And the chief priests and the leading men of the Jews brought charges against Paul, and they were urging him, requesting a concession against Paul, that he might have him brought to Jerusalem (at the same time, setting an ambush to kill him on the way). Festus then answered that Paul was being kept in custody at Caesarea and that he himself was about to leave shortly* (Acts 25:1-4).

Hendin, David. *Guide to Biblical Coins*, 5th ed. New York: Amphora, 2010.

HEROD AGRIPPA II

Coin of Agrippa II, bearing his name and featuring him riding a horse

Name: Herod Agrippa II (Marcus Julius Agrippa)

Time Period: 1st century AD (Roman Period)

Geographical Area: Galilee and Judea

Biblical Reference(s): Acts 25:13–26:32

Ancient Source(s): Josephus; coins; Beirut Inscription of Berenice and Agrippa

Identification Rating: Firm (A)

Coin of Agrippa II with his image, name, and title

Herod Agrippa II, also known as Marcus Julius Agrippa, was the son of Agrippa I and Cypros, and a great-grandson of Herod the Great. He was the last of the Herodian dynasty but spent much of his early life in Rome with future Emperor Claudius rather than in Judea. Around AD 48, Claudius appointed him as ruler over the areas surrounding Judea until his death around AD 94, while Judea Province continued to be ruled directly by a Roman governor (Josephus, *Antiquities* 19.360–20.159 and *Wars* 2.223-252). This included Chalcis initially, then after Batanea, Trachonitis, Abila, Iturea, Gaulanitis, Auranitis, and Paneas. At Caesarea Philippi, Agrippa II expanded the city and named it Neronias in honor of Nero.

Many scholars previously thought Agrippa II lived until about AD 100, but based on his coins, which cease during the reign of Domitian, he probably died earlier. A lead weight discovered near Tiberias in Galilee inscribed with the name Agrippa and the year 43 might indicate that he ruled until AD 96 or so, depending on how his regnal years were counted. Living and ruling through the reigns of multiple emperors, including Claudius, Nero, Vespasian, Titus, and Domitian, his lands expanded over time. Leading up to the Judean revolt against Rome, Agrippa II attempted to convince the people not to fight, but once the war broke

Ruins of the palace of Agrippa II at Caesarea Philippi

out, he sided with the Romans and even led his own troops against the rebels in the siege of Gamla, where he was wounded (Josephus, *Wars* 3.29–4.10 and *Life* 114).

The writings of Josephus dedicate significant space to Agrippa II, and indeed he was a major source of information (Josephus, *Life* 360–367). Agrippa II lived through the time of the early church, and along with his sister Bernice, he met the apostle Paul at the palace in Caesarea Maritima while Festus was the procurator of Judea, around AD 59 (Acts 25:13-14).

Outside the writings of Josephus, Agrippa II is attested on numerous coins he issued during his lengthy reign and an important inscription that also names his sister and grandfather. This Latin inscription found in Beirut, where he had built a theatre, names "the great King Agrippa friend of Caesar and Queen Berenice, children of the great King Agrippa...their ancestor King Herod." His coins occasionally bear the name Agrippa, and one type of coin even features his portrait, but most simply name a town and honor whichever emperor was in power at the time.

> *On the next day when Agrippa came together with Bernice amid great pomp, and entered the auditorium accompanied by the commanders and the prominent men of the city, at the command of Festus, Paul was brought in. Festus said, "King Agrippa, and all you gentlemen here present with us, you see this man about whom all the people of the Jews appealed to me, both at Jerusalem and here, loudly declaring that he ought not to live any longer. But I found that he had committed nothing worthy of death; and since he himself appealed to the Emperor, I decided to send him"* (Acts 25:23-25).

Hendin, David. *Guide to Biblical Coins*, 5th ed. New York: Amphora, 2010.

BERNICE II

Name: Bernice II (Julia Berenice)

Time Period: 1st century AD (Roman Period)

Geographical Area: Judea and Syria

Biblical Reference(s): Acts 25:13-23; 26:30

Ancient Source(s): Josephus; Tacitus; Suetonius; Cassius Dio; Beirut Inscription of Berenice and Agrippa; Statue of Bernice

Identification Rating: Firm (A)

Bernice, or Julia Berenice, was part of the Herodian dynasty as the daughter of Herod Agrippa I and a great-granddaughter of King Herod the Great (Josephus, *Antiquities* 20.140-147). Her siblings included Herod Agrippa II, Drusilla, and Mariamne.

Bernice married Herod of Chalcis, who was also her uncle, but he died not long after their marriage, and she chose to remain a widow. After this, Bernice lived with her brother Herod Agrippa II, but due to circulating rumors about an incestuous relationship with him, she briefly married Polemon, king of Cilicia (Josephus, *Antiquities* 20.145). Returning to the court of her brother, Bernice encountered the apostle Paul while he was imprisoned and interviewed at Caesarea Maritima (Acts 25:23).

Several years later, Bernice fell in love with Titus Vespasianus who was ten years younger than her, and she was an ardent supporter of the Romans and Vespasian in particular (Tacitus, *Histories* 2.2-81; Suetonius, *Life of Titus* 7). Bernice on her own was not powerful, but she was apparently quite wealthy and moved in the circles of kings and emperors. Although their affair lasted several

Queen Berenice and Agrippa II inscription

years, she was only ever his mistress, and after Titus became emperor in AD 79, Berenice was sent away in order to improve public perception of the new Caesar. Her fate is unknown.

In addition to four Roman historians mentioning Bernice, she is attested by two contemporary inscriptions in both Latin and Greek. A dedicatory Latin inscription was discovered in Beirut, part of Syria Province at the time, that mentions Bernice and her brother Herod Agrippa II, calling her "Queen Berenice" and making reference to their ancestry from King Herod the Great. Another inscription from Athens, written in Greek, appears on a statue of Bernice and identifies her as "Julia Berenice, great queen," while also associating her with Agrippa (IG III.556).

These inscriptions are undoubtably referring to the same Bernice, sister of Agrippa II, who Paul encountered when brought before the procurator Festus. Holding no political office and remaining unmarried for most of her life, Bernice is nevertheless one of the more thoroughly attested women of the Roman period.

> *On the next day when Agrippa came together with Bernice amid great pomp, and entered the auditorium accompanied by the commanders and the prominent men of the city, at the command of Festus, Paul was brought in* (Acts 25:23).

Macurdy, Grace. "Julia Berenice." *The American Journal of Philology* Vol. 56, No. 3 (1935).

APPENDIX

ARCHAEOLOGICAL PERIODS

Early Bronze I	3200–3000 BC
Early Bronze II	3000–2700 BC
Early Bronze III	2700–2200 BC
Early Bronze IV/Intermediate Bronze	2200–2000 BC
Middle Bronze I	2000–1750 BC
Middle Bronze II	1750–1650 BC
Middle Bronze III	1650–1500 BC
Late Bronze I	1500–1400 BC
Late Bronze II	1400–1300 BC
Late Bronze IIB	1300–1200 BC
Iron IA	1200–1150 BC
Iron IB	1150–1000 BC
Iron IIA	1000–925 BC
Iron IIB	925–722 BC
Iron IIC	722–587 BC
Babylonian Period	587–539 BC
Persian Period	539–332 BC
Hellenistic Period	332–63 BC
Roman Period	63 BC–AD 325
Byzantine Period	AD 325–638

INDEX OF PERSONAL NAMES

(Alphabetical Order)

OTHER GREAT BOOKS BY TITUS KENNEDY

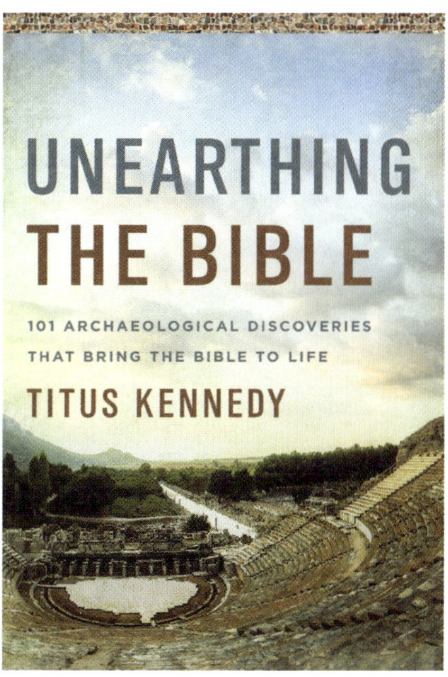

In *Unearthing the Bible*, Dr. Titus M. Kennedy presents 101 objects that provide compelling evidence for the historical reliability of Scripture from the dawn of civilization through the early church. Gathered from more than 50 museums, private collections, and archaeological sites, these pieces not only reinforce the reliability of the biblical narratives, but also provide rich cultural insights into the ancient world.

Using this visual guide, you can find context for your faith as you make your way through the Bible. Dr. Kennedy's photographs and detailed descriptions enable you to examine each piece of fascinating evidence for yourself.

From the earliest tablets of creation to artifacts connected with the life and resurrection of Jesus, *Unearthing the Bible* shows you can be confident there is an abundance of archaeological support for the history told in the Scriptures.

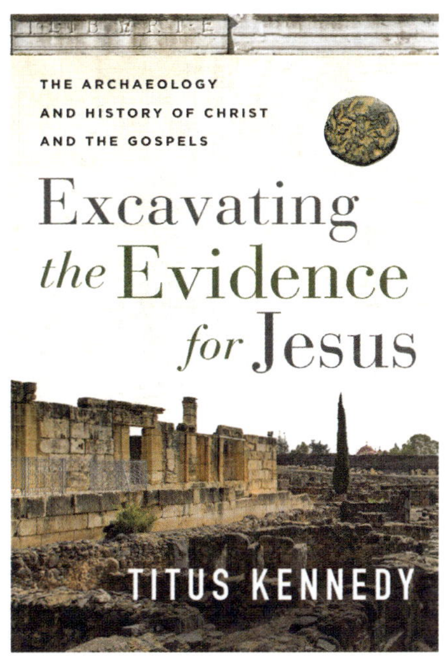

No other figure has impacted history like Jesus. Yet today, he's often seen as a mythical character whose legend increased over time. So what does the historical and archaeological evidence say about Jesus?

Archaeologist Dr. Titus Kennedy has investigated firsthand the discoveries connected to Jesus' birth, ministry, crucifixion, and resurrection. He has visited and excavated where Jesus walked, and examined the artifacts connected to Jesus' life. Here, he presents an up-to-date and comprehensive overview of the research and findings that illuminate the historicity of Christ as presented in the Bible.

Excavating the Evidence for Jesus progresses chronologically through the Gospels, noting the many relevant archaeological, historical, geographic, and literary findings. As you read, you'll be able to decide for yourself whether the evidence confirms the existence and story of Jesus, and determine whether the Gospels are worthy of being approached not as legends, but as history. Further, you'll gain a deeper understanding of the historic basis of Christianity, a richer knowledge of the ancient world, and an evidence-based perspective on the reliability of the Bible.

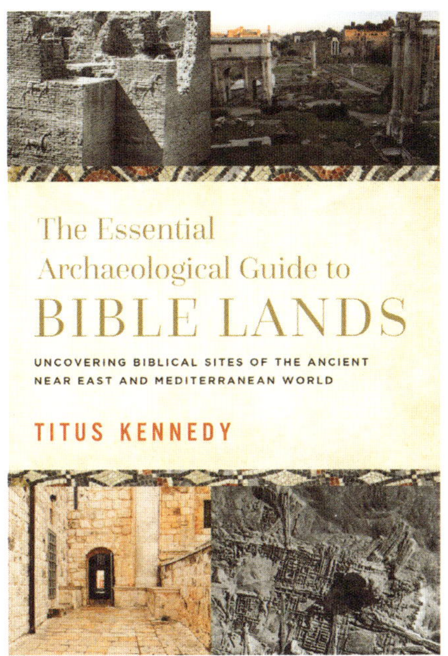

While the historical accuracy of the Bible has long been a topic of debate and has fallen under increased scrutiny in recent decades, new archaeological discoveries from an expanding host of ancient sites found in Bible lands continue to provide evidence pertinent to questions of reliability.

The Essential Archaeological Guide to Bible Lands offers the most geographically extensive overview of archaeological sites from all of the regions relevant to the biblical narratives. With information from excavations and research both old and new, this thorough guide from archaeologist and professor Dr. Titus Kennedy features

- more than 200 full-color photos that show ancient ruins and bring the Bible to life
- extensive exploration of archaeological discoveries from more than 70 key locations and historical sites stretching across Mesopotamia, Egypt, Anatolia, Greece, the Holy Land, and beyond
- expert research and analysis of archaeological evidence that illuminates and corroborates historical narratives of the Bible

The Essential Archaeological Guide to Bible Lands will aid in your search for answers, serving as a travel guide and a resource for investigating the context and historicity of the Bible while vicariously visiting many ancient biblical locations